AF269723

DUMBARTON OAKS
MEDIEVAL LIBRARY

Daniel Donoghue, General Editor

BIBLICAL AND PASTORAL POETRY

ALCIMUS AVITUS

DOML 74

Biblical and Pastoral Poetry

ALCIMUS AVITUS

Edited and Translated by

MICHAEL ROBERTS

DUMBARTON OAKS
MEDIEVAL LIBRARY

HARVARD UNIVERSITY PRESS
CAMBRIDGE, MASSACHUSETTS
LONDON, ENGLAND
2022

Library of Congress Cataloging-in-Publication Data
Names: Avitus, Saint, Bishop of Vienne, author. | Roberts, Michael,
    1947 September 16– editor, translator. | Avitus, Saint, Bishop of Vienne.
    De spiritalis historiae gestis. | Avitus, Saint, Bishop of Vienne. De
    consolatoria castitatis laude. | Avitus, Saint, Bishop of Vienne. De
    spiritalis historiae gestis. English. | Avitus, Saint, Bishop of Vienne.
    De consolatoria castitatis laude. English.
Title: Biblical and pastoral poetry / Alcimus Avitus ; edited and translated
    by Michael Roberts.
Other titles: Dumbarton Oaks medieval library ; 74.
Description: Cambridge, Massachusetts : Harvard University Press, 2022. |
    Series: Dumbarton oaks medieval library; DOML 74 | Includes
    bibliographical references and index. | Latin with English translation
    on facing pages; Introduction and notes in English.
Identifiers: LCCN 2021038116 | ISBN 9780674271265 (cloth)
Subjects: LCSH: Bible. Old Testament—History of Biblical events—
    Poetry—Early works to 1800. | Christian poetry, Latin (Medieval and
    modern)—Early works to 1800. | Virginity—Religious aspects—
    Christianity—Early works to 1800.
Classification: LCC PA6229.A9 D4513 2022 | DDC 873/.01—dc23/
    eng/20211222
LC record available at https://lccn.loc.gov/2021038116

Contents

Introduction

Poet and Poems

Alcimus Ecdicius Avitus was born probably some time in the mid-fifth century. His family belonged to the senatorial aristocracy of southern Gaul, in all likelihood tracing its descent from that Eparchius Avitus who was briefly emperor of Rome (455–456). He certainly was related to the distinguished public figure, poet, prolific letter writer, and churchman of the previous generation Sidonius Apollinaris, with whose homonymous son he exchanged correspondence, though the exact nature of the relationship is unclear. It has been attractively suggested that Avitus's mother, Audentia, was a sister of the elder Sidonius.[1] His father, Hesychius, had held public office but subsequently became bishop of Vienne, in the Rhone valley; Avitus was to succeed him in the episcopate, probably about 490.[2] The evidence suggests that Avitus died in 518.[3]

Avitus goes down in history as a vigorous defender of Christian orthodoxy. His extensive correspondence, over ninety items, includes a lively exchange with the Burgundian king Gundobad, an Arian, on matters of theology. In addition, some fragments of antiheretical writings and homilies survive. Avitus's most frequently read and most famous work, though, is his biblical epic, the *Spiritual History (De spiritalis historiae gestis),* which, along with a later work on virginity addressed to his sister Fuscina, represents the sum total of his surviving poetry.[4]

No precise date can be given for the composition of the *Spiritual History.* In the dedicatory letter to the work written to his brother Apollinaris, bishop of Valence, Avitus describes "find[ing] some books [that is, the *Spiritual History*] . . . with a friend." If the temporary loss of the poems can be attributed to the same disturbance that led to the permanent dispersal of a collection of his epigrams—the siege and capture of Vienne by Gundobad in 500[5]—that would push back the date of the *Spiritual History*'s composition to the last years of the fifth century. Publication, however, followed some years later. In a pair of letters of uncertain date, but before the Frankish defeat of the Visigoths in 507, Avitus complains that an incompletely revised manuscript of the poems has been taken from him against his wishes.[6] His dedicatory letter to his brother, the bishop of Valence, was to accompany the authorially sanctioned version of the text.

In writing to Apollinaris, son of Sidonius Apollinaris, to whom the stolen copy of the poem was passed at its author's request, Avitus describes his poem as "sport[ing] according to the law of poetry," that is, in meter, "on the events of spiritual history" (*de spiritalis historiae gestis . . . lege poematis lusi*).[7] It is from this characterization that the title now given to the whole work, *De spiritalis historiae gestis,* derives. The poet also equipped each book of his work with its own title, as he mentions in the dedicatory letter to his brother:[8] they appear in the manuscripts as "On the Beginning of the World" (*De initio mundi*), "On Original Sin" (*De originali peccato*), "On the Sentence Passed by God" (*De sententia Dei*), "On the Flooding of the World" *(De diluvio mundi),* and "On the Crossing of the Red Sea" *(De transitu Maris Rubri).* The titles to the individual books accurately reflect their subject matter: books 1–3 contain a continuous narrative of creation, the Fall, and the expulsion from paradise, based on Genesis 1–3; book 4 picks up again with the Flood story, covering Genesis 6–9; the last book skips over the rest of Genesis to describe in varying degrees of detail the Israelites' escape from Egypt, culminating in the miraculous events at the Red Sea (Exodus 1:1–15:1).

SPIRITUAL HISTORY

INTERPRETATION OF THE BIBLICAL NARRATIVE

This brief outline of the contents of the *Spiritual History* makes it clear that unlike its predecessors in the Old Testament biblical epic—the *Heptateuchos,* pseudonymously attributed to a Cyprianus Gallus, and the *Alethia* of Claudius Marius Victorius—the poem does not aspire to follow faithfully the sequence of the biblical narrative. While the events of books 1, 2, and 3 are continuous, books 4 and 5 contain discrete episodes without any immediate chronological relationship with what has gone before. Instead, the connection is thematic: the first three books pivot on the Fall and its consequences, the last two books present contrasting narratives of redemption. The connection is made explicit at the end of the *Spiritual History* (5.706–14): the stain of sin that humanity incurred by the crime of the first couple is washed away by baptism, symbolized by the waters of the Red Sea, and in book 4 by the waters of the Flood, from which a new offspring is born. The poem as a whole follows a cycle of original sin and redemption; it constitutes a history of Christian salvation, with the fortunes of the human race at its center.

Avitus's understanding of the biblical text depends primarily on the distinction between *historia* and *figura;* his poem is a *spiritalis historia,* alert to both levels of meaning. The distinction is drawn most fully in his poetry in the opening verses of book 5 of the *Spiritual History* (5.10–18).[9] There he speaks of the narrative sequence of the scripture (5.14), admiring the beauty of its historical record (5.15)—a beauty, though, that is surpassed by "the beauty of its form, prefiguring salvation" (5.16); "though in the historical account *(historiis)* the story is great, in its figural senses *(figuris)* it is greater" (5.17). In the Christian scheme of things, the circumstances Avitus describes were actual historical events, but their greater significance lies in their prefiguration of the future, whether the life of Christ, the history and practices of the Church, or the experiences of the individual Christian. In addition to providing a structural principle for the poem as a whole as an epic of salvation history, such figural interpretations inform the understanding of particular features of the biblical story, be it, for example, the creation of Eve from Adam's rib as a figure of the creation of the Church from the wounded side of Christ at the crucifixion (1.160–69), the ark as a figure of the Church buffeted by hostile forces (4.493–501), or the provision of manna to the Israelites in the desert as prefiguring the Eucharist (5.456–61).

Despite the centrality of figural interpretation to his poem, Avitus also contributes to the understanding of the biblical text at the literal/historical level. To some extent the simple act of rewriting that text as a poetic narrative is already an act of interpretation. But he also incorporates explanations of details that would otherwise be problematic. For example, the sleep that overcomes Adam when his rib is removed to create Eve is no ordinary sleep, but has anesthetic properties (1.149–53); the opening of the first couple's eyes after the Fall does not imply that they were previously blind, but only that now they are condemned to endure a fatal new way of seeing (2.263–72); and the animals that enter the ark, normally fierce and hostile to each other, will observe a pact of peace during the time of their confinement (4.269–74).[10] In particular, Avitus is adept at describing the psychology and mental processes of the actors in his poem, especially in his account of the Fall and his treatment of the pharaoh and his Egyptian people.

One last form of biblical exegesis in the poem might be called the homiletic, in which the Old Testament narrative plays an exemplary rather than a figural role, providing the poet with a source of moral instruction about the proper conduct of Christian life. The poet lays special emphasis on the need for penitence and the importance of not delaying repentance until it is too late: Adam and Eve's tears at their expulsion from paradise parallel the compunction that ordinary Christians will experience when too late, at their deaths, they review their past sinful lives (3.209–19). The story of Dives and Lazarus then serves as a cautionary tale, to illustrate the consequences of too-long delayed repentance (3.220–305). It concludes with an exhortation to humans to mend their ways and learn from the lesson of Adam, while tears still can be shed (3.306–10). The same theme recurs, though less emphatically, in book 4, in which the poet devotes thirty-one lines to a passage with no equivalent in the biblical text describing the various responses of the Flood generation to Noah's ark-building activities: some mock and continue to pursue worldly pleasures (4.306–14 and 4.327–36); others experience fear and wonder at the formidable construction of the ark, but are ignorant of the reason for its building (4.315–17). Their fear, a premonitory warning, does not induce them, however, to mend their ways (4.352–54). Like the inhabitants of Gomorrah (4.355–56), but unlike those of Nineveh, who heed Jonah's warning (4.357–90), they are exterminated. By their acts of penitence, their tears and lamentations, the Ninevites successfully persuade God to spare them. In this case, though repentance is late, it is heartfelt and timely.[11] The prayer to Christ that concludes book 3 similarly marshals a number of biblical examples of Christ's compassion and the efficacy of late repentance: the parables of the prodigal son (3.370–83) and the good Samaritan (3.396–406, identified by Avitus with Christ), and the conversion of the thief on the cross (3.409–19). Together they highlight the availability of Christ's mercy and the concomitant need to repent.[12]

For the most part Avitus's biblical interpretation conforms to the broad lines of the Western exegetical tradition and orthodox theology, as exemplified primarily in the writings of Ambrose and especially of Augustine.[13] In particular he follows the strict Augustinian line on the need for God's grace in order to achieve salvation, against contemporary Semipelagian teaching. The prayer to Christ that ends book 3 culminates with the wish that Christ's grace will prevail and "restore to their former abode those whom the enemy's jealous anger drove out from paradise": divine grace is a necessary prerequisite for overcoming the consequences of original sin.[14]

Genre, Composition, and Style

Despite the frequent presence of exegetical material, the *Spiritual History* remains a narrative poem, in which each section into which the poem falls (books 1–3, book 4, and book 5) owes its continuity to chronological progression, not to a sequence of argument. It tells of the *gesta* of spiritual history; that is, it is a biblical epic. The genre goes back to the Gospel biblical epic of the Spanish poet Juvencus in the early fourth century (ca. 329/30). Two other Old Testament poems, the *Heptateuchos* and Claudius Marius Victorius's *Alethia,* written earlier in the fifth century, were known to Avitus. In both the Old and the New Testament traditions, the trend is toward the increasing incorporation of exegetical material by various expedients into the biblical narrative, while preserving the distinctive idiom of Latin verse, modeled largely on Virgil. Avitus's assured handling of the demands of narration and interpretation marks his poem as a high point in the Old Testament biblical epic of late antiquity and arguably of the biblical epic of the period *tout court.*[15]

Avitus's treatment of his narrative shares features in common with much late Latin poetry. He makes extensive use of direct speech, and the speeches are often of some length, going well beyond what is in the biblical text. In some cases they have no equivalent in that text at all. The chronological sequence of events frequently slows for such a set speech or comes almost to a complete halt with passages of largely static description: for instance, of the Flood (4.429–92) or the battle array and destruction of the Egyptian forces at the Red Sea (5.501–18, 5.683–97). This tendency is especially evident in book 1. Avitus abandons the division by days of creation retained in the other Old Testament poets in order to describe the beauty and order of the newly created world.[16] The book is dominated by two extended descriptive passages—an anatomically detailed account of the creation and animation of man (1.73–127) and a richly colored evocation of paradise (1.193–259)—followed by an enumeration of the four rivers that flow from paradise, itself largely descriptive in nature (1.260–98). In total about two-thirds of the first book is given over to direct speech or description. Such a reliance on compositional set pieces and a concomitant reduction of space devoted to the chronological sequence of actions is characteristic of late Latin narrative poetry.

Naturally much of book 2 and the first part of book 3, recounting the sentence passed on the first couple by God, relies on a succession of speeches to provide the basic narrative core. Much of the content of the speeches, and even some entire speeches, are Avitus's elaborations on what is in Genesis. They concentrate on the motivation and cunning of the devil or illustrate the gullibility of Eve, who is twice described as *credula* ("trusting," 2.205 and 2.213). The devil/serpent's first address to Eve (2.145–60) is a masterpiece of calculated flattery and insinuation—it corresponds to eleven words in the Vulgate Genesis (3:1). Her naïve response (2.169–82) illustrates the *simplicitas* ("innocence," 2.99) that the devil had vowed to exploit. Throughout the account Avitus shows a keen interest in the psychological dynamics of the temptation and Fall, making his treatment a particular favorite of readers and attracting substantial scholarship.[17]

Book 5 shows a similar interest in the psychological dynamics of the narrative. Avitus extensively condenses and reworks the biblical account of events preceding the Israelites' expulsion from Egypt to focus on the conflict between Moses and the pharaoh.[18] That conflict concludes after the final plague with the pharaoh, despite his pride, admitting defeat (5.331–32). The same pattern repeats itself at the Red Sea. Avitus frames it as a military conflict—an unconventional epic battle narrative—with a succession of speeches tracing the fluctuating emotions of the participants, concluding once more with the pharaoh admitting defeat at the hand of God (5.672–75).[19]

The influence of classical poetry is omnipresent in the *Spiritual History*. The very idiom of late Latin dactylic poetry is heavily dependent on Virgil and bears strong affinities also to the Latin poets of the first century CE. Generations of scholars have compiled ample documentation of the classical influence on Avitus's language, material which is best accessed now in the listings provided in Nicole Hecquet-Noti's edition of the poem. Avitus can also call upon earlier Christian poets, of whom Prudentius is the most influential. While such coincidences with classical usage are not all distinctive or necessarily imply knowledge of the earlier writers, there are some striking examples of intertextuality. For instance, when God declares to the first couple before the Fall: "I have granted you unlimited offspring" (*progeniem sine fine dedi,* 1.175), the allusion to Jupiter's promise to Venus of the future greatness of Rome in the first book of the *Aeneid,*

"I have granted them empire without end" (*imperium sine fine dedi*, 1.279), is inescapable and prompts reflection on the different circumstances and outcomes of the two pledges.

Allusions to classical poetry may serve to prompt comparisons between figures or situations in that poetry and the events and personalities of the *Spiritual History*. The devil in book 2, for instance, takes on some of the coloring of the Virgilian Turnus and Allecto, and in his hostility to humanity he shares something of Juno's hostility to the Trojans.[20] The pharaoh too, also a diabolical figure, takes on qualities of Turnus when in his burning passion for battle he is described with the same phrase (*fervidus ardet*, 5.541) as that used of the doomed Turnus in a fleeting upsurge of confidence after the wounding of Aeneas (*Aeneid* 12.325).[21] Such intertextual allusions and parallels in content, not just with Virgil, but with Ovid and Lucan, suggest Avitus expects as audience for his poetry an educated readership, corresponding to the "few cognoscenti" (*paucis intelligentibus*) he refers to in the dedicatory letter to his poem on virginity, *In Consolatory Praise of Chastity*.

Stylistically Avitus shows himself to be a typical poet of late antiquity in his liking for paronomasia (play on words) and paradox, and his tendency to formulate ideas antithetically. To take a couple of examples from many, the sea monsters that come forth into the world with the creation are said to possess "misshapen (i.e., ugly) shapes" (*informes . . . formas*, 1.41); when the Red Sea opens up for the Israelites, an anonymous Egyptian describes it as "concealing dangers in the exposed seabed" (*nudo celans discrimina fundo*, 5.635—both paradox and antithesis).

One feature that is characteristic of Virgil's verse is "the expression of a sequence of events or a complex idea through reiterated parallel statements," instead of using the subordination more characteristic of Latin prose.[22] Virgil has a particular liking for the tricolon (three syntactically equivalent clauses in parataxis); often the constituent clauses do not trace a sequence of actions, but present complementary ways of viewing the same situation. In Avitus's poetry tricola regularly lack chronological progression; not surprisingly, given the recurrent emphasis of the *Spiritual History,* they often explore or dramatize an emotional or psychological situation or state. Here is Eve, hesitating to eat the fatal apple (2.217–19):

> O quotiens ori admotum compuncta retraxit
> audacisque mali titubans sub pondere dextra
> cessit et effectum sceleris tremefacta refugit!

> Oh, how often she felt qualms and drew back the fruit she had brought to her mouth, how often her hand shook and gave way under the weight of the bold transgression and, trembling, recoiled from performance of the crime!

The three main verbs, *retraxit* (drew back), *cessit* (gave way), and *refugit* (recoiled), all describe the same action; each clause provides a complementary perspective on Eve's mental state.

Metrically the *Spiritual History* largely conforms to classical norms. There are a few false quantities, but generally the Avitan hexameter presents little out of the ordinary. Avitus's placement of the caesura and preference for spondees over dactyls align him with Virgilian practice.[23]

In Consolatory Praise of Chastity
(On Virginity)

The majority of manuscripts of the *Spiritual History* conclude with what they identify as a sixth book of Avitus's poetry, addressed to his sister Fuscina, a consecrated virgin. Despite its numeration the poem is equipped with its own dedicatory letter, again to Avitus's brother, Apollinaris, bishop of Valence, and rather than being a continuation of the biblical poem it is clearly a separate work. The dedicatory letter shows that the poem was circulated later than the *Spiritual History,* but there is no reliable evidence for the date of its composition.

The title of the poem is something of a mystery. Most of the manuscripts give it as *De virginitate (On Virginity),* but in the dedicatory letter Avitus terms it *De consolatoria castitatis laude,* literally, "*On the Consolatory Praise of Chastity.*" Just as the title *De spiritalis historiae gestis* derives from the dedicatory letter to that poem, so *De consolatoria castitatis laude,* from the dedicatory letter to the later work, should be its authorially sanctioned title. It presents problems, however. What is "consolatory praise"?[24] The poem is neither a typical speech of praise *(laus)* nor speech of consolation *(consolatio).* It begins as though in praise of Fuscina, but at lines 112–14 the poet explicitly indicates such a *laus* would be premature before her death. As it goes on, the poem does contain some standard elements of treatises on virginity, but the praise of chastity does not play a formative role. As for consolation, the poem has little in common with the rhetorical *consolatio,* which typically consoles for someone's death. Instead *consolatoria* here apparently has its nontechnical sense: the poem serves in some way to assuage dissatisfaction or distress. And indeed, as Danuta Shanzer/Ian Wood, and Hecquet-Noti have all observed, the poem contains a number of references that can be interpreted as evidence of backsliding on Fuscina's part; she is urged, for instance, in the conclusion of the poem "never [to] fail to maintain the role [she] has chosen" (647).[25] Avitus's poem, in fact, is largely exhortatory in tone. He speaks of his "words of encouragement" (*hortantia dicta,* 117) and asks pardon for his exhortations (141). Many of the biblical examples he cites serve to bolster Fuscina's resolve, culminating in two examples of triumphs achieved by mental fortitude (*constantia mentis,* 502), in the stories of Eugenia (503–33) and Susanna (549–620).[26] Given the prevailing hortatory tone of the poem, a more accurate title for it might be *De hortatoria castitatis laude,* "In Hortatory Praise of Chastity."

In style, *In Consolatory Praise* is simpler than the *Spiritual History,* as befits its different genre. Narrative is confined to the biblical examples and parables and the episode from the life of Eugenia. In most cases these are told simply, in summary fashion, though there are exceptions. In the parable of the talents, two passages of direct speech (295–301 and 324–37) balance each other and frame the story. Ecphrasis is almost entirely absent; the one brief example is in the parable of the virgins, describing the flickering and dying flame of the foolish virgins' lamps (467–71). This contains, too, a rare example in *In Consolatory Praise* of tricolon. Speeches generally are in short supply in the poem. The longest example is that of Audentia to her daughter Fuscina (75–101). Its scenario, a parent speaking to her child, and the introduction to the speech, which describes the mother's mixed feelings of joy and anxiety, seem to prepare the way for an emotionally charged speech in the manner of an ethopoeia. In fact, it is largely protreptic in nature, culminating in the enumeration of the holy women in the family that Fuscina can look to for models. In general, *In Consolatory Praise* shows some propensity for such composition by enumeration, a common feature of late Latin poetry, whether in listing items of finery, jewelry, and dress (35–43), or in the extensive catalog of the books of the Bible, which are to serve as familiar reading for Fuscina (379–405).

TRADITION AND RECEPTION

Of the Old Testament poems composed in late antiquity, the *Spiritual History* is the only one to achieve canonical status in subsequent centuries. Already in the sixth century Avitus is the only Old Testament poet included in Venantius Fortunatus's list of his predecessors in Christian poetry with which he begins his *Vita sancti Martini* (1.24–25), written between 573 and 576. Avitus retains the same high status in similar lists provided by the Carolingian writers Alcuin and Theodulf of Orleans.[27] From the same Carolingian period (the ninth century) come the earliest manuscripts of Avitus's poems, and the same century saw the first appearance of the works in monastic library catalogs. The manuscript tradition of Avitus's poetry falls into two distinct families, originating from Gaul *(Gallicani)* and Germany *(Germanici)*, each represented among the earliest manuscripts.[28]

The first printed edition of the six books of the poems was published at Trier in 1507. The volume (59) of Migne's *Patrologia Latina* containing Avitus's poetry, appearing in 1847, reprinted a text that derived from the 1643 Paris edition of J. Sirmond and relied on a late and faulty representative of the Gallican family. The first fully critical edition of Avitus's writings is Rudolf Peiper's, produced in 1883 for the *Monumenta Germaniae historica* series, which was to remain the standard text of Avitus's poetry for over a century. It was not till the last years of the twentieth century and the first years of the twenty-first that a new edition of all of Avitus's poetry, equipped with a French translation and explanatory notes, appeared in the *Sources chrétiennes* series from Hecquet-Noti. In addition, texts with commentaries on individual books or parts of books have been appearing, most during the same period that Hecquet-Noti was working on or publishing her edition.[29] As a result, we are better informed about the nature of the *Spiritual History* and the sources of its inspiration. (*In Consolatory Praise* has received much less attention.) Further, Daniel J. Nodes in 1995 published a text of books 1, 2, and 3, based on an important early representative of the Gallican family of manuscripts, and in 1997 George W. Shea produced an English translation of Avitus's entire poetic corpus.[30]

In preparing this translation I have consulted all the scholarship listed above but must acknowledge a special debt to the full annotations and detailed introductory matter in Hecquet-Noti's three volumes. As always, my aim has been to produce a readable and accurate translation. In the interests of readability I have felt free to depart at times from the literal translation of Avitus's text, especially in matters of clause structure, in order to secure what to my ear is more natural English. The notes are intended to promote readability, providing information readers may need to understand the text or attempting to clarify the sequence of Avitus's thought when it may not seem immediately clear. I have indicated in all cases the biblical passages Avitus is versifying and have provided notice of other biblical references. In general, though, I have been sparing in listing parallels in language with classical texts unless they are especially striking or important.

I should like to express my gratitude to Daniel Nodes and Danuta Shanzer, whose careful reading of my manuscript in its final stages improved it in many ways. Needless to say, remaining errors and infelicities are all my own doing. My gratitude too to Jan Ziolkowski, whose urging and encouragement propelled me into this project. Finally, special thanks to Nicole Eddy, Managing Editor of the series, for her unfailing patience and helpfulness in bringing my manuscript to publication.

Notes

1 Ralph W. Mathisen, "Epistolography, Literary Circles, and Family Ties in Late Roman Gaul," *TAPA* 111 (1981): 100.

2 The date depends on a reference in a late life of Avitus, which speaks of him becoming bishop during the reign of Zeno, who died in April 491; see Rudolph Peiper, ed., *Alcimi Ecdicii Aviti Viennensis episcopi opera quae supersunt*, Monumenta Germaniae historica: Auctores antiquissimi 6, part 2 (Berlin, 1883), p. 177, line 7. He was certainly occupying the see by 494 or 496 (Ennodius, *Vita Epifani* 173).

3 See Danuta Shanzer and Ian Wood, trans., *Avitus of Vienne: Letters and Selected Prose*, Translated Texts for Historians 38 (Liverpool, 2002), 10.

4 In the dedicatory letter to the *Spiritual History*, he refers to a quantity of epigrams lost "in the pressing circumstances of that most notorious dis-

turbance" (*illa notissimae perturbationis necessitate*), generally identified with the capture of Vienne by Gundobad in 500.

5 Gregory of Tours, *Historiae* 2.33.

6 *Epistle* 43, to Eufrasius, bishop of Clermont (Peiper, *Aviti opera*, p. 72, line 31 to p. 73, line 3); *Epistle* 51, to Apollinaris, son of Sidonius Apollinaris (Peiper, *Aviti opera*, p. 80, lines 28–31).

7 Peiper, *Aviti opera*, p. 80, lines 21–22.

8 "They correspond to their own names and titles" (*nominibus propriis titulisque respondeant*).

9 See too *In Consolatory Praise of Chastity* 382.

10 See Ian N. Wood, "Avitus of Vienne," in *Society and Culture in Late Antique Gaul: Revisiting the Sources,* ed. Ralph W. Mathisen and Danuta Shanzer (Aldershot, 2001), 265, for further examples. Augustine discusses the sense of *aperti sunt oculi amborum* ("the eyes of them both were opened," Genesis 3:7) in *De Genesi ad litteram* 11.31, to which Avitus's account broadly conforms.

11 Avitus emphasizes that God had allowed the Flood generation too plenty of time to repent, (4.133–36 and 4.153–54), but to no avail.

12 Christ is addressed in the first line of this prayer as "you . . . who are always quick to show mercy" (*Sed tu . . . cui semper parcere promptum est,* 3.362). Both the prodigal son (3.377) and the thief on the cross (3.415) must confess or atone for their sins.

13 Wood, "Avitus of Vienne," puts special emphasis on the influence of Augustine's *De Genesi ad litteram.*

14 *Livida quos hostis paradiso depulit ira, / fortior antiquae reddat tua gratia sedi* (3.424–25). Daniel J. Nodes, "Avitus of Vienne's *Spiritual History* and the Semipelagian Controversy: The Doctrinal Implications of Books I–III," *Vigiliae Christianae* 38 (1984): 185–95, analyzes the role of grace in the series of examples of divine mercy contained in the prayer to Christ. *In Consolatory Praise* 284 also emphasizes the necessity for grace.

15 For a collection of admiring comments, see Michael Roberts, *Biblical Epic and Rhetorical Paraphrase in Late Antiquity* (Liverpool, 1985), 103n163.

16 Roberts, *Biblical Epic,* 123–24. The effect is to throw into greater relief the creations of man and woman; the fortunes of humankind are central to Avitus's conception of his epic.

17 See Paul-Augustin Deproost, "La mise en scène d'un drame intérieur

dans le poème 'Sur la péché originel' d'Avit de Vienne," *Traditio* 51 (1996): 43–72; Sigmar Döpp, *Eva und die Schlange: Die Sündensfallschilderung des Epikers Avitus im Rahmen der bibelexegetischen Tradition* (Speyer, 2009); Helge Hanns Homey, "Evas Schuld (Alcimus Avitus *De spiritalis historiae gestis* 2,145–182)," *Hermes* 137 (2009): 474–97.

18 Roberts, *Biblical Epic,* 124–25 and 132–33, and Nicole Hecquet-Noti, ed., *Histoire spirituelle,* 2 vols., Sources chrétiennes 444 and 492 (Paris, 1999–2005), vol. 2, pp. 121–23.

19 See Michael Roberts, "Rhetoric and Poetic Imitation in Avitus' Account of the Crossing of the Red Sea (*De spiritalis historiae gestis* 5.371–702)," *Traditio* 39 (1983): 29–80.

20 See Deproost, "Mise en scène," 48–49 and 54–56; Hecquet-Noti, *Histoire,* vol. 1, pp. 68–73.

21 Roberts, "Rhetoric and Poetic Imitation," 65–66.

22 Kenneth Quinn, *Virgil's Aeneid: A Critical Description* (London, 1968), 420.

23 I rely for the characterization of Avitus's metrics and prosody on Hecquet-Noti, *Histoire,* vol. 1, pp. 83–85. For metrical irregularities, see also Peiper, *Aviti opera,* 362, under *metrica et prosodiaca.*

24 Jacques Fontaine, *Naissance de la poésie dans l'occident chrétien: Esquisse d'une histoire de la poésie latine chrétienne du IIIe au VIe siècle* (Paris, 1981), 273, describes the title as "curious" and "scarcely translatable." I have tentatively preferred "In Consolatory Praise of Chastity," though I was unable to find any entirely satisfactory translation.

25 Shanzer and Wood, *Letters and Selected Prose,* 262–63; Nicole Hecquet-Noti, ed., *Éloge consolatoire de la chasteté (Sur la virginité),* Sources chrétiennes 546 (Paris, 2011), 56. Lines 115–21, 132–37, 425–39, and 500–502 deal with the dangers of backsliding and the need for constant application.

26 For instance, the parable of the talents teaches the need to be assiduous in the struggle for virtue (*In Consolatory Praise* 290–337), the figure of Deborah the need for martial resolve in that struggle (338–62), and the parable of the withered fig tree the importance of remaining true to one's vows in actions, not just in name (417–27).

27 See Alcuin, *Versus de patribus, regibus, et sanctis Euboricensis ecclesiae* 1551; Theodulf of Orleans, *Carmina* 45.13 (Ernst Dümmler, ed., *Poetae Latini*

Aevi Carolini, vol.1, Monumenta Germaniae historica, Poetae Latini medii aevi, vol. 1 [Berlin, 1881], p. 543).

28 On the manuscript tradition and references in medieval library catalogs, see Hecquet-Noti, *Histoire,* vol. 1, pp. 89–105.

29 Book 1: Abraham Schippers, *De mundi initio* (Kampen, 1945); Luca Morisi, *Alcimi Aviti "De mundi initio"* (Bologna, 1996). Book 3: Manfred Hoffmann, *"De spiritalis historiae gestis," Buch 3: Einleitung, Übersetzung, Kommentar* (Munich, 2005. Portions of books 4 and 5: Alexander Arweiler, *Die Imitation antiker und spätantiker Literatur in der Dichtung "De spiritalis historiae gestis" des Alcimus Avitus, mit einem Kommentar zu Avit. carm. 4,429–540 und 5,526–703* (Berlin, 1999). For scholarship on book 2, see above, note 17.

30 Daniel J. Nodes, *The Fall of Man: De spiritalis historiae gestis libri I–III* (Toronto, 1985); George W. Shea, *The Poems of Alcimus Ecdicius Avitus* (Tempe, 1997).

SPIRITUAL HISTORY

Prologus Alcimi Aviti episcopi
ad Apollinarem episcopum

Domino sancto in Christo piissimo et beatissimo Apollinari episcopo Alcimus Ecdicius Avitus frater.

Nuper quidem paucis homiliarum mearum in unum corpus redactis hortatu amicorum discrimen editionis intravi. Sed adhuc te maiora suadente in coturnum petulantioris audaciae durata fronte procedo. Iniungis namque ut si quid a me de quibuscumque causis metri lege conscriptum est, sub professione opusculi vestro nomini dedicetur. Recolo equidem nonnulla me versu dixisse, adeo ut, si ordinarentur, non minimo volumine stringi potuerit epigrammatum multitudo. Quod dum facere servato causarum vel temporum ordine meditarer, omnia paene in illa notissimae perturbationis necessitate dispersa sunt. Quae quoniam singillatim aut requiri difficile, aut inveniri impossibile foret, abieci ea de animo meo, quorum mihi vel ordinatio salvorum, ne dicam dispersorum reparatio, dura videretur. Aliquos sane libellos apud quendam familiarem meum postea repperi, qui licet nominibus propriis titulisque respondeant, et alias tamen causas inventa materiae opportunitate perstringunt. Hi

Prologue of Bishop Alcimus Avitus
to Bishop Apollinaris

Alcimus Ecdicius Avitus, his brother, to his saintly lord and the most holy and blessed bishop Apollinaris.

It is true that at the urging of friends I recently compiled a few of my homilies into a single volume and incurred the risk of publishing them. But since you are still urging me to greater things, I am steeling myself to venture on flights of still more shameless boldness. For you are proposing that whatever has been written by me on any subject according to the laws of meter be dedicated to your name in the guise of a minor work. And indeed I recall that I have composed some works in verse in such numbers that, if they were brought together, the quantity of epigrams could only be contained in a not inconsiderable volume. But when I was thinking of doing this, maintaining the sequence of their subjects and chronology, almost all of them were dispersed in the pressing circumstances of that most notorious disturbance. And since they would be difficult to search out or even impossible to discover individually, I put all thought of them out of my mind. Even arranging those that survived seemed difficult, quite apart from the recovery of what had been dispersed. I did certainly find some books later with a friend, which, although they correspond to their own names and titles, yet also touch on other matters when their subject matter presents the opportunity. These, then, although

ergo, quia iubes, etsi obscuri sunt opere meo, tuo saltem nomine inlustrabuntur. Quamquam quilibet acer ille doctusque sit, si religionis propositae stilum non minus fidei quam metri lege servaverit, vix aptus esse poemati queat, quippe cum licentia mentiendi, quae pictoribus ac poetis aeque conceditur, satis procul a causarum serietate pellenda sit. In saeculari namque versuum opere condendo tanto quis peritior appellatur, quanto elegantius, immo, ut vere dicamus, ineptius falsa texuerit. (Taceo iam verba illa vel nomina, quae nobis nec in alienis quidem operibus frequentare, ne dicam in nostris conscribere licet, quae ad compendia poetarum aliud ex alio significantia plurimum valent.) Quocirca saecularium iudicio, qui aut imperitiae aut ignaviae dabunt non uti nos licentia poetarum, plus arduum quam fructuosum opus adgressi divinam longe discrevimus ab humana existimatione censuram. Quoniam in asserendis quibuscumque rebus vel etiam, prout suppetit, explicandis si quacumque ex parte peccandum est, salubrius dicenti clerico non impletur pompa quam regula et tutius artis pede quam veritatis vestigio claudicatur. Non enim est excusata perpetratione peccati libertas eloquii. Nam si pro omni verbo otioso quod locuti fuerint homines rationem redhibere cogentur, agnosci in promptu est illud periculosius laedere quod tractatum atque meditatum, anteposita vivendi legibus loquendi lege, praesumitur.

they derive no light from my writing, will at least, since you bid it, be lent luster by your name. However shrewd and learned a man may be, if in the expression of his Christian belief he observes the law of faith no less than the law of meter, he can hardly be true to poetry, since the seriousness of his subject requires that the freedom to lie, which is granted to painters and poets alike, be utterly banished. For in the composition of secular poetry the more artistically, or rather, to tell the truth, the more improperly, a man has introduced falsehoods, the more skilled he is acclaimed to be. (I make no mention now of those words or names that we may not even peruse in the works of others, much less include in our own writings, which because of a transference of meaning are a very great convenience for poets.) Therefore, since in the judgment of laymen, who will attribute my failure to employ poetic license to a lack of skill or application, I have undertaken a task more difficult than rewarding; I have far preferred the appraisal of God to the opinions of men. For if there is to be a fault of some kind in setting forth any subject matter or even, where possible, explaining it, for a speaker who is a cleric it is more beneficial that the demands of correctness be met rather than those of stylistic display and safer to limp in a metrical foot than on the path of truth. Stylistic freedom does not acquit one of committing a sin. For if men will be made to render account for every idle word they have spoken, it is easy to see that what is chosen after consideration and thought and with preference given to the law of eloquence over the laws of right living is particularly hazardous and damaging.

De initio mundi

Quidquid agit varios humana in gente labores,
unde brevem carpunt mortalia tempora vitam,
vel quod polluti vitiantur origine mores,
quos aliena premunt priscorum facta parentum,
5   addatur quamquam nostra de parte reatus,
quod tamen amisso dudum peccatur honore,
ascribam tibi, prime pater, qui semine mortis
tollis succiduae vitalia germina proli.
Et licet hoc totum Christus persolverit in se,
10   contraxit quantum percussa in stirpe propago,
attamen auctoris vitio, qui debita leti
instituit morbosque suis ac funera misit,
vivit peccati moribunda in carne cicatrix.
    Iam Pater omnipotens librantis pondere Verbi
15   undique collectis discreverat arida lymphis
litoribus pontum constringens, flumina ripis.
Iam proprias pulchro monstrabat lumine formas
obscuro cedente die varioque colore
plurima distinctum pingebat gratia mundum.
20   Temporibus sortita vices tum lumina caelo
fulsere alterno solis lunaeque meatu.
Quin et sidereus nocturno in tempore candor
temperat horrentes astrorum luce tenebras.
Actutum suavi producens omnia fetu

The Beginning of the World

All the causes of the manifold troubles of the human race, the reason why the span of mortal life is brief, our corrupt behavior, perverted from the start and oppressed by deeds not our own, but by those of our distant parents—though guilt has accrued from our part too—and the long continuance of sin once high status was lost, all this I will attribute to you, first father, who by sowing the seed of death deprived successive generations of growth and life. And although Christ in his own person redeemed all that the human race contracted in the blasting of its stock, yet because of the fault of its founder, who incurred a debt to death and transmitted disease and mortality to his children, the scar of sin still lives in mortal flesh.

Already the almighty Father by the weight of the stabilizing Word had gathered together the waters from every source and separated out dry land, confining seas with shores and rivers with riverbanks. Already as the darkness of day retreated before the radiant light, a great many beauties were revealing their distinctive forms and bringing adornment to a dappled and multicolored world. Then the luminous heavenly bodies, sharing out the time between them, shone with alternating course, now of the sun, now the moon. In addition, in the nighttime the brilliance of stars moderated the oppressive darkness with their astral light. At once the earth gave birth to everything in alluring

25 pulchra repentino vestita est gramine tellus.
Accepere genus sine germine iussa creari
et semen voluisse fuit. Sic ubere Verbi
frondescunt silvae; teneris radicibus arbor
duravit vastos parvo sub tempore ramos.
30   Protinus in taetras animalia multa figuras
surgunt et vacuum discurrunt bruta per orbem.
Elatae in altum volucres motuque citato
pendentes secuere vias et in aere sudo
praepetibus librant membrorum pondera pinnis.
35 Post etiam clausi vasto sub gurgite pisces
respirant lymphis flatusque sub aequore ducunt,
quaeque negant nobis, illis dant umida vitam.
Nec minus in pelago vivescunt grandia cete
accipiuntque cavis habitacula digna latebris,
40 et quae monstra solet rarus nunc prodere pontus,
aptat ad informes condens Sollertia formas,
quodque hominum falso credit mens nescia foedum,
per propriam speciem natura iudice pulchrum est.
    Ergo ubi completis fulserunt omnia rebus,
45 ornatuque suo perfectus constitit orbis,
tum Pater omnipotens aeterno lumine laetum
contulit ad terras sublimi ex aethere vultum,
illustrans quodcumque videt. Placet ipsa tuenti
artifici factura suo laudatque creator
50 dispositum pulchro, quem condidit, ordine mundum.
Tum demum tali Sapientia voce locuta est:
"En praeclara nitet mundano machina cultu
et tamen impletum perfectis omnibus orbem
quid iuvat ulterius nullo cultore teneri?
55 Sed ne longa novam contristent otia terram,

profusion and took on beautiful clothing from the instant 25
vegetation. Plants bidden to grow without germination
formed a species; their seed was divine will alone. In this
way forests filled out with leaves, with the Word as their
nurturer; the tree from tender roots hardened in a short
time into widely spreading branches.

Soon many animals arose to take on threatening shapes 30
and brute creatures roamed the empty world. Birds
mounted on high, cleaving with rapid motion an aerial path
and in the clear air suspending the weight of their limbs by
the swift movement of their wings. Next fish, enclosed in 35
the vast ocean, inhaled underwater and drew breath below
the sea; moisture provided them the life that it denies to us.
There lived also in the deep huge sea creatures who found
their proper homes in hollowed-out lairs; these monsters
that the sea now rarely displays their creator Wisdom en- 40
dowed with misshapen shapes. But what the ignorant mind
of man falsely considers ugly, in its own kind is beautiful in
the judgment of nature.

And so, when with the completion of the universe all
was resplendent—the world brought to perfection in its 45
finery—then the almighty Father turned his countenance,
radiant with eternal light, from the height of heaven to the
earth, illuminating whatever he saw. His creation pleased its
author as he looked on, and the creator praised the beauti- 50
fully ordered world he had fashioned. Then finally Wisdom
spoke the following words: "See, now the universe is refined,
its construction outstanding in its splendor. And yet what
satisfaction can there be in a world that is full of every per-
fection but still occupied by no inhabitant? Instead, so that 55
long idleness not deface this new-formed land, let a human

nunc homo formetur, summi quem tangat imago
numinis, et nostram celso donatus honore
induat interius formonsa in mente figuram.
Hunc libet erectum vultu praeponere pronis,
60 qui regat aeterno subiectum foedere mundum,
bruta domet, legem cunctis ac nomina ponat,
astra notet caelique vias et sidera norit,
discat et inspectis discernere tempora signis,
subiciat pelagus saevum, ingenioque tenaci
65 possideat quaecumque videt; cui bestia frendens
serviat et posito discant mansueta furore
imperium iumenta pati iussique ligari
festinent trepidi consueta in vincla iuvenci.
Quoque magis natura hominis sublimior extet,
70 accipiat rectos in caelum tollere vultus,
factorem quaerat proprium cui mente fideli
impendat famulam longaevo in tempore vitam."
    Haec ait et fragilem dignatus tangere terram
temperat umentem consperso in pulvere limum
75 orditurque novum dives Sapientia corpus,
non aliter quam nunc opifex cui est artis in usu
flectere laxatas per cuncta sequacia ceras
et vultus implere manu seu corpora gypso
fingere vel segni speciem componere massae.
80 Sic Pater omnipotens victurum protinus arvum
tractat et in lento meditatur viscera caeno.
Hinc arcem capitis sublimi in vertice signat
septiforem vultum rationis sensibus aptans
olfactu, auditu, visu, gustuque potentem.
85 Tactus erit solus, toto qui corpore iudex

now be shaped who will receive the impress of the highest divinity and, endowed with high honor, take within himself our profile in his well-formed mind. It is my pleasure to bestow on him precedence with his upright countenance over the downward-looking, to rule the subject world in an eternal covenant, to tame the savage, to give law and names to all, to observe the stars and know the paths of heaven and the constellations, to learn to distinguish the seasons by the observation of signs, to bring into subjection the cruel sea, and to possess with his unyielding intellect whatever he observes. Let wild animals, despite their raging, be his servants, and beasts of burden, tamed, their fierceness set aside, learn to endure his command; let bullocks, when ordered to be yoked, hurry in fear to their accustomed restraints. And so that human nature be still more exalted, let him receive an upright countenance to raise up to heaven, and let him seek out his own maker to devote to him with faithful spirit a life of obedience in the long course of time."

With these words resourceful Wisdom, deigning to lay hands on brittle earth, combined moist mud with a scattering of dust and began to frame a new body in just the same way as in the present day a craftsman does, whose artistic practice is to mold pliant wax into every configuration, to shape faces with his hand or delineate bodies from plaster, or to impress form on a recalcitrant mass. In this way the almighty Father shaped the earth, soon to be brought to life, and envisaged flesh in the supple mud. And so on the highest point he marked out the citadel that is the head, adapting the face with its seven openings to the sensations of consciousness, with control over smell, hearing, vision, and taste. Touch would be the only one that feels and passes

sentiat et proprium spargat per membra vigorem.
Flexilis artatur recavo sic lingua palato,
pressus ut in cameram pulsantis verbere plectri
percusso resonet modulatus in aere sermo.
90 Exim succiduum porrecto in corpore pectus
spargit ramosas post brachia fortia palmas.
Succedit stomacho medius, qui tegmine molli
inter utrumque latus foveat vitalia, venter.
Dividuam partem femur excipit, aptius ut se
95 alternum moveat duplicato poplite gressus.
At parte ex alia, fingit quam conditor unus,
occipiti submissa suo descendere cervix
incipit et vastos compagibus addere nervos.
Spina rigens crebris inter commercia nodis
100 diffundit duplicem costarum ex ordine cratem.
Pars interna novos vitae formatur ad usus,
naturale parant tegmen vitalia cordi,
massaque congestis pendens absconditur extis.
Additur et tenui pascendus ab aere pulmo,
105 qui concepta trahens lenti spiramina flatus
accipiat reddens, reddat quas sumpserit auras,
inque vicem crebro pellatur anhelitus haustu.
Dextra tenet iecoris vegetandum sanguine fontem,
quo clausum venae spargant per viscera flumen.
110 Lienis laevam sortitur regula partem,
qua crines perhibent unguesque recrescere sectos;
quae vivunt sensuque carent in corporis usu
nec abscisa dolent, hinc nunc augmenta resumunt.

judgment throughout the entire body and disperses through every limb its native powers. The pliable tongue was enclosed within the hollow palate in such a way that when confined in that chamber and impelled by the tongue's pulsing plectrum, the voice sounds out in articulate speech in the agitated air. Next in progression downward, on the front of the body the chest sends out branching hands on the end of strong arms. In the middle below the esophagus comes the belly, which between both flanks protects the vital organs with its soft covering. Then the thigh divides into two so that the body can more readily advance with bent knees and alternating steps. But on the other side, as the work of the same single creator, set below the back of the head the neck begins its descent and attaches a web of sinews to the structure. The rigid spine, while joined together by multiple vertebrae, sends out on either side the regular sequence of the rib cage. The internal structure is shaped to meet the new requirements of life: the vital organs provide natural protection for the heart, and its suspended form is concealed by a mass of entrails. Lungs too take their place, to feed upon the insubstantial air: by drawing the breaths they have received in slow drafts they are reciprocally to inhale and to exhale the air they have taken in, and respiration is to be driven by the recurrent alternating intake of breath. The right side is occupied by the liver, a spring that derives vigor from blood; veins distribute through the body the stream that is contained therein. The fixture of the spleen takes up the left side, by means of which, it is said, hair and nails, when cut, grow back; they live but have no physical sensation, they do not feel pain when trimmed, but proceed to grow back once more.

Postquam perfectae iacuit novitatis imago
115 formatumque lutum speciem pervenit in omnem,
vertitur in carnem limus durataque molles
visceribus mediis traxerunt ossa medullas.
Inseritur venis sanguis vivoque colore
inficit ora rubor. Toto tum corpore pallor
120 pellitur et niveos depingit purpura vultus.
Inde ubi perfectis consuescit vivere membris
totus homo et fumant calefacta ut viscera, solam
expectant animam, puro quam fonte Creator
promat et erectos recturam mittat in artus.
125 Lenem perpetuo flatum profundit ab ore
inspiratque homini, quem protinus ille receptum
attrahit et crebri discit spiraminis auras.
    Postquam nascentem sollers prudentia sensum
imbuit et puro rationis lumine fulsit,
130 surgit et erectis firmat vestigia plantis.
Tum varias mundi species caelumque refulgens
mirantem tali compellat voce Creator:
"Haec quae mundanis cernis pulcherrima rebus
incrementa novis ornatum tensa per orbem,
135 solus habe totisque prior dominare fruendo.
Tu mihi, cuncta tibi famulentur; maximus ordo
te parere pio, qui subdidit omnia, patri.
Non species ullae nec numina vana colantur,
non si quid caelo sublime novumque coruscat,
140 non quae vel terris vivunt formata vel undis
nec quod forte premens prohibet natura videri.

After the pattern of this new being lay prone but complete, and after the clay, now shaped, took on its full dimensions, the mud changed into flesh, and in the midst of the body bones grew hard and acquired soft marrows. Blood was introduced into the veins, and a flush tinged the face with the color of life. Then pallor was banished from the whole of the body, and a rosy tint adorned the snow-white countenance. Next the entire human being, its frame complete, grew accustomed to life; its flesh gave off steam as it grew warm. All then that was needed was a soul for the Creator to furnish from a pure source and introduce as ruler over the upright limbs. He produced from his eternal mouth a gentle breath and breathed it into man, who immediately received and inhaled it, learning thereby the regular respiration of air.

After ingenious Wisdom inspired his newborn senses and shone with the pure light of reason, he rose up to his feet and secured his upright stance. Then as he was marveling at the various sights of the world and the brilliant heavens, the Creator addressed him in the following words: "These finest of ornaments that you see disposed over the richly furnished earth in this new world retain for yourself alone; have dominion over them all as their superior and enjoy them to the full. You be my servant, but let everything else serve you. The highest obligation is to obey your holy father, who has subjected all things to you. Let no images or false gods receive worship, neither any new body that shines aloft in the sky, nor what is formed to live on earth or in the water, nor even what nature keeps hidden from sight. Remember that

Usibus ista tuis, non cultibus, esse memento;
praecellens factis factorem pronus adora."
　　Interea sextus noctis primordia vesper
145　rettulit alterno depellens tempore lucem,
dumque petunt dulcem spirantia cuncta quietem,
solvitur et somno laxati corporis Adam.
Cui Pater omnipotens pressum per corda soporem
iecit et immisso tardavit pondere sensus,
150　vis ut nulla queat sopitam solvere mentem,
non si forte fragor securas verberet aures,
nec si commoto caelum tunc intonet axe,
sed nec pressa manu rupissent membra quietem.
Tum vero cunctis costarum ex ossibus unam
155　subducit laevo lateri carnemque reponit.
Erigitur pulchro genialis forma decore
inque novum subito procedit femina vultum.
Quam Deus aeterna coniungens lege marito
coniugii fructu pensat dispendia membri.
160　　Istius indicium somni mors illa secuta est,
sponte sua subiit sumpto quam corpore Christus.
Qui cum passurus ligno sublimis in alto
penderet nexus, culpas dum penderet orbis,
in latus extensi defixit missile lictor.
165　Protinus exiliens manavit vulnere lympha,
qua vivum populis iam tum spondente lavacrum
fluxit martyrium signans et sanguinis unda.
Inde quiescenti, gemina dum nocte iaceret,
de lateris membro surgens Ecclesia nupsit.

these exist for your use, not your worship; take precedence over what is created, but bow down and worship their creator."

Meanwhile the evening of the sixth day summoned again the beginnings of night, driving off the sunlight in the regular cycle of time, and as all breathing things were seeking out the sweetness of rest, Adam too with recumbent body was relaxed in sleep. The almighty Father instilled sleep deep in his heart and dulled his sensations by the heaviness he induced, so that no force could release his mind from drowsiness, not if some crash should assail his heedless ears, nor if the heavens should then thunder and the sky be shaken; still, even then his limbs, subdued by the divine hand, would not have broken off their sleep. Next, of all the bones God removed one of the ribs from Adam's left flank, then put his flesh back in place. A figure of charm and beauty rose up, worthy of marriage; in a moment woman took on a countenance never before seen. By joining her in eternally sanctioned marriage to a husband God compensated for the loss of a body part by the benefits of wedlock.

The death that Christ endured of his own free will when he took on a body followed the pattern of this sleep. When for his suffering he was suspended on high, bound to a tall gibbet of wood, when he was paying off the sins of the world, an attendant drove a spear into his taut and exposed flank. Immediately a spring of water gushed from the wound, which already then promised to Christian peoples life-giving baptism, and with it too came a flow of blood, prefiguring martyrdom. Then, while he lay at rest for two nights, the Church arose from his flank to become his wedded bride.

170 Principio Rector tanti sacrare figuram
 disponens vincli nectit conubia verbo:
 "Vivite concordi studio mundumque replete;
 crescat longaevum felici semine germen,
 non annis numerus vitae nec terminus esto.
175 Progeniem sine fine dedi, quam tempore toto
 aspicies, generi primus qui poneris auctor.
 Pronepos eductos spargens per saecla nepotes
 viventes numeret proavos inque ora parentum
 ducant annosos natorum pignora natos.
180 Tum lex coniugii toto venerabilis aevo
 intemerata suo servabitur ordine cunctis.
 Femina persistat de viscere sumpta virili
 coniugio servare fidem, nec separet alter
 quod iungit sociatque Deus; cum patre relinquat
185 et matrem iusto constrictus amore maritus.
 Ista parentales non rumpant vincula curae,
 vita sed amborum carnem teneatur ad unam."
 Taliter aeterno coniungens foedere vota
 festivum dicebat hymen castoque pudori
190 concinit angelicum iuncto modulamine carmen.
 Pro thalamo paradisus erat mundusque dabatur
 in dotem et laetis gaudebant sidera flammis.
  Est locus eoo mundi servatus in axe
 secretis, Natura, tuis, ubi solis ab ortu
195 vicinos nascens aurora repercutit Indos.
 Hic gens ardentem caeli subteriacet axem
 quam candor fervens albenti ex aethere fuscat.
 His semper lux pura venit caeloque propinquo

In the beginning the Sovereign, determining to sanctify 170
the symbolism of so important a bond, confirmed the ties of
marriage with these words: "Live in harmonious devotion
and fill the world with people; let your progeny grow from
a prosperous seed through the long course of time; let the
count of your years be unnumbered and your life be without
end. I have granted you unlimited offspring, yours to view 175
for all time, for you are chosen to be first parent of the hu-
man race. Let great-grandchildren, multiplying from cen-
tury to century the grandchildren they have brought up,
number still living great-grandfathers and let offspring bring
before the eyes of their parents their children's aged chil-
dren. Then the honorable law of marriage will be preserved 180
inviolate by all in due order for all time. Let the woman,
taken from man's flesh, continue to keep faith in wedlock,
and let no one else part what God brings together in union.
Let the husband, possessed by a righteous love, leave both 185
his father and mother. No concern for parents should break
the ties of marriage, but the life of the couple should be
united in one flesh." In sealing wedding vows in an eternal
compact with these words, God pronounced a festive mar-
riage hymn, while an angel choir joined in harmonious song 190
in honor of chaste modesty. Paradise was the couple's bridal
chamber, the world was given them as their dowry, and the
stars with exultant flames were filled with joy.

There is a place under the world's eastern skies kept
secure for your secrets, Nature, where the dawn in its 195
birth at the rising of the sun meets neighboring India. Here
below the burning arc of the heavens a people dwells whom
the white and scorching heat blackens under the glaring
skies. Here the light always comes unclouded, and with the

nativam servant nigrantia corpora noctem.
200 Attamen in taetris splendentia lumina membris
captivo fulgore micant visuque nitente
certior accrescit collatis vultibus horror.
Caesaries incompta riget, quae crine supino
stringitur, ut refugo careat frons nuda capillo.
205 Sed magnum nostros quidquid perfertur ad usus,
his totum natura dedit telluris opimae;
quidquid odoratum pulchrumque allabitur, inde est.
Concolor his ebeni piceo de fomite ramus
surgit et hic, eboris munus quae porrigit orbi,
210 informis pulchros deponit belua dentes.
     Ergo ubi transmissis mundi caput incipit Indis,
quo perhibent terram confinia iungere caelo,
lucus inaccessa cunctis mortalibus arce
permanet aeterno conclusus limite postquam
215 decidit expulsus primaevi criminis auctor,
atque reis digne felici ab sede revulsis
caelestes haec sancta capit nunc terra ministros.
Non hic alterni succedit temporis umquam
bruma nec aestivi redeunt post frigora soles,
220 excelsus calidum cum reddit circulus annum,
vel densante gelu canescunt arva pruinis.
Hic ver adsiduum caeli clementia servat:
turbidus auster abest semperque sub aere sudo
nubila diffugiunt iugi cessura sereno.
225 Nec poscit natura loci quos non habet imbres,
sed contenta suo dotantur germina rore.
Perpetuo viret omne solum terraeque tepentis

proximity of the heavens the people's blackened bodies preserve a native darkness. Yet in their swarthy bodies their gleaming eyes flash with imprisoned radiance, and because of the brilliant visage they inspire all the greater dread from the contrast of body and faces. Their hair is stiff and unkempt, the locks tightly pulled back so that the bare forehead is free of the secured hair. But every choice item that is imported for our enjoyment the nature of their rich land has bestowed on these people; whether scented or beautiful to look at, all flow to us from there. There a branch of ebony grows from a pitch-black trunk, in color like these Indians, and there the ugly creature that supplies the gift of ivory to the world sheds its beautiful tusks.

Then beyond India, where the summit of the world begins and where they say the earth is in close proximity to the sky, a grove exists, its heights inaccessible to all mortals, shut off by an everlasting boundary ever since the originator of the first crime fell and was expelled from there; and now, since the culprits have rightly been driven from that happy abode, this sacred land gives accommodation to heaven's ministers. Here winter never take its place in the alternation of the seasons, nor do summer suns return after the cold, when the heavenly cycle brings back the warmth of the year or ice thickens and fields grow white with frost. Here the mildness of the climate maintains perpetual spring: there is no place for the south wind's violence, but always in the bright air clouds disperse, giving way to continually clear skies. Nor does the nature of the place have any need of the rains that it lacks, but it is sufficient for the vegetation to be endowed with its own special dew. The entire ground is perpetually green, and the aspect of the warm earth entices

blanda nitet facies; stant semper collibus herbae
arboribusque comae, quae cum se flore frequenti
230 diffundunt, celeri confortant germina suco.
Nam quidquid nobis toto nunc nascitur anno,
menstrua maturo dant illic tempora fructu.
Lilia perlucent nullo flaccentia sole,
nec tactus violat violas, roseumque ruborem
235 servans perpetuo suffundit gratia vultu.
Sic cum desit hiems nec torrida ferveat aestas,
fructibus autumnus, ver floribus occupat annum.
Hic, quae donari mentitur fama Sabaeis,
cinnama nascuntur, vivax quae colligit ales
240 natali cum fine perit nidoque perusta
succedens sibimet quaesita morte resurgit.
Nec contenta suo tantum semel ordine nasci,
longa veternosi renovatur corporis aetas
incensamque levant exordia crebra senectam.
245 Illic desudans fragrantia balsama ramus
perpetuum pingui promit de stipite fluxum.
Tum si forte levis movit spiramina ventus,
flatibus exiguis lenique impulsa susurro
dives silva tremit foliis ac flore salubri
250 qui sparsus terris suaves dispensat odores.
Hic fons perspicuo resplendens gurgite surgit;
talis in argento non fulget gratia, tantam
nec crystalla dabunt nitido de frigore lucem.
Margine riparum virides micuere lapilli
255 et, quas miratur mundi iactantia gemmas,
illic saxa iacent; varios dant arva colores
et naturali campos diademate pingunt.

with its brilliance; grass always grows on the hills and foliage on the trees, which, while a mass of abundant blossom, rein- 230 force their growth with swift-running sap. For all that now comes to birth for us in an entire year takes just a month to reach full fruition there. Lilies spread light that no sun can fade, violets suffer no violence from taint, and the beauty 235 that colors the face of the rose retains its redness forever. Accordingly, since there are neither winters nor the scorching heat of summer, autumn fills the year with fruits, and spring with its flowers. On one side grows cinnamon, which report falsely claims as property of the Sabaeans, and which the long-lived bird collects when it perishes, its end a new birth, and though burned up in its nest in a death it has 240 courted, is born once again as heir to itself. Not content to be born only once in its life's course, its body, enfeebled over a long period of time, wins renewal and repeated new beginnings relieve old age in a conflagration. On another side a 245 tree branch sweats fragrant balsam and produces a continual flow from its resinous trunk. Then if a light wind happens to have stirred a breeze, moved by the gently whispering weak currents of air, the rich grove is aquiver in its foliage and in the healthful flowers that cover the ground, 250 spreading sweet perfumes. In another place a spring rises up, shimmering with translucent spray; silver's gleam is not as beautiful, nor will crystal produce as much light from its chill splendor. On the edge of riverbanks green emeralds glitter, and the jewels the vanity of the world admires lie 255 there as simple rocks; the fields are a pattern of multiple colors and bedeck the landscape with a natural coronet.

Eductum leni fontis de vertice flumen
quattuor in largos confestim scinditur amnes.
260 Euphraten Tigrinque vocant, qui limite certo
longa sagittiferis faciunt confinia Parthis.
Tertius inde Geon, Latio qui nomine Nilus
dicitur, ignoto cunctis plus nobilis ortu,
cuius in Aegyptum lenis perlabitur unda
265 ditatura suam certo sub tempore terram.
Nam quotiens tumido perrumpit flumine ripas
alveus et nigris campos perfundit harenis,
ubertas taxatur aqua caeloque vacante
terrestrem pluviam diffusus porrigit amnis.
270 Tunc inclusa latet lato sub gurgite Memphis
et super absentes possessor navigat agros.
Terminus omnis abest; aequatur iudice fluctu
annua suspendens contectus iurgia limes.
Gramina nota videt laetus subsidere pastor
275 inque locum pecorum viridantis iugere campi
succedunt nantes aliena per aequora pisces.
At postquam largo fecundans germina potu
lympha maritavit sitientis viscera terrae,
regreditur Nilus sparsasque recolligit undas.
280 Fit fluvius pereunte lacu; tum redditur alveo
pristina riparum conclusis fluctibus obex,
donec dividuum spargens per devia finem
gurgite septeno patulum percurrat in aequor.
Sed cur dicatur tantum mundana latere
285 vertex, Nile, tuus? Nam qui nesciris ab ortu,
non solus, sed quartus eris diffusus ab illo,
despicit excelso qui flumina cuncta meatu

From the gentle source of the spring a river issues forth to
quickly divide into four full streams. Those that with a long   260
and clearly marked border delimit the territory of the ar-
cher Parthians are called the Euphrates and the Tigris. The
third of these is Geon, named in Latin the Nile, more fa-
mous than all others because of the mystery of its source,
whose waters flow gently into Egypt to enrich the land it   265
passes through at a fixed season. For whenever it bursts its
banks with swelling current and the riverbed spreads black
silt over the landscape, fertility is enhanced by the water,
and under a cloudless sky the expanding river provides a ter-
restrial inundation. Then Memphis lies hidden, submerged   270
under the wide-spreading wave, and the landowner sails
over his invisible fields. All boundary markers are gone; un-
der the flood's jurisdiction land demarcations are concealed
and so nullified, thereby suspending each year's disputes.
The shepherd rejoices to see his familiar pasturage disap-
pear under water; fish take the place of sheep on the acres of   275
green farmland, swimming through waves, an alien expanse.
But after the water, by fertilizing new growth with its abun-
dant drafts, has quickened the womb of the thirsty earth,
the Nile draws back and gathers to itself again its straying
waves. It becomes a river once more, its flooding subsiding;   280
then the obstacle the banks presented in the past to the riv-
er's channel is restored, and its course remains confined un-
til it splits up in different directions at its mouth and with
seven streams empties into the open sea. But why should
your source, Nile, be declared so much of an earthly mys-
tery? For you whose origin is unknown will not be the only   285
one, but one of four, flowing from that stream that looks

ipsius atque pater pelagi supereminet omnes,
quas montes, quas plana vomunt, quas nubila lymphas?
290   Quartus Physon erit, quem possidet India Gangen,
motus odorifero quotiens qui vertice crevit,
deciduas pulchro quas spargunt flamina luco,
praelabens furatur opes et gurgite nostrum
ducit in exilium. Nam ripa largus utraque,
295   amnibus ut nostris enodes ferre papyros
aut scirpos algasque leves deducere mos est,
excrementa trahens magnus sic ditia Ganges
hoc etiam donat mundo, quod proicit alveo.
     Interea primi, Summus quos iunxerat Auctor,
300   in paradisiaca ponuntur sede beati.
Tum Rector tali proponit praemia lege:
"O summum factoris opus, quos sola creavit
nostra manus nasci cum cetera voce iuberem,
aspicitis quanto pulcherrimus ubere lucus
305   per multas famuletur opes. Haec cuncta dabuntur
ad vestros sine fine cibos, hinc esca petatur:
sumite concessas fruges et carpite poma.
Hic operis dulci studio secura quiescat
deliciisque fruens longaevo in tempore vita.
310   Est tamen in medio nemoris, quam cernitis, arbor
notitiam recti pravique in germine portans.
Huius ab accessu vetitum restringite tactum,
nec vos forte premat temeraria discere cura
quod doctor prohibet; melius nescire beatis
315   quod quaesisse nocet. Testor quem fecimus orbem,
quod si quis vetitum praesumpserit arbore pomum,

down upon all other rivers from its lofty course and as father of oceans overtops all the waters that mountains, plains, or clouds pour forth.

The fourth river is Physon, claimed by India as the Ganges. Whenever it wells up in motion from its fragrant source, its stream steals the wealth that breezes spread as aroma in that beautiful grove, to carry it off on its wave to exile in our world. For just as it is the custom for our rivers to produce smooth papyrus, rushes, and worthless water plants, so the great Ganges, spreading bounty on both its banks, carries along precious flotsam and bestows on the world what it ejects from its waters.

And so the first couple, whom the Highest Creator had joined, were granted the bliss of a dwelling in paradise. Then the Sovereign laid out the prizes before them, but with this stipulation: "O greatest work of your creator, whom alone my hand fashioned when I bid all else come to birth with my voice, you see with what bounty this fairest of groves offers up an abundance of riches. All this will be yours to feed on for all time, from this you are to receive your sustenance: take up the crops I have granted you and pick the fruits. Here let your life with sweet devotion experience repose untroubled by labor, enjoying these delights over the long course of time. There is, however, in the middle of the grove a tree, as you see, carrying in its stock the knowledge of good and of evil. Keep your hand from reaching for this, for it is forbidden; let no rash curiosity impel you to learn what your instructor prohibits. For your happiness it is better to be ignorant of what harms if discovered. I call to witness the world I have created, that if anyone ventures to pick the forbidden fruit from that tree, he will pay for his daring crime

audax commissum mortis discrimine pendet.
Non immensa loquor; facilis custodia recti est.
Servator vitam, finem temerator habebit."
320 Accipiunt iuvenes dictum laetique sequuntur,
spondentes cuncto servandam tempore legem.
Sic ignara mali novitas nec conscia fraudis
incautas nulla tetigit formidine mentes.
At Pater instructos sacrata in sede relinquens
325 laetus in astrigeram caeli se sustulit aulam.

with the penalty of death. It is no very great thing I am saying; to observe what is right is easy. He who keeps to this will have life, but its violator death." The young couple paid   320 heed to these words and joyfully followed their precepts, promising the law would be maintained for all time. So ignorant of evil and innocent of deceit was their naivete that it inspired no inkling of fear in their carefree minds. At this the Father, joyfully leaving those he had instructed in that sacred abode, ascended to the starry court of heaven.   325

De originali peccato

Utitur interea venturi nescia casus
libertas secura bonis fruiturque beata
ubertate loci. Largos hinc porrigit illis
tellus prompta cibos; fruticis quin alter opimi
5   sumitur assiduus tenui de caespite fructus.
At si curvati fecundo pondere rami
mitia submittunt sublimi ex arbore poma,
protinus in florem vacuus turgescere palmes
incipit inque novis fetum promittere gemmis.
10   Iam si praedulces delectat carpere somnos,
mollibus in pratis pictaque recumbitur herba,
cumque voluptati sacrum nemus offerat omnes
delicias opibusque novis se praebeat amplum,
sic epulas tamen hi capiunt escamque requirunt,
15   compellit quod nulla fames nec lassa fovendo
indigus hortatur compleri viscera venter.
Et nisi concessum libuisset noscere pastum,
esuries ignota cibos non posceret ullos
nullaque constantem fulcirent pabula vitam.
20   Corpora nuda vident et mutua cernere membra
non pudet atque rudis foedum nil sentit honestas.
Non natura hominis, vitii sed causa pudori est.

Original Sin

For the time being in their freedom, unaware of the catastrophe to come, the couple made untroubled use of the good things at their disposal and enjoyed the blessings of the place's fertility. There the earth readily provided them food in abundance; one crop after another was continually harvested from teeming bushes, however small the plot of land. If branches, bending under the weight of their fertility, lowered to the ground from the tops of trees their ripe fruits, immediately then the stripped vine tendrils began once more to swell into flower and with fresh buds promise new produce. Then if at any time the desire took them to enjoy the sweetness of sleep, they took their rest on soft meadows and spangled grass, and though the holy grove offered for pleasure every delight and proved itself richly endowed with ever-new resources, yet they still took in food and sought out nourishment, though no hunger compelled them, and no importunate belly clamored for a weary stomach to be filled with sustenance. Indeed if it had not given them pleasure to experience the food available to them, hunger, because foreign to them, would have made no demands for nourishment, and no meals would have been needed to maintain the tenor of life. They saw their naked bodies but felt no shame to look at each other's limbs; innocent virtue found nothing foul. It is not the nature of man that brings shame, but the guilt of wrongdoing. For only

Nam quaecumque bonus formavit membra Creator
ut pudibunda forent, carnis post compulit usus.
25 Tunc mens intactos servabat candida visus,
angelicae qualis narratur gloria vitae
sidereas habitare domos qualemque redemptis
spondet reddendam mortis post tempora Christus,
quis neque coniugium curae nec foedere turpi
30 miscebit calidos carnalis copula sexus.
Cessabit gemitus, luxus, metus, ira, voluptas,
fraus, dolor atque dolus, maeror, discordia, livor.
Nullus egens, nullus cupiens, sed pace sub una
sufficiet cunctis, sanctorum gloria, Christus.
35   His protoplastorum sensum primordia sacra
continuere bonis donec certamine primo
vinceret oppressos fallacem culpa per hostem.
Angelus hic dudum fuerat, sed crimine postquam
succensus proprio tumidos exarsit in ausus,
40 se semet fecisse putans, suus ipse creator
ut fuerit, rabido concepit corde furorem
auctoremque negans: "Divinum consequar," inquit,
"nomen et aeternam ponam super aethera sedem,
excelso similis summis nec viribus impar."
45 Talia iactantem Praecelsa Potentia caelo
iecit et eiectum prisco spoliavit honore.
Quique creaturae praefulsit in ordine primus
primas venturo pendet sub iudice poenas,
quandoquidem gravior talem sententia punit
50 quem mirum cecidisse putes. Nam crimen acerbat
auctor; in ignoto minor est peccante reatus,

later did the pursuits of the flesh compel the limbs that the beneficent Creator fashioned to be a cause of shame. At that time in its innocence the mind retained its purity of vision in a life like the glorious existence attributed to angels in their starry habitations and like the one that Christ promises to grant the redeemed after the moment of death, when they will have no thought of marriage and no carnal coupling will bring them together in a debased union of sexual arousal. Then lamentation, indulgence, fear, anger, pleasure, deceit, grief, treachery, sadness, disharmony, jealousy, all will come to an end. No one will feel need, no one desire, but in a shared peace Christ, the glory of the saintly, will be sufficient for all.

With this bounty the original divine state of things satisfied the senses of the first-created couple until in their very first contest wrongdoing overcame them, defeated by a treacherous enemy. He had in the past been an angel, but after he had flared up in an arrogant act of daring, inflamed by his own wrongdoing, thinking that he had fashioned himself, that he was his own creator, he was possessed by frenzy in his raging heart and denying his maker said: "I will attain to the title of god and set up my eternal throne above the heavens, a match for the most high and not inferior to the greatest in strength." When he made these boasts, the Sublime Power threw him from heaven and stripped him as an exile of his former station. And he who outshone all as first in the hierarchy of creation will be the first to pay the penalty in the judgment to come, since a more severe sentence punishes anyone whose fall can be considered exceptional. For the identity of the criminal intensifies the crime; in the case of a humble sinner the guilt is less, while the evil

durius atque malum quod maior fecit habetur.
Sed quod vivaces pertendit in abdita sensus
quodque futura videt rerumque arcana resignat,
55 angelici fervens superest natura vigoris,
horrendum dictu signisque notabile monstrum.
Nam quidquid toto dirum committitur orbe,
iste docet scelerumque manus ac tela gubernat
pugnat et occultus per publica crimina latro.
60 Et nunc saepe hominum, nunc ille in saeva ferarum
vertitur ora novos varians fallentia vultus.
Alitis interdum subito mentita volantis
fit species habitusque iterum confingit honestos.
Apparens nec non pulchro ceu corpore virgo
65 protrahit ardentes obscena in gaudia visus.
Saepe etiam cupidis argentum immane coruscat
accenditque animos auri fallentis amore,
delusos fugiens vano phantasmate tactus.
Nulli certa fides constat vel gratia formae,
70 sed quo quemque modo capiat teneatque nocendo,
opportuna dolis clausaeque accommoda fraudi
sumitur exterior simulata fronte figura.
Maior adhuc etiam saevo permissa potestas,
ut sanctum fingat. Dudum collata creato
75 sic natura valet, rectam quam condidit Auctor,
sed post ad pravos subversor transtulit usus.
    Vidit ut iste novos homines in sede quieta
ducere felicem nullo discrimine vitam,
lege sub accepta famulo dominarier orbi
80 subiectisque frui placida inter gaudia rebus,

done by a more eminent person is judged more harshly. But he retained the forceful nature of his angelic powers, to penetrate with his vigorous senses into what is concealed, to see into the future, and to unlock the secrets of the world, a prodigy fearful to speak of and infamous for the signs he works. For every terrible act in the whole world is from his teaching: he directs men's hands and weapons in crime and wages his battles as a stealthy thief through open wrongdoing. To deceive he often changes his appearance to the countenance of humans, at other times to the fierce features of wild animals, adopting a variety of new guises. From time to time he takes on the false aspect of a flighted bird or on the other hand pretends a respectable demeanor. He appears too as a virgin of beautiful body and attracts gazes that burn for indecent pleasures. Often also he appears to the avaricious as the fearful gleam of silver and inflames minds with love for illusory gold, only to flee their deluded grasp as an empty phantom. There remains no true consistency or charm to any of his manifestations, but he adopts an outer form best suited to capturing and keeping a person in thrall with the harm he works, assuming a counterfeit guise appropriate for his scheming and well suited to his secret deceit. But an even greater power continued to be granted to that cruel creature, to represent himself as holy. In this way the nature bestowed on him in the past when he was created holds good, but what the Creator established as virtuous its perverter has afterward turned to wicked uses.

But when he saw the new humankind spending a happy life in a peaceful abode, free from all peril with authorization to lord it over the world their servant and to enjoy with untroubled pleasure subservient nature, a spark of jealousy

commovit subitum zeli scintilla vaporem
excrevitque calens in saeva incendia livor.
Vicinus tunc forte fuit, quo concidit alto,
lapsus, et innexam traxit per prona catervam.
85 Hoc recolens casumque premens in corde recentem
plus doluit periisse sibi quod possidet alter.
Tum mixtus cum felle pudor sic pectore questus
explicat et tali suspiria voce relaxat:
"Pro dolor, hoc nobis subitum consurgere plasma
90 invisumque genus nostra crevisse ruina!
Me celsum virtus habuit, nunc ecce reiectus
pellor et angelico limus succedit honori.
Caelum terra tenet, vili compage levata
regnat humus nobisque perit translata potestas.
95 Non tamen in totum periit; pars magna retentat
vim propriam summaque cluit virtute nocendi.
Nec differre iuvat. Iam nunc certamine blando
congrediar, dum prima salus experta nec ullos
simplicitas ignara dolos ad tela patebit.
100 Et melius soli capientur fraude, priusquam
fecundam mittant aeterna in saecula prolem.
Immortale nihil terra prodire sinendum est;
fons generis pereat, capitis deiectio victi
semen mortis erit. Pariat discrimina leti
105 vitae principium. Cuncti feriantur in uno;
non faciet vivum radix occisa cacumen.
Haec mihi deiecto tantum solacia restant:
si nequeo clausos iterum conscendere caelos,
his quoque claudantur. Levius cecidisse putandum est

roused instantaneous heat, and the warmth of his envy grew into a savage conflagration. At that time it happened that his fall was still fresh, when he tumbled from on high and carried with him in his downward career a host loyal to him. Remembering this and brooding in his heart over his recent demise, he grieved all the more that he had lost what another was possessing. Then a mixture of chagrin and bitterness gave expression to these heartfelt complaints, and he vented his grievances with the following words: "Alas, this upstart creation is rising up at our expense, and a hateful race has benefited from our downfall! My powers once gave me lofty station, but now I am driven into exile, and mere mud succeeds to my status as an angel. Earth possesses heaven, clay reigns supreme, exalted in a worthless composition, and power has changed hands and is lost to us. Yet it is not entirely lost; a large part retains its native force and is distinguished by its supreme ability to harm. I have no wish to delay. I will engage right now in a contest of sweet words, while their welfare is new and their unthinking innocence, wholly inexperienced in deceit, will be vulnerable to my weapons. They will be more easily taken in by trickery when on their own, before they bequeath their prolific offspring to all ages to come. Nothing immortal must be allowed to come from earth; let the source of the race perish, then in defeat the overthrow of the first begetter will sow the seed of death. Let the origins of life give birth to the perils of mortality. In a single person let all be condemned; a root that is cut down will not produce a living canopy of branches. In my demise this consolation alone remains to me: if I cannot once more ascend to the heaven that is shut off to me, let it be shut off to these beings too. My fall is

110 si nova perdatur simili substantia casu.
    Sit comes excidii, subeat consortia poenae
    et quos praevideo nobiscum dividat ignes.
    Sed nec difficilis fallendi causa petetur;
    haec monstranda via est dudum quam sponte cucurri
115 in pronum lapsus. Quae me iactantia regno
    depulit, haec hominem paradisi limine pellet."
    Sic ait et gemitus vocem clausere dolentis.
        Forte fuit cunctis animantibus altior astu,
    aemulus arguto callet qui pectore, serpens.
120 Huius transgressor de cunctis sumere formam
    eligit aerium circumdans tegmine corpus
    inque repentinum mutatus tenditur anguem.
    Fit longa cervice draco; splendentia colla
    depingit maculis teretisque volumina dorsi
125 asperat et squamis per terga rigentibus armat.
    Qualis vere novo, primis cum mensibus aestas
    praemittit laetos post frigora pigra tepores,
    evadens veterem reparatis motibus annum
    et siccum nitido discingens corpore tegmen
130 procedit coluber terrarumque abdita linquens
    perfert terribilis metuendum forma decorem.
    Dira micant oculi; tum lumine visus acuto
    laetior optatum discit consuescere solem.
    Nunc simulat blandum, crebro ceu carmine fauces
135 ludunt et trifidam dispergunt guttura linguam.
        Ergo ut vipeream malesuada fraude figuram
    induit et totum fallax processit in anguem,
    pervolat ad lucum; nam forte rubentia laeti

easier to contemplate if this new creature perishes in a simi- 110
lar downfall. Let him be my companion in destruction, par-
ticipate in my punishment, and share with me the fires that
I foresee will come. Nor will the means to deceive be diffi-
cult to find; I must show the path that in the past I pursued
of my own free will in my headlong fall. The pride that drove 115
me from the heavenly kingdom will drive humankind from
the threshold of paradise." These were his words; sobs con-
cluded his painful speech.

There happened to be a creature that was advanced in
cunning above all others, the snake, subtle in rivalry and de-
vious of heart. The rebel, cloaking his airy body in a disguise, 120
chose of all animals to take this creature's form and with a
sudden change extended himself into a snake. He became a
serpent with long neck; its brilliant nape he picked out with
markings, made rough the coils of the snake's arched back, 125
and armed its body with rigid scales along the spine. Just so
at the beginning of spring, when in the first months the
warm season sends out welcome heat after the enervating
cold, the snake ventures forth, taking leave of the old year
by resuming its movements and sloughing off its dry coat
for a shining new body; on quitting its hidden lair in the 130
earth its awful appearance conveys a terrible beauty. Its eyes
have a fearful gleam; it is then that its sharp-eyed vision is
learning to accustom itself with growing contentment to
the long-awaited sun. Then it pretends to be harmless, its
jaws quiver as if in repeated song, and its throat flicks out a 135
three-forked tongue.

And so when the false one with treacherous deceit had
assumed serpentine form and had completely turned into
a snake, he hastened to the grove, for the young couple

carpebant iuvenes viridi de palmite mala.
140 Tum veritus serpens, firma ne mente virili
non queat iniecto subvertere corda veneno,
arboris erectae spiris reptantibus alto
porrigitur tractumque suum sublimibus aequans
auditum facilem leni sic voce momordit:
145 "O felix mundique decus pulcherrima virgo,
ornat quam roseo praefulgens forma pudore,
tu generi ventura parens, te maximus orbis
expectat matrem, tu prima et certa voluptas
solamenque viri, sine qua non viveret ipse—
150 ut maior, sic iure tuo subiectus amori—
praedulcis coniunx reddes cui foedere prolem.
Vobis digna datur paradisi in vertice sedes,
vos subiecta tremit famulans substantia mundi:
quod caelum, quod terra creat, quod gurgite magno
155 producit pelagus, vestros confertur in usus.
Nil natura negat; datur ecce in cuncta potestas.
Nec equidem invideo, miror magis ut tamen una
contineat liber dulci super arbore tactus.
Scire velim: quis dura iubet, quis talia dona
160 invidet et rebus ieiunia miscet opimis?"
Haec male blanditam finxerunt sibila vocem.
Quis stupor, O mulier, mentem caligine clausit?
Cum serpente loqui, verbum committere bruto
non pudet, ut vestram praesumat belua linguam?
165 Et monstrum pateris responsumque insuper addis?

chanced to be happily plucking ruddy apples from a green bough there. Then, fearing that because of the man's reso- 140 lute spirit he could not corrupt that heart by the injection of his poison, the snake, writhing his coils round the length of a tall-standing tree, stretched himself up till he reached to the top and bit with coaxing words his susceptible listener as follows: "O happy and most fair virgin, glory of the world, 145 whom radiant beauty adorns with the blush of modesty, you are destined to become parent of the human race, you the whole expanse of the world awaits as its mother, you the first sure pleasure and comfort for your husband, without whom he could not live—though your superior, he is rightly 150 in thrall to your love; in the bond of marriage you will present him with children as his dearly beloved wife. To the two of you a fitting abode is granted in the heights of paradise; before you all that exists in the world trembles in servitude as your subject: whatever sky, whatever earth creates, what- 155 ever sea brings forth from its vast flood, all is devoted to your use. Nature denies you nothing; behold, power over everything is granted to you. For my part I feel no envy, but rather marvel at the fact that the freedom to touch should be excluded in the case of one sweet tree alone. I should like to know: who gives such harsh orders, who begrudges such 160 gifts and mingles fasting with abundant provisions?" With these hissed words he fashioned a dangerously seductive speech. What folly, O woman, befogged your understanding? Are you not ashamed to speak with a serpent, to exchange words with an insensate creature, so that a wild animal lays claim to your language? Do you tolerate such a 165 prodigy and, what is more, return a reply?

Ergo ubi mortiferum seductilis Eva venenum
auribus accipiens laudi consensit iniquae,
tunc ad serpentem vano sic ore locuta est:
"Suavibus O pollens coluber dulcissime dictis,
170   non, ut rere, Deus nobis ieiunia suasit
nec prohibet largo curari corpora pastu.
Ecce vides epulas totus quas porrigit orbis.
Omnibus his licito genitor promptissimus uti
praestitit et totas vitae laxavit habenas.
175   Haec sola est nemoris medii quam perspicis arbor
interdicta cibis, haec tantum tangere poma
non licitum; dives praesumit cetera victus.
Nam si libertas temeraret noxia legem,
iurans terribili praedixit voce Creator
180   quadam nos statim luituros morte reatum.
Quid vocitet mortem, tu nunc, doctissime serpens,
pande libens, quoniam rudibus non cognita res est."
Callidus inde draco et leti tum sponte magister
interitum docet et captas sic fatur ad aures:
185   "Terroris vacuum formidas, femina, nomen.
Non veniet vobis rapidae sententia mortis,
sed pater invisus sortem non contulit aequam
nec vos scire dedit sibimet quae summa reservat.
Quid iuvat ornatum comprendi aut cernere mundum
190   et caecas misero concludi carcere mentes?
Corporeos pariter sensus oculosque patentes
sic brutis natura creat, sol omnibus unus
servit, et humano non distat belua visu.
Consilium mage sume meum mentemque supernis
195   insere et erectos in caelum porrige sensus.
Namque hoc quod vetitum formidas tangere pomum

And so when the susceptible Eve, taking in with her ears the deadly poison, succumbed to the malicious praise, she addressed the snake with naïve words as follows: "O sweetest snake, excelling in charm of language, God did not, as you think, urge us to fast, nor does he forbid us to nurture our bodies with abundant foodstuffs. Behold, you see the rich fare, the produce of all the world. All this a most generous father has granted us the license to enjoy, relaxing all restrictions on our way of life. This tree alone, which you see in the middle of the grove, is forbidden for our food, this fruit alone we are not allowed to touch; everything else our rich diet can enjoy. For if injurious freedom should violate the law, the Creator, voicing a terrible oath, declared that we would immediately pay for our crime with something called death. What he means by death, most learned snake, be good enough to explain now, for it is not something known to us in our innocence."

Then the cunning serpent, a willing instructor on the subject of death, gave Eve a lesson in mortality, addressing her spellbound ears as follows: "Woman, you fear a name that is devoid of threat. No sentence of swift death will overtake you, but your jealous father has bestowed on you a fortune unequal to his and has not allowed you to know the highest secrets he keeps for himself. What pleasure is there in experiencing and perceiving the world in all its finery when your minds are blind, enclosed in a miserable prison? Nature bestows such physical senses and wide-open eyes on brute creatures too, one sun ministers to all, and there is no distinction in vision between man and animal. Rather be advised by me, direct your mind to what is above, raise up your senses and extend them to heaven. For this forbidden fruit

scire dabit quaecumque pater secreta reponit.
Tu modo suspensos tantum ne contine tactus,
nec captiva diu frenetur lege voluptas.
200 Namque ubi divinum libaveris ore saporem,
mox purgata tuo facient te lumina visu
aequiperare deos, sic sancta ut noxia nosse,
iniustum recto, falsum discernere vero."
    Talia fallaci spondentem dona susurro
205 credula submisso miratur femina vultu,
et iam iamque magis cunctari ac flectere sensum
incipit et dubiam leto plus addere mentem.
Ille ut vicino victam discrimine sensit,
atque iterum nomen memorans arcemque deorum
210 unum de cunctis letali ex arbore malum
detrahit et suavi pulchrum perfundit odore.
Conciliat speciem nutantique insuper offert
nec spernit miserum mulier male credula munus,
sed capiens manibus pomum letale retractat.
215 Naribus interdum labiisque patentibus ultro
iungit et ignorans ludit de morte futura.
    O quotiens ori admotum compuncta retraxit
audacisque mali titubans sub pondere dextra
cessit et effectum sceleris tremefacta refugit!
220 Dis tamen esse cupit similis serpitque venenum
ambitione nocens. Rapiunt contraria mentem
hinc amor, inde metus. Pulsat iactantia legem
interdumque etiam lex subvenit. Aestuat anceps
dividui cordis dura inter proelia fluctus.

that you fear to touch will grant you knowledge of all the se-
crets your father keeps to himself. Only cease to hold back
your hesitant grasp, and do not let your pleasure be reined in
for long in bondage to a law. For when you have tasted the   200
divine flavor with your mouth, immediately your eyes will
be cleansed and will make you in vision the equal of the
gods, to know holy and harmful, to distinguish wrong from
right, false from true."

With lowered gaze the gullible woman marveled at him
and the gifts he promised with such treacherous insinua-   205
tion. Increasingly she began to hesitate, to waver in her re-
solve, and incline her uncertain mind more toward death.
When her tempter realized that she was vanquished and the
crisis was imminent, invoking again the title and high abode
of the gods, he plucked from the fatal tree one single apple   210
from all the fruit and imbued its beauty with a sweet per-
fume. He made it enticing in appearance and, as she contin-
ued to hesitate, proceeded to hold it out to the woman. She,
too trusting, did not reject the cursed gift, but took and
played with the deadly fruit in her hands. Without thinking,   215
from time to time she put it to her nostrils or to her open
lips and all unaware sported with death to come.

Oh, how often she felt qualms and drew back the fruit
she had brought to her mouth, how often her hand shook
and gave way under the weight of the bold transgression
and, trembling, recoiled from performance of the crime! Yet   220
she wished to be like the gods, and the poison, made viru-
lent by ambition, seeped its way in. Opposing forces seized
control of her mind, on one side love, on the other fear. Her
pride pushed the law aside, but the law too sometimes stole
in again. In the bitter conflict the swell of her divided heart

225 Nec tamen incentor desistit fallere serpens
ostentatque cibum dubiae queriturque morari
et iuvat in lapsum pendentis prona ruinae.
    Ut tandem victae gravior sententia sedit
aeternam temptare famem per criminis escam,
230 serpentem satiare cibo quem sumeret ipsa,
adnuit insidiis pomumque vorata momordit;
dulce subit virus, capitur mors horrida pastu.
Continet hic primum sua gaudia callidus anguis
dissimulatque ferum victoria saeva triumphum.
235   Ignarus facti diversa parte revertens
Adam diffusi laetus per gramina campi
coniugis amplexus atque oscula casta petebat.
Occurrit mulier, cui tunc audacia primum
flabat femineos animosa in corda furores,
240 et sic orsa loqui, semesum namque gerebat
adservans misero pomum exitiale marito:
"Sume cibum dulcis vitali ex germine coniunx,
quod similem summo faciet te forte Tonanti
numinibusque parem. Non hoc tibi nescia donum,
245 sed iam docta feram. Primus mea viscera gustus
attigit audaci dissolvens pacta periclo.
Crede libens, mentem scelus est dubitasse virilem,
quod mulier potui. Praecedere forte timebas,
saltim consequere atque animos attolle iacentes.
250 Lumina cur flectis? Cur prospera vota moraris
venturoque diu tempus furaris honori?"

surged now this way, now that. But still her tempter, the ser- 225
pent, did not stop his deceits, but as she hesitated showed
her the food, complained of her delay, and prompted her to
succumb to the imminent headlong fall.

When finally she was vanquished, and the ominous deci-
sion was taken to risk eternal hunger for the sake of a forbid-
den mouthful and to satisfy the serpent's appetite with food 230
she ate herself, she acceded to his wiles and bit on the fruit,
only to be swallowed herself; the sweet venom stole upon
her, and the horror of death was ingested along with that
feeding. At this the guileful snake initially concealed his joy,
and cruel victory disguised its savage triumph.

Adam was returning in high spirits from a different area 235
of paradise over the green turf of a wide-spreading plain
and, all unaware of what had happened, was seeking the em-
braces and modest kisses of his wife. That woman ran to
meet him; then, for the first time daring was fanning female
frenzy in an emboldened heart. She was still carrying the
deadly fruit, only half-eaten, that she had kept back for her
unfortunate husband, and so began to speak to him these 240
words: "Sweet husband, take nourishment from this life-
giving tree, for perhaps it will make you like the almighty
Thunderer and equal to the gods. This gift I bring you not in
ignorance but already with full knowledge. When the first 245
taste reached my stomach, that dangerous venture annulled
the pact we had pledged. Believe me without reserve, it is
a crime for manly resolution to hesitate to do what I, a
woman, was capable of. Perhaps you were afraid to go first;
still take my lead and rally your failing courage. Why do you 250
turn your gaze aside? Why delay the prosperity you aspire to
and persist in stealing time from the glory to come?"

    Haec effata dabat victurae fercula mortis,
intereunte anima letum dum crimina pascunt.
Accipit infelix malesuadi verba susurri
255 inflexosque retro deiecit ad ultima sensus.
Non illum trepidi concussit cura pavoris,
nec quantum gustu cunctata est femina primo,
sed sequitur velox miseraeque ex coniugis ore
constanter rapit inconstans dotale venenum
260 faucibus et patulis inimicas porrigit escas.
    Vix uno pomum libaverat horrida morsu
ingluvies summumque dabat vix esca saporem,
ecce repentinus fulgor circumstetit ora
lugendoque novos respersit lumine visus.
265 Non caecos natura dedit nec luminis usu
privatam faciem peperit perfectio formae.
Nunc mage caecus eris, cui iam non sufficit illud
noscere quod tantus voluit te nosse creator.
Ad vitam vobis cernendi facta facultas;
270 vos etiam letum vestra sed sponte videtis.
    Tum patuisse gemunt oculos, nam culpa rebellis
fulsit et obscenos senserunt corpora motus.
Tum primum nudos—dubium quid dicere possim
extinctus natusne—pudor circumspicit artus.
275 Erubuit propriae iam mens sibi conscia culpae
pugnavitque suis carnis lex indita membris.
Namque hinc posteritas vitiato germine duxit
artibus illicitis cognoscere velle futura

With these words she served up death, securing its victory, when sinfulness fostered mortality at the cost of the soul. Unhappy man, he took in her words with their treacherous insinuations, and at the last his senses were swayed 255 and brought low. No anxiety, quaking, or dread shook his resolve, not even for as long as the woman hesitated before the first taste, but he quickly followed her example and in response to his unfortunate wife's urging, betraying his past pledge, unwaveringly snatched hold of the poison she brought as her dowry and reached the noxious mouthful to 260 his wide-open jaws.

Scarcely had his doomed appetite taken a single bite of the fruit, scarcely was that food beginning to impart its flavor, when, lo, a sudden brightness surrounded his countenance and with its mournful light shed on it a new way of seeing. Nature did not create humans blind, and their physi- 265 cal perfection did not produce a face deprived of vision. In fact it is rather now, Adam, that you will be blind, since you are not content with knowing only what your mighty creator wanted you to know. The faculty of vision was granted you for the purpose of life, but by your voluntary act you are 270 both also looking at death.

Then they lamented that their eyes had been opened, for their sinful rebellion brought a flash of illumination and their bodies began to feel indecent impulses. For the first time then they were either ashamed or shameless—I hesitate which to say—as they looked at their naked limbs. Now 275 the mind, conscious of its fault, felt a blush, and was in conflict with the law of the flesh dwelling in the body. For from this defective stock future generations derived the desire to discover the future by forbidden arts and enter with their

arcanisque sacris tardos immittere sensus,
280 edita vel caelo vel taetro mersa profundo
rimari et cautas naturae irrumpere leges;
quaerere nunc astris quo quisquam sidere natus,
prospera quam ducat restantis tempora vitae,
dissimilem paribus proventum discere signis;
285 nec non et geminos uno sub tempore fusos,
quos indiscretus luci produxerit ortus,
motibus adversis varia sub sorte notare;
indigetes quosdam stellis adscribere divos,
iunior antiquis aetas quos protulit astris,
290 atque infernali iam dudum nocte sepultis
vana per immensum disponere nomina caelum.
    Iam magicam digne valeat quis dicere fraudem
occultas tacito temptantem pectore vires
divinis iungi virtutibus et cupientem?
295 Legifer ut quondam vates sub rege superbo,
dum nova monstraret iussi miracula signi,
commovit livore magos ut talia temptent
accumulentque suas zelo fervente ruinas.
Illis suppeteret recta si sorte potestas,
300 demere, non etiam festinent addere monstra,
aemula sed signis tantum, non viribus aequa,
quod removere nequit, duplicavit iustius ira.
Hinc est laudato possunt quod crimine Marsi,
cum tacita saevos producunt arte dracones
305 absentes et saepe iubent confligere secum.
Tunc ut quisque gravem bello persenserit hydrum

sluggish senses into the secrets of the divine, to scan the   280
heights of heaven and the depths of the fearsome abyss, and
to break free from the restrictions the laws of nature im-
posed; now they desired to find out from the stars under
what constellation each person was born and what prosper-
ity he could enjoy during the remaining course of his life, to
search for differing outcomes, though the signs coincide,
and furthermore by the observation of contrary motions to   285
assign different fates to twins born at the same moment,
with no distinction in the time that they came forth to the
light. They sought too to enlist among the heavenly bodies
native divinities whom an age more recent than the an-
tiquity of the stars gave birth to and to distribute through-
out the immensity of the heavens the empty names of those   290
long buried in infernal night.

Who could adequately describe the deceitfulness of
magic, as it seeks to evoke secret forces in the silence of the
heart and to secure for itself divine powers? So in the past   295
during the reign of an arrogant ruler, the prophet and law-
giver Moses, when he was displaying new and miraculous
signs as God had instructed, aroused the envy of magicians
to attempt the same, only for them to enhance their own
downfall with their impassioned rivalry. If they had laid
claim to legitimate power, they would be eager to reduce,   300
not add to such prodigies. Their anger competed in signs
only, but was unequal in powers, justly redoubling the por-
tents it could not remove. From this source too comes the
power that the Marsi possess, winning applause for their
crime, when with a secret skill they summon up dangerous
snakes and often command those creatures even from a dis-   305
tance to enter a contest with them. Then when an individual

aspidis aut durae clausas cognoverit aures,
concutit interius secreti carminis arma.
Protinus et lassis verbo lactante venenis
310 mox impune manu coluber tractatur inermis
et morsus tantum, non virus in angue timetur.
Interdum perit incantans, si callida surdus
adiuratoris contempsit murmura serpens.
Hoc quoniam de matre trahunt et origine prima,
315 anguinae fraudis quod sic linguaeque periti,
mutua per carmen reddunt commercia fandi.
    Nec minus his pulsat contraria cura saluti,
angit praescitus ducti quos terminus aevi,
cum tamen eductas infernis sedibus umbras
320 colloquium miscere putent et nota referre.
Spiritus erroris sed qui bacchatur in illis
ad consulta parat vanis responsa figuris.
Et ne porrecto dicantur singula verbo,
praesenti illusus damnabitur ille perenni
325 iudicio quisquis vetitum cognoscere temptat.
    Nec iam sola fuit scrutatrix Eva malorum.
Dicam nunc aliam tali quae peste laborans
et coniuncta viro proprium non vicerit Adam.
Peccandi quasdam fervor succenderat urbes
330 civica permittens laxatis crimina frenis.
Incestus pro lege fuit totumque libido
ius habuit, regni sedem metata voluptas
indigenas populos domina sub carne tenebat,

has detected a water snake, dangerous in warfare, or identi-
fied the cruel asp with its closed-off ears, he calls up from
within the secret weapon of his spell. Immediately with the
enchantment of the language the venom loses its strength,
and right away the serpent, now disarmed, can freely be 310
handled; only its bite, not its poison, gives cause for fearing
the snake. Occasionally, though, the charmer meets his end,
if the serpent turns a deaf ear to the practiced incantations
of his would-be enchanter. Since these people have inher-
ited from the first mother and the very beginnings of things
this knowledge of the deceitfulness and the language of 315
snakes, by their spells they can communicate in mutual ex-
change of speech.

Equally, those who are tortured by the foreknowledge
that their lives will end suffer from anxiety at odds with
their salvation, when they expect ghosts called up from the
depths of the underworld to join in conversation with them 320
and tell them what they know. But instead the spirit of false-
hood which runs riot among those shades gives answers to
their questions with specious riddling. In sum, to avoid a
long and detailed speech, whoever attempts to discover
what is forbidden will be deluded in the present and judged 325
and condemned for eternity.

Nor was Eve the only woman to seek after evil. I shall tell
of another who suffered from the same malign forces, but,
though married to a husband, did not get the better of her
Adam. A passion for sin had inflamed certain cities, allowing 330
their citizens to give rein to unbridled wickedness. Indecent
lust took the place of law, holding sway over everything,
and pleasure rife throughout the realm kept the native
population in subjugation to the flesh. In their devotion to

et scelerum studio fida quod plebe localis
335   dudum parendi promptis res publica iussit,
abstinuisse nefas et non peccasse pudendum
credebant omnes, facinus quos iunxerat omne.
Talibus offensus iudex atque arbiter orbis
cum fureret flammasque loco finemque pararet,
340   quendam dissimilem cunctis tectoque latentem,
qui tunc forte fuit propria peregrinus in urbe,
atque inter multos solum sic alloquitur Loth:
"Oppida lascivo iam dudum plena furore
respergunt caelum maculis nostrasque fatigant
345   quamvis obstructas scelerum clamoribus aures.
Imminet exitium, tellus succensa reatu
ignibus ardebit, restinguet fulminis imber
quae non extinxit ferventia crimina fletus.
Ipsa in perpetuas solvetur terra favillas,
350   quae vivos cineres et post incendia servans
sicque solum fingens, leviter si calce teretur,
ad minimum fugiens discedet pallida tactum.
Tu nunc linque domum, perituras desere terras,
et rea cum dignis subsidant arva colonis.
355   Nec tete impendens letum coniunxerit illis
non iunxit quos vita tibi. Solacia coniunx
praebeat; hac tantum socia contentus abito.
Adcelerate fugam, tendatur tramite recto,
neu subvertendas quisquam respexerit urbes.
360   Vos nescite malum; poenas quicumque subibit
aspiciat mortisque suae spectacula secum,
qui meruere ferant. Salvandis terror abesto."

evildoing all of them believed it a disgrace to abstain from wrongdoing and shameful not to commit a sin, in accordance with the commands of their home state, which as a loyal people they were long disposed to obey; all their criminality united them as one. But when the judge and ruler of the world, offended by such acts, was enraged and preparing a fiery end for that place, there was one man different from all the others, who, keeping to his own house, was then an alien in his own city; this man, Lot, alone among so many, he addressed as follows: "These cities, long full of wanton frenzy, bespatter heaven with their pollution and assail my ears with the cries of their criminality, however much I block them off. Destruction is at hand; for their sinfulness the earth will catch fire and go up in flames, and a torrent of lightning will eliminate the cauldron of crimes that tears did not extinguish. The earth itself will crumble into perpetual ash; even after the fire it will retain live cinders, mimicking real soil, and if lightly trodden underfoot, at the slightest touch it will fly up and disperse in a pale spray. But you now must quit your house, abandon the doomed land, and leave its guilty fields to their destruction along with their cultivators, as they deserve. Do not share the impending death with those whose life you have not shared. Let your wife provide you with consolation; with her alone as companion readily depart this place. Hurry to make your escape, keep directly on your course, and let no one look back at the cities doomed to destruction. You must remain ignorant of the disaster; let only the ones who suffer this punishment be the ones to see it, and only those who have deserved this end endure the spectacle of their death. But let those to be saved have no fear." These were the words of the Father.

Haec Pater. Ast illi properant abscedere terra
inciduntque moras crudeliaque arva relinquunt.
365   Coeperat obduci victum caligine densa
atque ignota prius demittere murmura caelum.
Nec sic ut tonitru crebro cum percitus aether
ostentat pavidis innoxia fulmina terris,
sed prorsus finale malum stridore minaci
370 taetra per aerios mittebat signa tumultus.
Tendebant moniti simul et mandata tenentes
concessam rectis ad sedem vultibus ibant.
Callidus alta petens sed qui subverterat Evam
serpens femineam consuetus tangere mentem,
375 hic quoque formidans animum temptare virilem
coniugis inspirat votis ut nosse ruinas
vellet et evasas visu deprendere clades.
O demens animi! Cur iam non sufficit unam
subcubuisse dolo? Caruit iam parte bonorum,
380 qui mala cognovit. Si non exempla priorum
terrent, exemplum fies nostroque timori,
vel post te pereat secreti dira cupido.
Illicitum quod scire fuit vetitumque tueri,
respiciens tantum nec narratura videbis.
385   Ergo ubi maiorem vicina ex urbe tumultum
accepit mulier, vultum tunc flexa retortum
vix primo in visu restrictis motibus haesit,
cernere desistens cum coeperat. Inde gelato
sanguine marmoreus perfudit viscera torpor;

They in response hurried to quit the land, and without a moment's delay they left behind them that cruel country.

Already the heaven had begun to be obscured under a thick pall of darkness and to emit rumblings never known before. It was not like when the sky is shaken by recurrent thunderclaps and makes a show of harmless lightning to the fearful earth, but rather the last and final catastrophe with threatening howls was producing awful forewarnings in the chaos of the heavens. Lot and his wife continued on together as instructed and in obedience to their orders came to the home allotted them, keeping their faces turned straight ahead. But the cunning serpent who in raising himself up had ruined Eve, well versed in swaying the female mind, on this occasion too, fearing to test male resolution, inspired in Lot's wife the wish to witness the destruction and catch sight of the disaster she had escaped. What madness and folly! Why is it not enough for you that one woman already has succumbed to deceit? Whoever has come to know evil has already left the ranks of the good. If the example of those preceding you does not inspire fear in you, you yourself will become an example for our fear; after you, at least, may the cursed desire for secret knowledge come to an end. You only caught sight of what was unlawful to know and forbidden to look at; you will not be able to go on to tell what you have seen.

And so when the woman heard the mounting roar from the nearby city, she turned her gaze back, but hardly had she taken a first look when her movement was paralyzed and she came to a halt, ceasing to look the moment she had begun to do so. Right then her blood grew icy and a heaviness like that of marble pervaded her frame;

390 diriguere genae, pallor novus inficit ora.
Lumina non clausit, non saltim concidit illo
pondere quo pulsant demissa cadavera terram,
sed stetit horrendo perlucens massa nitore
servavitque suam species decepta figuram,
395 nec facile ut nosses, vitrum, lapis, anne metallum
succedens homini, si non sal fauce notetur.
Ex tunc insipido mulier praeventa reatu
plus salsum sine mente sapit, quae pungere sensus
exemplique potest salibus condire videntes.
400 Hoc tamen hic magnum, quod non inflectitur iste
nec sequitur sociam fortis nec vincitur Adam.
Credo equidem melius, quod non occurrerit uxor
enarrare viro, nam si comperta referret,
forsan et hunc visu suasisset temnere iussa,
405 ceu proprium gustu fecit primaeva virago.
Quae postquam sese pariter comitemque fefellit,
et nondum natam percussit vulnere prolem.
    Tum victor serpens certamine laetus ab ipso,
puniceam crispans squamoso in vertice cristam,
410 iam non dissimulans quem presserat ante triumphum
acrior insultat victis et taliter infit:
"En divina manet promissae gloria laudis.
Quidquid scire meum potuit, iam credite vestrum est.
Omnia monstravi sensumque per abdita duxi
415 et quodcumque malum sollers natura negabat
institui dextrisque dedi coniungere laevum.
Istinc perpetua vosmet mihi sorte dicavi.

her cheeks grew stiff and a new pallor suffused her face. She 390
did not close her eyes, nor even fall with the weight with
which dead bodies collapse and strike the ground, but stood
a shimmering block of terrible brilliance, and her tainted
appearance retained its former shape, so much so that you 395
could not easily tell whether glass, stone, or metal had re-
placed the human form, unless you identified the salt by
tasting it. From that moment the woman whose life had
been cut short for her unseasonable crime, though sense-
less, gained seasoning from the salt, and won the power to
stimulate the senses and to season with the salt of her ex-
ample those seeing her. But in this case it is important that 400
the Adam was not persuaded, nor followed or succumbed
to his partner. In fact I think it was better that the wife did
not encounter her husband to tell him her tale, for if she
had told her experiences, perhaps she would have persuaded
him too to contravene his instructions by looking, as the 405
first woman caused her husband to do by tasting. In that
case after she was deceived and went on to deceive her part-
ner, she inflicted a wound on generations not yet born.

Then the victorious serpent, rejoicing in the result of the
contest, raised up on his scaly head the scarlet crest, and no 410
longer disguising the triumph he had suppressed before, ex-
ulted more fiercely over the vanquished, beginning to speak
as follows: "See now, the divine glory of the renown I prom-
ised is yours. All my knowledge could give you, you can be
sure, is now in your keeping. I have shown you everything
and led your senses through all that is hidden; I have taught 415
you every evil that nature in its wisdom denied you and
given you the power to commingle wrong with right. In so
doing I have acquired a claim over you that will forever be

Nec Deus in vobis, quamquam formaverit ante,
iam plus iuris habet: teneat, quod condidit ipse;
420   quod docui, meum est—maior mihi portio restat.
Multa creatori debetis, plura magistro."
Dixit et in media trepidos caligine linquens
confictum periit fugiens per nubila corpus.

your fate. God himself does not have more of a claim over you, though he shaped you first: let him keep what he fashioned; what I taught belongs to me—the greater part that is left is mine. You owe a great deal to your creator, but more to your teacher." He finished speaking and left behind the fearful couple in a pall of mist. Meanwhile, as he fled through the clouds, the bodily shape he had assumed vanished from sight.

420

De sententia Dei

Tempus erat quo sol medium transcenderat axem
pronus et excelsi linquens fastigia centri
vicina iam nocte leves permiserat auras.
Illis sed maior curarum volvitur aestus
5 ferventesque tenent male conscia corda dolores.
Utque pudor capto detorsit lumina sensu
reppulit et miseros alterno a corpore visus
nec iam secura praestatur luce tueri
signatam fixo peccati stigmate carnem,
10 indumenta petunt, foliis ut mollibus ambo
membra tegant nudumque malum de veste patescat.
Umbrosis propter stabat ficulnea ramis
frondentes diffusa comas, quas protinus Adam
umentem capiens raso de cortice librum
15 adsuit et viridi solatur veste ruborem.
Induitur simili mulier lacrimabilis arte.
Quosque pavit misero fallax insania pomo
vestivit folio; saeva quos arbore nudos
reddidit, hos gravius tenui super arbore texit.
20 Et tamen adveniet tempus cum crimina ligni
per lignum sanet purgetque novissimus Adam
materiamque ipsam faciat medicamina vitae,
qua mors invaluit. Leto delebere, letum.

The Sentence Passed by God

It was that time of day when the sun had passed the middle of the heavens and in its downward course was leaving behind the high summit of its midcareer, stirring up light breezes as night was already approaching. But for the first parents a greater tide of cares broke upon them, and seething sorrows gripped their conscience-stricken hearts. With their senses now in thrall, shame caused them to look away and in their misery made them shun the sight of each other's bodies. They could no longer contemplate with carefree vision flesh branded with the permanent mark of sin, but they sought out clothing, so that the two of them could cover their bodies with soft foliage, thereby laying bare their wretchedness by their attire. Nearby stood a fig tree with spreading branches, clothed in a rich growth of leaves, which Adam quickly sewed together, using the moist inner fiber of the tree after scraping away the bark, and with this cloak of greenery covered up his blushes. In the same way the unhappy woman clothed herself too. That mad delusion that caused them to eat the cursed fruit now dressed them in foliage; those whom that madness made naked by means of a cruel tree, it now ominously cloaked in a light covering from a tree. But a time will come when the latest Adam will expiate and heal the crime of the wood with wood and will make from the same material that gave death its power a life-bringing remedy. Death, you will be destroyed by a

Aereus excelso pendebit stipite serpens,
25 cumque venenatum simulaverit, omne venenum
purget et antiquum perimat sua forma draconem.
    Interea Genitor viridis per mollia luci
rorantes sudo capiebat ab aere ventos.
Protinus attonitis senserunt auribus ambo
30 praesentem Dominum. Tristi tum luce perosa
expavere diem detecto in crimine testem.
Illos nam, vastis specubus si forte baratrum
panderet aut subitum tellus monstraret hiatum,
non pigeat prono trepidos descendere saltu,
35 et si suppeteret iam tum sententia leti,
hanc etiam raperet solandi cura pudoris;
se flammis lymphisve darent vel pectora ferro
appeteret vindex crudeli vulnere dextra.
Sic miseri mortem nondum discrimine notam,
40 cum primum meruere, volunt.
                              Exordia finem
signant et similes praedicunt adfore luctus,
ultima cum mundi senium consumpserit aetas
cumque repentinus percusserit omnia fulgor
caelorum clangente tuba, qua nuntius ante
45 Iudicis adventu concussum terreat orbem,
tunc cum sinceros pastor discreverit agnos,
haedis disparibus diversa in parte locatis,
per medium dirimente chao, quod fluctibus implet
sulphureis volvens undosa incendia gurges,
50 flammarum stagnante lacu, quo fervida quondam

death. A brazen serpent will be suspended on a high stake, and though it makes a pretense of being poisoned, it will ac- 25 tually purge all poison and by its form will destroy the ancient serpent's power.

Meanwhile the Father was on his way over the soft turf of the verdant grove, taking in the dewy breezes in the clear air. Immediately the first couple, their hearing alert, recog- 30 nized the Lord's presence. They hated then the day's oppressive light and feared it as witness to the crime it revealed. Indeed if a chasm of yawning expanse were to open up before them or the earth suddenly to gape wide, in their fear they would have had no compunction about plunging headlong down, and if a sentence of death had been already 35 passed on them, in their eagerness to assuage their shame they would have seized on that course, they would have surrendered themselves to water or to flames, or in requital grasped a sword and with a merciless wound plunged it into their breasts. In this way, no sooner had they deserved it than the unhappy couple longed for death, though as yet 40 they had no experience of what it was.

These first days prefigure the end of time and foretell that there will be similar grief when the last age brings the decaying world to a close and a sudden lightning bolt lays everything waste to the clamor of the heavenly trumpet, with which at the Judge's arrival a herald will give forewarning, 45 inspiring fear in the stricken world. Then the shepherd will separate out the unblemished sheep, while setting aside in a different location their opposites, the goats, with a gulf between the two to keep them apart, a gulf that a sea of billowing waves of fire fills with its sulfurous swell, in a pooling 50 lake of flames like that with which a burning cloud over

dicitur attracto nubes Sodomitica nimbo
guttatim sparsum fudisse in crimina fulmen,
cum plueret nox taetra focos caeloque caducae
aera per calidum stillarent undique mortes.
55 Taliter ignifero missi de fonte gehennae
fluxerunt tristes aliena in saecula rivi.
At quem terribili Iudex decreverit hora
vivere post mortem poenaque ardere perenni,
subtrahet optato gravior sententia leto,
60 cumque foret melius dispersis corpora membris
carpere perpetuum dura sub morte soporem,
invitos tamen urna vomet, quis sola voluntas
rursus posse mori sensuque carere dolendi.
Sed sic accipiet ferventis flamma camini
65 ambustura suas, ut numquam finiat, escas.
   At primi interea iuvenes conamine casso
per deserta ruunt tutoque abscondita furto
facta putant, caecis optant latuisse tenebris.
Quid iuvat, infelix? Oculos a Iudice flectis,
70 te Iudex cernit. Nolis cur ipse videre,
cum videare palam? Solem non fuscat amoenum,
si depressa gravem formidant lumina lucem
debilis et sanum visus non sustinet orbem.
   Tum sic terribili primum Deus increpat ore
75 atque, ubi sit, miserum noscens interrogat Adam.
Qui trepidam pavido producens pectore vocem
vix haec pauca refert: "Tuus, O celsissime, terror
mentibus insidens latebram temptare coegit.

Sodom is said once to have punished sin from a looming storm cloud in a widespread downpour of lightning, when the acrid night rained fire and death fell everywhere from the sky in showers in the sweltering air. In the same way, streams flowing from the fiery font of hell have brought misery to generations of unbelievers. But for anyone who at that terrible hour the Judge decrees must go on living after death and burn in eternal punishment, that sentence will be all the heavier in depriving him of the death he longs for. Although it would be better for their bodies, with the dissolution of their limbs, to enjoy eternal sleep in the harsh conditions of death, yet the burial urn will spew them out against their will, when their only wish is to be able to die once more and be free from the feeling of pain. But instead the flames of a boiling-hot furnace will receive them to feed its fire, so that it never fails.

At first then the young couple made a futile attempt to take themselves off far away in solitude; they thought their actions would be safely concealed by this stratagem and wished to remain hidden in impenetrable darkness. But, wretch, what is the point? You may avert your eyes from the Judge, but the Judge sees you. Why avoid seeing when you are clearly seen? It does not darken the beauty of the sun if eyes look downward in fear of its oppressive light and if feeble vision cannot endure its wholesome orb.

Then God first rebuked the wretched Adam with his fearsome voice and asked him where he was, though he knew the answer full well. In response, though fearful in heart, Adam managed with a trembling voice to stammer out these few words: "Dread of you, most high one, possessed my spirit and compelled me to attempt concealment.

Nam quia nuda forent inopertis corpora membris,
80 erubui, fateor, caelumque per abdita fugi."
"Et quis," ait, "subitum concussit corde pudorem?
Visus et unde novus? Nam te nec vellera dudum
nec contexta prius velavit tegmine vestis.
Forma rudis proprio melius contenta decore
85 iudice se placuit, sed postquam foedere rupto
interdicta tuus perstrinxit germina gustus,
naturale tibi tegmen non sufficit unum
hactenus et nudis nunc denudata patescunt,
arguit obscenus quae turpia corpora motus."

90   Ille ubi convictum claro se lumine vidit
prodidit et totum discussio iusta reatum,
non prece submissa veniam pro crimine poscit,
non votis lacrimisve rogat nec vindice fletu
praecurrit meritam supplex confessio poenam.
95 Iamque miser factus nondum miserabilis ille est:
erigitur sensu tumidisque accensa querellis
fertur in insanas laxata superbia voces:
"Heu male perdendo mulier coniuncta marito,
quam sociam misero prima sub lege dedisti,
100 haec me consiliis vicit devicta sinistris,
haec sibi iam notum persuasit sumere pomum.
Ista mali caput est, crimen surrexit ab ista.
Credulus ipse fui, sed credere tu docuisti
conubium donans et dulcia vincula nectens.
105 Atque utinam felix quae quondam sola vigebat,
caelebs vita foret talis nec coniugis umquam
foedera sensisset comiti non subdita pravae."

For I was ashamed, I confess, because our bodies were naked, with limbs exposed, and so I fled from the sight of heaven to seek seclusion." To this God said, "Who roused in your heart this sudden sense of shame? Where did this new power of sight come from? You have not long worn skins; no woven garments cloaked you in the past. Your primal appearance, rightly content with its natural grace, was pleasing in its own judgment, but after the pact was broken and you tasted the forbidden fruit, nature's covering alone does not suffice and only now is the nakedness of your bodies apparent to you, when indecent impulses argue their shamefulness, though you were naked before this."

When Adam saw that he had been proved guilty in the clear light of day and a well-merited examination had revealed all his guilt, he did not seek pardon with suppliant prayers for his crime, nor petition with tears and with vows; no humble confession anticipated his well-deserved punishment with penitent weeping. Although he was piteous, he was not yet deserving of pity: he gave himself airs and, inflamed by an inflated sense of injustice, his arrogance was given full rein in flights of unrestrained language: "Alas, the woman joined to me in marriage has caused my utter ruin, the woman you gave me to my cost in your first dispensation to be my partner. Succumbing to evil counsel, she got the better of me; she it was who persuaded me to take the fruit whose effect she already knew. She is the source of the evil, the sinfulness derived from her. I was too trusting, but you taught me to trust with your gift of marriage and the sweet bonds you wove. If only the happy single life I once enjoyed alone still existed and that my life had never experienced the wedding compact in subjugation to a corrupt mate."

Hac igitur rigidi commotus mente Creator
maerentem celsis compellat vocibus Evam:
110 "Cur miserum labens traxisti in prona maritum
nec contenta tuo deceptrix femina casu
sublimi sensum iecisti ex arce virilem?"
Illa pudens tristique genas suffusa rubore
auctorem sceleris clamat decepta draconem,
115 qui pomum vetito persuasit tangere morsu.
Post haec finalem promit sententia legem
serpentemque reum prima sic voce notavit:
"Tu, coluber, cuius peccavit femina fraude
errorisque virum consortem reddidit ipsa,
120 propter utrumque reus pendes quod fecit uterque,
nec tibi sublimi constabit corpore vertex,
callida sed pronus per terram pectora volves,
utque fuga trepido sinuosa volumina currant,
non gressus, sed lapsus erit teque ipse sequeris
125 flexibus et spiras viventia vincula nectent.
Tum pro persuasa miserorum cordibus esca
tellurem captans pastu vesceris inani,
mensibus et certis supero depulsus ab orbe
inclusus terris communi sole carebis.
130 Inter cuncta replent quae nunc animantia mundum
auctor mortis eris, fies gravis omnibus horror.
Praecipue infelix mulier cum prole futura
sic inimicitias odio currente reponat,

The Creator, stirred by the impenitent Adam's senti-
ments, addressed the grieving Eve in heightened tones:
"Why in your fall did you drag your unhappy husband down   110
after you and, not satisfied with your own demise, but play-
ing the part of a deceitful woman, cast manly reason down
from its lofty seat?" She was mortified and ashamed; a blush
spread over her cheeks, and she declared that she was a vic-
tim of deceit and that the snake was the originator of her
sin, since he persuaded her to take a bite of the forbidden   115
fruit.

After this God's verdict pronounced a final decree, cen-
suring the guilt of the serpent in his first speech, as follows:
"You, snake, by whose treachery the woman fell into sin and
in turn caused her husband to share in her error, you are   120
guilty and will pay for both of the crimes the two of them
committed: your head will not be set on top of an upright
body, but flat on the earth you will slither on your cunning
belly, and to make sure your undulating coils move quickly
in flight when you are afraid, you will slide along, not walk;
your body will curve in pursuit of itself, and you will perma-   125
nently be confined to a writhing motion. Further, in retribu-
tion for the food that in swaying their hearts you persuaded
this unfortunate couple to eat, you will seek out and feed on
the earth with its meager subsistence, and in specific
months of the year you will be exiled from the world above
and imprisoned under the earth, will be deprived of the sun
that is common to all. Of all the creatures that now populate   130
the world you will be the bringer of death and will inspire
grave dread in all of them. In particular the unhappy woman
and all her future offspring are to establish such an enmity
with you, with a long-lasting hatred, that each successive

semina seminibus mandent ut vota nocendi.
135 Insistens semper pavidae sectabere calcem;
conterat illa caput victoremque ultima vincat."
    Post haec attonitam Iudex commotus in Evam:
"At tu, quae primam violasti femina legem,
accipe succiduum vitae quod restat in aevum.
140 Imperium patiere tori dominumque timebis
quem socium dederam; parebis subdita iussis
et curvata caput libitus assuesce viriles.
Moxque ubi concipiens fetum persenserit alvus,
ventris onus gemitu testaberis ac tibi clausum
145 anxia crescentem portabunt viscera fascem,
donec transacto fastidia tempore complens
naturale malum partu sub vindice pendas
producens vitam prolis; sic poena parentis.
Quid diversa loquar post iam discrimina matri?
150 Nam cum praeduro mulier confecta labore
optatam subolem tali produxeris ortu,
lugebis vacuos nonnumquam orbata dolores."
    Interea trepidus iam dudum sustinet Adam
quid sibi terribilis tandem sententia servet.
155 Cui Pater, "Attentis," inquit, "nunc auribus et tu
accipe quid mereare, levis quem femina vicit.
Impolluta prius pulchro sub germine tellus
non iam fida satis nec puro semine simplex

generation bequeaths to the next the desire to do you harm. You will always harass her, to her alarm, and keep close at   135
her heel, but she will crush your head and at the last will conquer her conqueror."

After this in his anger the Judge turned to the dumb-founded Eve: "As for you, the woman who first transgressed my law, listen to the kind of life that remains for you in the time to come. You will suffer domination in your marriage   140
and will fear as master the man I gave you to be your part-ner; you will obey him in subjection to his commands and with bowed head accommodate yourself to his masculine desires. Soon when your womb conceives and finds itself with child, with groans you will bear witness to the load in your belly, and your anguished flesh will carry a growing bur-   145
den enclosed within you, until, when the time has come and the weary wait is over, you suffer nature's travail with the punishment of childbirth, bringing forth life for your off-spring; such is the penalty of parenthood. And why should I go on to say that the trials of a mother are any different thereafter? For when as a woman, exhausted by the harsh   150
pangs of labor, you have brought forth the child you longed for in such a birth, often you will lose that child and lament that your suffering all was in vain."

Meanwhile for some time Adam was awaiting with trepi-dation what punishment the fearful sentence was keeping to the end for him. The Father said to him, "You too, listen   155
with keen attention now to the punishment you have earned for coming under the sway of a too-credulous woman. The earth that was previously unsullied, clothed in beautiful vegetation, no longer will be wholly true to you, nor in the now-corrupt world will it innocently display the vista it did

pristina monstrabit corruptum terga per orbem
160 exemploque tuo semper tibi terra rebellans
vepribus ac tribulis armata resistere discet.
Aut si frangenti cedens succumbet aratro
vomeris et fixo mordaci dente subacta est,
pinguia decipient mentito germine culta.
165 Nam pro triticeo lolium consurgere fructu
et fictas segetes vacuasque dolebis avenas.
Sic vix extortum producent iugera panem
sudore adsiduo nitens quem sumat egestas,
illecebramque cibi poenalis vindicet esca.
170 Aequalem brutis facient tibi pabula vitam
et simul herbarum sucos pastumque requirens
stercore consimili depressa gravabitur alvus.
Aerumnosa diu volvetur talibus aetas,
donec praescriptum ponant tibi saecula finem
175 et compacta luto solvantur tempore membra.
Limo formatus rursus redigeris in arvum.
Ante tamen proprium nati praecurrere letum
conspicies poenasque tuas in prole videbis,
ut metuenda magis cernatur mortis imago,
180 peccasse agnoscas quid sit, quid mortua fleri
quidve mori. Ac ne quid desit tibi forte malorum
quae castigandis corruptus parturit orbis,
acrior immenso miscebitur ira dolori.
Nam cum prima tibi producent tempora natos,
185 livor edax arto certabit limite mundi.
Nec iam sufficiet vacuus qua tenditur orbis
totaque germanis stringetur terra duobus.

before when its seed was unblemished, but following your   160
example it will continually rebel against you and, armed
with thorns and brambles, will learn to resist. Or if it yields
in submission to the plow that breaks through its surface
and is subdued by the penetrating and incisive bite of the
plowshare, its rich lands will cheat hopes with counterfeit
growth. For you will lament that instead of a crop of wheat   165
darnel will grow, and with it a sham harvest, stalks empty of
grain. In this way the bread your fields will produce will be
wrung with difficulty from the soil, and grinding poverty
will acquire it only by the continual sweat of the brow; food
will act as a punishment, requiting the allure your appetite
exerted on you. Your diet will make your life the equal of   170
brute beasts', and the stomach, in seeking nourishment
from the juices of plants, will be weighed down by a burden
of excrement as theirs is. Long will your life be plagued by
such woes, until succeeding ages bring it to a preordained
end and limbs compact of mud in time dissolve again.   175
Formed of clay, you will once more be reduced to tilth. But
before then you will see your son's death take place before
your own and observe in your own child the punishment you
incurred, so that the fearful specter of death will present it-
self more clearly to you, and you will recognize what it   180
means to sin, to weep for mortal things, and to die. And so
that you are spared none of the evils that the corrupt world
brings forth for those deserving of punishment, untold grief
will be mingled with still keener anger. For when first the
passage of time produces children for you, corrosive jeal-   185
ousy will compete over the reduced confines of the world.
No longer will the unpopulated extent of all the lands suf-
fice for them, and the whole earth will be too constrained

Alter in alterius consurget funera frater
telluremque novam cognato sanguine tinguet.
190 Exim posteritas varios passura labores
casibus in multis mortalia debita pendet,
dum veterem ductus dissolvat terminus orbem,
occidat omne vigens finisque redarguat orta."
Audierat motumque dedit conterrita tellus.
195   His Pater exactis haedorum pellibus ambos
induit et sancta paradisi ab sede reiecit.
Tum terris cecidere simul mundumque vacantem
intrant et celeri perlustrant omnia cursu.
Germinibus quamquam variis et gramine picta
200 et virides campos fontesque ac flumina monstrans,
illis foeda tamen species mundana putatur
post, Paradise, tuam; totum cernentibus horret
utque hominum mos est, plus quod cessavit amatur.
Angustatur humus strictumque gementibus orbem
205 terrarum finis non cernitur et tamen instat.
Squalet et ipse dies, causantur sole sub ipso
subductam lucem, caelo suspensa remoto
astra gemunt, tactusque prius vix cernitur axis.
  Tunc inter curas permixti felle doloris
210 affectus sensere novos et pectora pulsans
nondum compertas prorumpit fletus in undas
attentisque genis iniussus defluit umor.
Haud aliter vivax deceptus mole caduca
spiritus, impleto venit cum terminus aevo,

for a pair of brothers. One will rise up and murder the other and in so doing taint the new earth with family blood. Thereafter your descendants will suffer various hardships and pay the debt of mortality in repeated misfortunes, until the end comes and dissolves the aging world, when every living thing will die, and the last times convict all that has come into being." The earth had heard all this and trembled in terror.

After this the Father clothed them both in goatskins and cast them out of their blessed abode in paradise. Their fall took them both to a new land to enter an unpopulated world; there they rapidly surveyed all their surroundings. The appearance of that world, although it was colorfully adorned with various plants and grasses and presented to view green plains, springs, and rivers, yet seemed ugly to them in comparison with your beauty, Paradise; everything was repulsive in their sight and, as is human nature, what had gone was loved the more. The land closed in on them and in their grief at their reduced world the limits of earth, though not visible, seemed to press hard on them. Even the daylight itself was dimmed and, though the sun was out, they complained the light had been taken away; they lamented that the sky where the stars were hanging was now far removed and that the heavens, previously in their reach, were scarcely to be seen.

Then in their anxiety they felt new emotions of grief mixed with bitterness; tears burst from them in never-before-experienced floods, shaking them to the core, and, unbidden, moisture streamed down their now-receptive cheeks. No differently the living spirit, led astray by the transitory burden of the flesh, when its life is over and the

215 post obitum peccata dolet. Tum quidquid iniquum
gesserit in mentem revocat, tum paenitet omnis
errorum lapsus, semet quos iudice damnat,
et si praeteritae reddatur copia vitae,
sponte ferat quoscumque dabunt mandata labores.
220   Sanctus namque refert de quodam divite Lucas,
quem nimio luxu dissolvens vita fovebat.
Ipse coturnatus gemmis et fulgidus auro
serica bis coctis mutabat tegmina blattis.
Inde ut bacchantem suasissent tempora mensam,
225 currebant epulae totus quas porrigit orbis,
cumque peregrinus frugem misisset acervus,
fervebat priscum crystallo algente Falernum.
Vivida quin etiam miscebant cinnama turi
et suffita domus pingui fragrabat amomo.
230 Quod pelagus, quod terra creat, quod flumina gignunt,
certatim mensis cedentibus undique lassus
portabat pallens auri cum fasce minister.
Languidus ante fores pauper tunc forte iacebat
divitis obstrictis resoluto corpore membris
235 et supplex poscebat opem, non munera captans,
reliquias tantum sed si quas copia iecit,
has tunc opperiens alvus ieiuna rogabat.
Sed proclamanti dives non addidit aurem
nullaque languentem pietas respexit egenum,
240 nec quae completis cecidere superflua mensis
pauperis ad victum quisquam dedit. Insuper aegri
despicitur facies et putria vulneris horrent.
Cumque canes miti perlambant ulcera lingua

end has come, grieves after death for its sins. Then it calls to
mind whatever wrong it has done, then it regrets all its fail-
ings and errors, which as its own judge it condemns, and if
the opportunity were given to relive its past life, it would
readily endure all the hardships God's commandments en-
join.

The saintly Luke tells the story of a certain rich man
who reveled in a dissolute life of extreme luxury. His shoes
flashed with jewels, he shone with gold, and his silk gar-
ments were colored with purple, twice dyed. When the
moment called for a riotous feast, foodstuffs flocked to his
table from the whole world; and after such foreign bounty
had contributed its fruits, vintage Falernian began to spar-
kle in chill crystal goblets. Moreover, the strong scent of
cinnamon mingled with incense; the house had a fragrant
odor, perfumed with rich balsam. From every direction
weary attendants, pale with the weight of the gold platters
they were carrying, served on sagging tables all that sea and
earth create and rivers bring forth. At that time it so hap-
pened that a poor invalid was lying before the rich man's
doors, his limbs paralyzed and his body in a state of collapse.
Humbly he was begging for aid, but not looking for hand-
outs. His starving belly asked only to be allowed to wait for
any scraps that fell from the fine fare. But the rich man did
not lend an ear to these cries and without any compassion
showed no regard for the other's weakness and need; no one
gave the poor man the leftover food that had fallen from the
tables to eat when the courses were finished. What is more,
the appearance of the sick man aroused their disgust, and
they were repelled at his suppurating sores. When dogs,
showing greater sympathy, were gently licking his ulcers

blandior et fesso feritas medicabilis adsit,
245   sola hominum nescit mens semper dura moveri.
    Haec sed diversa penitus dum sorte geruntur,
impendens obitus pariter pulsavit utrumque
divite praevento, numquam qui credidit istud.
Optatam pauper longo vix tempore mortem
250   pervenit et victor morbos artusque relinquit.
Ille quidem, celsa qui dudum floruit arce,
fletibus ad tumulum stipato funere fertur
auratoque datur conditus membra sepulchro
et pretiosa tegunt elatum lintea marmor.
255   Spiritus abstruso sed mox demissus Averno
incidit aeternas per saeva incendia poenas.
E quarum medio sublimi sede locatum
haud procul (hoc certe censetur, nam procul inde
ut docet eventus) sinibus conspexit ovantem
260   Abrahae iusti mutatum in paupere vultum
nec eius similem, quem dudum luce receptum
quarto forte die vix quisquam largus humandi
ne per dispersum naturae lege cadaver
dira frequentatae contagia mitteret urbi,
265   obtectum laceris tenui velamine pannis
naribus astrictis nuda tellure locavit.
Angelicis manibus tunc in sublime levatus
iam dives, iam sanus erat: contraque superbi,
qui congesta tenens opibus diffluxerat amplis,
270   arida sic flammis mendicant guttura guttas:
"O Pater, electas animas qui sede beata

with their tongues and despite their fierceness bringing re- 245
lief to his weary state, only the minds of men, always hard-
hearted, were incapable of being moved.

While these two were experiencing such very different
circumstances, the threat of death struck both of them
down. The rich man was taken by surprise; he had never
given a thought to such a thing. But the poor man finally af- 250
ter a long struggle achieved the death he longed for and in
triumph quit his disease-ridden body. The first, it is true,
who had long enjoyed high status, was conducted to his
tomb to the accompaniment of weeping by a crowded cor-
tege, and his embalmed body was laid in a gilded sepulcher,
where precious linen draped the grand marble. But as soon 255
as his spirit descended to the depths of Avernus, in its cruel
fires he became subject to eternal punishment. In the midst
of that suffering, from not far away (at least it seemed so,
but actually far from there, as the outcome shows) he caught
sight of the poor man's changed visage, enthroned on high
and rejoicing in the bosom of Abraham the righteous, and 260
not at all like the one who, though recently received into
the light of God, even by the fourth day scarcely anyone
was ready to bury; it was only to prevent his corpse in the
natural process of decomposition spreading a terrible plague
through the populous city that someone, holding his breath, 265
set the body, shrouded in a thin covering of torn rags, in the
bare earth. But now he was raised up on high by the hands of
angels, now he was rich, now in full health; on the other
hand, for the proud man who had been awash with abun-
dant riches which he hoarded for himself, his throat, seared 270
by the flames, could only beg for drops of water with these
words: "O Father, who gather to yourself the souls of the

colligis ct mcritis dispensas praemia iustis,
haec ego non mereor, sed saltim deprecor unum,
Lazarus ut missus veniat digitoque levatum
275 afferat huc labris ardentibus inde liquorem
quique refrigerio, si non extinxerit omnes,
ad tempus saltem tantos vel mitiget aestus,
donec fessa brevi respirent membra quiete."
    Taliter immixto lacrimis stridore rogantem
280 magnanimus tandem compellat sic patriarcha:
"Desine iam seras in cassum fundere voces
et vacuas miscere preces. Haud talia dudum
dicta dabas, foribus cum te prandente iaceret
ipse ignotus, egens, aeger, ieiunus, inanis,
285 cum tua non caperet congestos mensa paratus
pauperis atque tuas non iret clamor ad aures.
Quapropter tandem librato examine veri
praeteritae vitae sortem deponis. Uterque
permutate vices. Et te iam sufficit amplis
290 exundasse bonis; laetetur fine malorum
qui doluit coeptis. Non est iam terminus ultra.
Insuper horrendo currit qui tramite limes
et chaos obiectum lato distinguit hiatu
non sinit abiunctas misceri foedere partes
295 accessumque negat, sic vobis semper ut istis."
    Ille gemens vanum repetita voce precatur:
"Si nil post obitum prodest commissa fateri
nec tua mutatur fixis sententia verbis,
hoc concede mihi, nulla quod lege vetatur.
300 Fratres quinque domo discedens luce reliqui.

chosen in your happy abode and reward the just as they de-
serve, rewards which I do not merit, I make this one plea at
least, that you dispatch Lazarus to come and bring water   275
from there on his finger to my burning lips here, for that will
bring relief and for a time at least lessen the intense heat, if
it cannot entirely extinguish it, while my weary limbs enjoy
a brief respite."

Finally, in response to these tearful pleas intermingled
with cries the noble patriarch answered as follows: "Stop   280
now—it's too late—making such futile speeches and min-
gling in them empty pleas. You said nothing like this in the
past, when, while you were feasting, this man was lying at
your door, unrecognized, needy, sick, hungry, and bereft,
when your board could not accommodate all the good   285
things piled on it, but the cries of the poor man did not
reach your ears. For that reason, now that your case has fi-
nally been weighed on the balance of truth, you are to give
up of the conditions of your past life. The two of you must
exchange your positions. It is enough for you now to have   290
once been rolling in great riches; let the one who initially
knew only pain rejoice at the end of his suffering. From
now on there is no endpoint for you. Moreover, there is a
dividing line, marking a fearsome trail, that cuts off hell's
abyss, demarcating it by a wide gulf. It does not permit the
separate regions to strike a pact and forever prevents all   295
interaction, for you as well as for those others."

Then with a groan the rich man began again to speak
with the following vain entreaty: "If it profits nothing to
confess one's sins after death, and your sentence, once irre-
vocably spoken, is not subject to change, grant me at least
this request, which no law forbids. When I departed the   300

His peto mittatur, qui vivos corrigat, ante
in tormenta cadant quam talia carne soluti.
Nam quamvis duro persistant corde rebelles,
si tamen obstructa quisquam de morte rediret,
305 credent experto poenasque intrare timebunt."
Ille quidem poscens effectum non capit ullum,
nos autem, dum vita manet, dum luce vigemus,
olim defuncti perterret nuntius Adam,
dum locus est flendi, dum non iniussa petuntur
310 nec obduratis pulsatur ianua serris.
    Novimus en cuncti quid primus planxerit ille
qui pulsus prisca nescivit sede reverti.
Namque obitum quendam casu tum pertulit ipso,
perdita ne precibus lacrimisve reduceret ullis.
315 Ex tunc paulatim retro sublapsa referri
vita prior coepitque malis laxata potestas.
Tum tristes morbi et varii subiere dolores
et corrupta satis dira pinguedine tellus
letali quaedam suffudit germina suco.
320 Inde truces saevire ferae dudumque timentes
excitat ad pugnam tum primum conscia virtus
reddit et armatas unguis, dens, ungula, cornu.
Ipsa etiam leges ruperunt tunc elementa
et violare fidem mortalibus omnia certant.
325 Inflatur ventis pelagus, volvuntur et undae,
excitusque novum turgescit pontus in aestum.
Tunc primum tectis taetra caligine caelis
ingratos hominum castigatura labores

light, I left five brothers at home. I request that someone be sent to them to reform them while they are still living, before they fall victim to torments like these when they take their leave from the flesh. For although their hearts are hardened and they continue to resist, yet if someone were to return from death's shuttered realm, they will believe him   305
because of his own experience, and they will fear to incur punishment." He, it is true, achieved no effect with his plea, but as for us, as long as life remains and we flourish in this light, the example of Adam, who died long ago, fills us with fear, while there still is an opportunity for weeping, provided that nothing forbidden is sought and the door that we   310
knock on is not barred fast.

To be sure, we all understand the grief he first felt who was expelled from his former abode and could no longer return. For by that fall he then endured a kind of death, in that neither by prayers nor tears could he win back what had been lost. From that moment the former way of life began   315
gradually to slip away and the power of evil to be released. Then grievous diseases and a host of different sorrows came on the scene; the earth, thoroughly tainted, with baneful fertility infused a deadly sap in certain plants. From then on   320
wild animals were savage and violent; then for the first time a sense of their strength roused them, long fearful, to battle, and claws, tooth, hoof, and horn supplied them with arms. Then also the very elements transgressed their covenant, and all of them vied to break faith with mortal humankind. The ocean was scoured by winds, waves began to roll and   325
surge, and the sea in its agitation was swollen with new billows. Then for the first time the sky was covered with lowering darkness, clouds poured hailstorms on the terrified

grandineos pavidis fuderunt nubila nimbos
330 atque polus discors invidit germina terris.
Quin magis ipsa sibi tellus adversa negavit
seminis excepti vertens mentita nitorem.
   Haec gemini primum senserunt tunc protoplasti.
Posteritas nam quanta ferat dispendia rerum,
335 non cui vel centum linguae vel ferrea vox est
enumerare queat, nec si quem Mantua misit
Maeoniusve canant diversa voce poetae.
Quis tales referat motus? Quis denique fando
evolvat totos, qui volvunt saecula, fluctus:
340 arma fremunt, crebra quatitur formidine mundus,
funditur irriguus sanguis maiorque sititur?
Quid dicam celsas praeclaris coetibus urbes
in deserta dari, populos populante rapina
dispergi et lacerum vacuari partibus orbem?
345 Servitio subdi dominos famulosque vicissim
praeferri dominis et belli sorte perire
sors generis claro quondam quos sanguine misit?
At si forte brevi requiescant tempore bella,
legibus armatas furere in certamina lites,
350 ius anceps pugnare foro, quo iurgia fratrum
non levius votis feriunt quam proelia telis?
Sed quis vota notet, clament cum facta nocentum?
Quis fraudes et furta gemat gaudente rapina?
Quisve minora fleat—stringi nec maxima possunt?
355 Inde minora tamen, si summis iuncta notentur,

people to thwart their unrewarding labors, and the hostile 330
heavens begrudged vegetation to the earth. What is more,
earth became its own enemy: deceitfully it refused to pro-
duce a splendid crop from the seed it had received by spoil-
ing it.

This was the first time that the original couple experi-
enced things like this. But not even if he had a hundred
tongues or a voice of steel could anyone list all the harm 335
later generations were to suffer; not even the poet from
Mantua or from Maeonia could do so, if they sang of that
subject in their different languages. Who could tell of such
convulsions? Who could recount in speech all the tides that
agitate the world from age to age: the clash of weapons, a 340
world shaken by recurrent fears, and streams of blood, with
a thirst for more to come? What need to mention glorious
cities with their famous inhabitants reduced to desolation,
or populations ravaged and scattered far and wide, a world
torn apart with whole regions a desert? Or masters becom- 345
ing subjects to slaves and slaves in turn being preferred to
their masters; those whom once the fortune of birth en-
dowed with brilliant ancestry now perishing in the fortunes
of war? But if perhaps wars for a brief period come to a
halt, then lawsuits flare into conflict with the laws as their
weapons, and disputes over rights are fought out in the fo- 350
rum, where quarrels between brothers deal no less telling
blows with their pleading than are dealt with weapons in
battle. But who would censure their pleas, when the deeds
of the guilty cry out? Who would bewail dishonesty and
theft when brigandage goes scot-free? Who would weep for
lesser crimes—not even the greatest ones can be checked?
But they are only lesser if judged by comparison with the 355

nam per se nullum facinus sub Iudice parvum est.
Nec refert cunctas percurri carmine causas.
Hoc parvo sermone loquar, post damna priorum
nil superesse mali, quod non vel perpetret orbis
360   vel toleret plenus scelerum pariterque laborum,
in casu discrimen habens et crimen in actu.
      Sed tu, Christe potens, cui semper parcere promptum est,
tu figulus massam potis es reparare caducam
et confracta diu resolutaque fingere vasa.
365   Qui dudum multo latitantem pulvere dragmam
invenis accensis verbi virtute lucernis.
Linquentem caulas turpique errore vagantem
pastor ovem celeri dignatus quaerere gressu
subvehis, utque suo gaudens reddatur ovili,
370   sarcina fit quae cura fuit. Sic filius ille
iunior, exhaustos postquam dispersit acervos
vitaque consumpto mutata est prodiga censu,
turpia porcorum digne convivia sectans
optavit siliquis compleri vilibus alvum,
375   donec saeva fames longo discrimine victum
cogeret offenso tandem se reddere patri
confessumque reum laxato crimine solvi.
Denique prostratum mitis pater allevat ultro
et trepidum blanda solatur voce pudorem.
380   Ornatus reduci vestis dat prima secundos
laetaque sollemnis celebrat convivia coetus,
quod rediviva suis quodam de funere proles

greatest, for no misdeed is small in itself in the eyes of the Judge. But it is pointless to enumerate in verse every single form of crime. In brief I will only say this, that after the first parents' punishment there was no wickedness that the world did not either perpetrate or permit, teeming as it was with wrongdoing and suffering, exposed to the perils of chance and disposed to evil in its actions.

But you, all-powerful Christ, who are always quick to show mercy, you have the power as a potter to repair fragile matter and reshape shattered vessels that have long been broken into pieces. You discover the coin, long deeply concealed in dust, by the light that is kindled with the power of your word. As a shepherd you take it upon yourself to seek out with all haste and take up in your arms the sheep that has wandered from its fold and strayed into wickedness; in order to return it happy to its sheep pen, you make your burden what was your concern. In the same way that younger son, after he wasted in extravagance his accumulated riches and his spendthrift life had suffered a change when his wealth was exhausted, deservedly shared the demeaning diet of pigs, seeking out coarse husks to fill his stomach, until merciless hunger compelled him to succumb to his protracted hardship and finally to return to the father he had offended, to confess his guilt, be forgiven his wrongdoing and be absolved. In fact, the gentle father, when his son fell before him, spontaneously lifted him to his feet and with soothing words allayed his hesitance and shame. On his return the finest of clothing arrayed him for the second time in splendid attire, and a festive company marked the occasion with a joyful celebratory banquet, because a son had risen up from a kind of death and returned to his own,

surgat et orbato redeant nova lumina patri.
At tu, praepollens hominum rerumque creator,
385   quamquam cuncta velis fidae constare saluti,
nulla tamen pateris nostrae dispendia mortis
nec quoquam pereunte tuis contingere damnum
divitiis poterit. Nescis decrescere, nescis
augeri et pleno perstat tibi gloria regno.
390   Sed famulis tu redde tuis quod perdidit Adam
quodque tulit primum vitiatae stirpis origo
ortu restituat melior iam vita secundo.
Sorduerit nimium lacero circumdata peplo
forma vetus; scissam ponens cum crimine vestem
395   pallia prima, Pater, redeunti porrige proli,
seminecem quondam miserans qui forte repertum
proiectumque via, quem saevi caede latrones
impositis cuncto spoliarant tegmine plagis.
Sed tu, sancte, viam sumpto dum corpore curris,
400   invenis allisum nec praeteris; insuper aegrum
iumento carnis propriae sub tecta reportas.
Nos fuimus quondam rabido data praeda furori,
sed si nunc medico percurrat vulnera fotu
gratia producens oleum, sapientia vinum,
405   commendet stabulo Samaritis dextera curam,
pelletur validus medicato corpore languor.
    Suscipe, qui non vis moriendi crescere causas,
quos confessa tibi gemitus pia pectora fundunt,
ut quondam tecum passae sub tempore carnis
410   proximus immani dependens stipite praedo,
quem non culpa tibi similem, sed poena tenebat.
Ille tamen nexus membris nec corde ligato,
etsi confixas clavis extendere palmas

bringing back to his bereaved father new light. In your case, however, all-powerful creator of the world and of human- 385 kind, although you desire that all things enjoy the assurance of salvation, yet you will suffer no loss at our death nor, if someone perishes, will your riches suffer any decrease at all. You are incapable of diminishing or of increasing; your glory endures forever in the fullness of your kingship.

But restore to your servants what Adam lost; let a better 390 life now bring back with a second birth what the origins of a corrupt race first took away. In the past man's figure was very mean in appearance, dressed only in a torn cloak; set aside this tattered clothing along with his sin and give your 395 returning offspring, Father, his first mantle again, as you once felt pity for a man you chanced on, half-dead, prostrate on the roadway, whom murderous robbers had beaten and stripped of all of his clothing. But you, holy one, as in human form you went on your way, came upon the maimed victim 400 and did not pass him by; what is more, you brought the injured man back to shelter on the pack animal that is your flesh. Once we were abandoned as prey for raging fury, but if now grace, bringing oil, and wisdom, bringing wine, tend our wounds with their healing balm, if the hand of the 405 Samaritan convey its patient to a lodging, our violent sick- ness will be dispelled and our bodies cured.

You who do not wish occasions for dying to multiply, give kindly hearing to the laments that righteous spirits pour forth in confession to you, as you did once in the case of the thief who hung next to you at the time of your body's pas- 410 sion on the cruel tree, sharing the same punishment as you, but unlike in his guilt. Though bound fast in his limbs, his heart was unconstrained, and though he could not reach out

non potuit, liber mentem cum voce tetendit.
415 Sicque reus scelerum, dum digna piacula pendit,
martyrium de morte rapit, cui fine sagaci
maxima cura fuit tales non perdere poenas.
Praeripuit scandens aditum caeloque levandus
ardua sublimi tenuit compendia saltu.
420 Porrige sic nobis celsam, Pater inclite, dextram.
Nos quoque perpetuae conquirat vita saluti
atque profanati deceptis fraude latronis
ceu tibi compasso miserans succurre latroni.
Livida quos hostis paradiso depulit ira,
425 fortior antiquae reddat tua gratia sedi.

his hands that were held fast by nails, he was free to reach
out his spirit and give it voice. In this way, despite the guilt   415
of his crimes, as he paid the penalty that was his due, he
seized hold of martyrdom by his death; showing good sense
at the last, it was his greatest concern not to let that punish-
ment he suffered go unrewarded. In his elevation he lay
claim to admittance to paradise; assured of mounting to
heaven, he secured profit on high with one bound to the
skies. In the same way, glorious Father, stretch out to us your   420
hand on high. Let life win us too for eternal salvation; show
pity and come to the aid of those deceived by the treachery
of the wicked robber, as you did for that robber who suf-
fered with you. May your grace prevail and restore to their
former abode those whom the enemy's jealous anger drove   425
out from paradise.

De diluvio mundi

Infectum quondam vitiis concordibus orbem
legitimumque nefas laxata morte piatum
diluvio repetam, sed non quo fabula mendax
victuros lapides mundum sparsisse per amplum
5   Deucaliona refert, durum genus unde resumpti
descendant homines cunctisque laboribus apti
saxea per duram monstrent primordia mentem,
sed veri compos fluctus nunc prosequar illos
per quos immissus rebus vix paene creatis
10   lactantem velox praevenit terminus orbem.
    Extulerat mortale genus crudelibus ausis
ingentes animos: licitum quod quisque liberet,
credidit et propria valuit pro lege voluntas.
Ius adeo nullum, sic nil distare putatum
15   fasque nefasque inter, recti custodia nusquam,
non iudex, non testis erat, non denique rector,
arbiter aut morum vel qui suaderet honestum,
sed princeps sibi quisque fuit virtute nocendi
nec meritis sed mole potens. Qui fortior esset,
20   hic melior sibimet, sed se censore, placebat.
Sic hominum vitam brutorum more tenebat
motibus addicens mens inclinata ferinis.
Sanguine potus erat, caesorum viscera passim
indomitis laceras praebebant faucibus escas.

The Flooding of the World

I will describe how the corrupt world, once united in wickedness with sin as its law, was purged by a flood and the death it let loose—but not in that flood when the lying tale declares Deucalion scattered over the expanse of the earth stones soon to receive life, because of which the restored 5
humanity from generation to generation is a hard race, well suited to every toil, and demonstrates its mineral origin by the hardness of its mind. Rather, in full knowledge of the truth, I will now recount that inundation by which a sudden end was imposed on a scarcely yet complete creation, to cut 10
short the world still in its infancy.

The mortal race had acquired an arrogant spirit in acts of savage recklessness; they believed that what anyone desired was permissible and that a person's will was his law. In fact, there was no justice, no distinction was recognized between 15
right and wrong, nowhere was proper behavior observed, there was no judge, no witness, in sum no director or arbiter of morals, or anyone to urge propriety, but everyone was a law to himself, deriving power not from his virtues but from his physical strength and capacity to do harm. The stronger anyone was, the better pleased he was, at least in his own 20
judgment. In this way their debased minds, in thrall to bestial emotions, constrained men to live in the manner of brute animals. Blood was their drink, the flesh of the slaughtered everywhere provided gobbets of food for their savage

25 Insuper et quadrupes, propria qui morte necatus,
saevior aut certe quem vincens bestia cepit,
pastus erat, quem nulla fides, lex nulla vetabat.
Ut vero pecorum ritu permissa voluptas
et diffusa palam ruptis lascivia frenis
30 luxuriaeque forum atque obsceni nundina mundi
fervuerit, casto fas non est dicere cantu.
Talibus ac tantis hominum gens improba gestis
silvestres animos naturae foedere rupto
induerat pulsaque simul ratione furebat
35 et deserta iacens Domini caelestis imago
omne decus mentis turpi deiecerat actu.
Haut secus ac pulchri cum fertilis area campi,
quam succisa dedit purgato robore silva,
dum colitur, iusto paret fecunda labori,
40 subicitur rastris, respondet frugibus ac se
servat composito ruralis gratia vultu.
Agricola oblitus si bracchia forte remisit
laxavitque manus fessoque quievit aratro,
pigrescit primum durato caespite tellus.
45 Mox rudibus ramis atque aspera palmite crebro
disciplinatos dissuescit promere fructus,
effundit frutices vacuos silvamque minatur,
quam si nec sera succisor falce repurget,
non iam virgultis sed denso stipite lucus
50 texitur et steriles diffundit in aera frondes,
donec conclusa ramis currentibus umbra

gullets. What is more, they fed on four-footed creatures 25
that had died a natural death or that some fiercer animal had
overcome and carried off, which no item of faith, no pro-
hibition yet forbade. In a modest song, however, it is not
proper to describe how they abandoned themselves to lust
in the manner of animals, and how wantonness openly pre-
vailed, bursting free of restraints, how their public spaces 30
seethed with luxury and their world was a frenzied market-
place of lust. By their many actions of this kind the sinful
race of men had transgressed the compact of nature and
taken on the character of the wild. Throwing off reason,
they surrendered themselves to madness. The image of our 35
heavenly Lord lay abandoned, all decent feeling discarded in
such vile behavior. In no different way, a fertile expanse of
fine flatland that has been cleared by cutting down a forest
and stripping away the tree trunks when cultivated responds
productively to the proper exercise of labor; it is mastered 40
by the hoe and provides a return in crops — the beauty of the
countryside is maintained by its well-ordered appearance.
But if the farmer negligently happens to slacken his physical
toil, to relax the work of his hands, and to take a rest from
the weary plow, the earth first grows unresponsive and the
soil hardens into clumps. Soon, as it becomes overgrown 45
with fresh branches and a multitude of suckers, it loses the
habit of bringing forth regular crops, throws up sterile
shrubs in abundance, and threatens to revert to forest. If a
woodcutter does not, however belatedly, clear it again with
his scythe, a copse grows up from what are no longer bushes
but densely interwoven tree trunks, spreading its unproduc- 50
tive foliage up into the air, until, when the branches run
together to enclose an area in shade, soon the welcome

mox opportunae depulso sole tenebrae
iam secura feras invitent credere lustra.
Taliter humani generis, non ordine recto
55 perdita mandatae iam post primordia legis
in pravum labens paulatim vita tetendit
proficiens peiore via, constantior ipso
iam paribus studiis nutriti criminis usu.
Et tamen auctorem vitii culpaeque magistrum
60 doctior errorum lapsuque peritior omni
succiduae prolis crescens audacia vicit.
  Ut fluvius parva primum diffusus ab urna
perspicuum leni promittit gurgite fontem,
tramite quem summo facili transmittere saltu
65 quisque potest, mox irriguo deductus ab ortu
viribus augetur subitis ripasque retrorsum
pellens crescentes tendit per plana liquores
occupat et spatium pereuntique imminet arvo,
tum circumfusos vicinis vallibus amnes
70 sorbet praeteriens externasque incipit undas
augmento finire suo mixtasque sub uno
nomine cum rasis diffuso gurgite terris,
cum trabibus stabulisque boum lustrisque ferarum,
saevior accessu longoque furore potitus,
75 tandem desistens pelagi transportat in undas;
hos inter motus similisque ad turbinis instar
humanum vitiis ibat genus. Et tamen ipsa
longior insanas mentes dissolverat aetas.
Centenos novies crebro cum duceret annos
80 vita tenax, tanto suspensi tempore leti
nullus terror erat. Sors si quem sera tulisset,

darkness, from which the sun is banished, attracts wild animals to believe there are now safe haunts for them there. In this fashion the life of the human race, on a wayward course after the first law that had been given them had already been transgressed, gradually degenerated into wickedness and, advancing onward on a still worse track, showed increasing persistence in the practice of the criminality that all nurtured now with equal intensity. And indeed the mounting boldness of this successor generation surpassed the originator of sin and the exemplar of guilt, being more refined in its wrongdoing and more versed in every crime.

It was like a stream that, issuing first from a small pitcher, sends out a clear spring with gentle current, which anyone can easily leap over at the beginning of its course; but soon, as it makes its way from the source of its waters, it is suddenly increased in strength and, expanding its banks, spreads its mounting waters over the flatlands, taking up more territory, and threatening to swamp the fields. Then in its course it absorbs rivers that flow on either side of it in neighboring valleys and begins to encompass in its enlargement waters not its own, combining them in its widespread flood under a single name, and with them the devastated land, the timber, cattle stalls, and the haunts of wild beasts. As it proceeds it increases in violence, acquiring a far-reaching fury, until finally brought to a halt when it empties into the sea's waves. In a progression like this, like an irresistible flood, the human race advanced in sin. What is more, their very length of life had reduced their minds to madness. Since life for them endured, frequently lasting nine hundred years, they felt no fear of death, postponed as it was for so long a time. If belatedly fate did carry anyone

ceu qui nec natus fuerit numquamque levandus
morte putabatur. Sic cunctis nulla futuri
spes inerat solusque sibi fundaverat omnem
85   sensibus in caecis periturum mundus amorem.
    Tempore quin etiam peccatrix terra sub ipso
nutribat saevos, immania monstra, gigantes,
nec tamen effari licitum quo semine cretos.
Communem cunctis ortum de matre ferebant,
90   qui genus, unde patres, prohibent arcana fateri.
Si speciem quaeras, humani corporis illis
plus vultus quam forma fuit; sic linea membris
conveniens hominem monstrabat, dissona molem.
Quam propter deinceps commentis Graecia fictis
95   dedecus infandum massis informibus auxit
et portentosis descripsit corpora membris:
pube tenus quod forma viris, cum corporis ima
supplerent vasto mixti pro crure dracones,
artus semihominum patulis qui faucibus atri
100   ferrent et verso praeberent vertice gressus.
Tunc etiam solitos iusso terrore Tonanti
blasphemis caelo convicia mittere plantis
mordacesque pedes moto fremuisse veneno.
Hos similis mendax Phlegraei fabula belli
105   excussas finxit iecisse per aera rupes,
pro telis spatiosa manus quod turbine montes
sparserit et missis caelum quassaverit arvis.
    Haec sunt priscorum quae de terrore gigantum
carmine mentito Grai cecinere poetae.

off, he was thought of as someone who had never been born and so never subject to being taken off by death. So no one held out any expectations for the future, and in their blind delusion this world alone formed the basis for all their de- 85
sires.

What is more, at this time earth in its sinfulness gave nurture to cruel giants, huge monsters of whom no one can say from what seed they arose. The story was they were all born from a common mother, but the obscurity of their ori- 90
gins prevents determining what their ancestry was and what their paternity. If you ask what species they were, they possessed the appearance of a human body rather than its physique; they conformed in the outline of their limbs to and gave the appearance of humans, but differed in their bulk. For this reason, subsequently Greece in its lying fictions ex- 95
aggerated with grotesque shapes this monstrous deformity and told of bodies with freakish limbs: as far as the groin they were shaped like men, while to serve as massive legs black snakes conjoined made up the lower part of the body and supported the hybrid humans' limbs, with gaping jaws and downturned heads imparting movement. Then too, it is 100
said, with a natural urge to terrorize they were accustomed to hurl insults heavenwards against the high Thunderer from their sacrilegious feet, which hissed aggressively as their venom was aroused. A similar lying tale about the Phlegrean war claimed that the giants tore crags from the 105
ground and tossed them through the air, and that their huge hands in place of weapons launched mountains in spiraling flight and shook the heavens with whole fields as missiles.

Such are the stories about the terror the ancient race of giants inspired, that Greek poets gave voice to in lying song.

110 Et tamen audaci voluit contendere pugna
quisque rebellis erat. Qui cum confligere telis
non potuit, saevis concepit proelia votis.
Montibus impositos fas non est credere montes,
hoc tamen et deinceps illos temptasse putabo,
115 qui coctos lateres lentoque bitumine iunctos
in sublime rati manibus sic posse superbis
sustolli et celsas in sidera surgere moles,
cum fureret mortale genus cassoque labore
irrita transcensis caementa inferret in altum
120 nubibus et refugum sequeretur machina caelum,
non prius absistens, subitas discordia linguas
quam daret et varius confunderet omnia sermo.
    Hinc sparsum foedus, scissa sic lege loquendi
consensum scelerum turbata superbia rupit,
125 dum se quisque suis possit quem noscere verbis
aggregat atque novas sequitur gens quaeque loquellas.
Sic interruptae perierunt culmina massae
effectuque carens cessavit in aethere turris.
Haec post Diluvium. Nam quantas tempore prisco
130 pressa giganteas tellus produxerit arces
atque lacessitis contemptum miserit astris,
abstergente Deo sat nostra silentia damnent.
    Cernebat patiens iam dudum insana frementes
terrarum populos hominum rerumque creator

Yet in reality all who were rebellious in spirit did want to engage in a venturesome conflict, but because they could not fight with weapons, their aggression found expression in their unbridled desires. It is wrong to imagine that mountains were piled on mountains. Instead I will contend that the men who subsequently attempted this were those who thought that baked bricks with a binding of viscous pitch could be raised up on high by their arrogant handiwork in a similar way, and that their lofty construction could rise to the stars, at the time when the race of mortals, in the grip of a passion, was with unavailing labor fruitlessly piling rubble up beyond the clouds and pursuing with the edifice they built the retreating heavens, only abandoning their endeavor when disharmony suddenly produced multiple languages, and the variety of tongues threw everything into confusion.

Because of this a compact was dissolved and, when conformity of speech was broken in this way, the proud were thrown into confusion and cast off their unanimity in crime, since everyone allied himself to whoever he could understand in his own language, and each nation adopted new ways of speaking. In this way the massive construction was broken off, and its high turrets came to nothing; the tower stopped in midair without being completed. All this was after the Flood. Let it be enough, however, that we condemn with our silence all the strongholds of the giants that the oppressed earth gave rise to in former times and built up in scornful challenge to the stars, since God has washed them away.

For a long time already the creator of mankind and all nature was watching the mad frenzy of the peoples of earth,

135 expectans, si quem vani consortia mundi
     linquentem melior moneat resipiscere cura.
     Sed coniuratus postquam percurrere coeptum
     perditionis iter statuit sensumque per omnem
     obtinuit victor peccati insignia mundus
140 nec revocare gradum quisquam gressumque referre
     praecipiti iam mente potest, exhorruit Auctor
     paenituitque videns totum, quod fecerit, orbem.
     Tum tales tonuisse minas commotus ab alto
     fertur et excitas laxasse his vocibus iras:
145 "O nullis attracta bonis nullisque repressa
     legibus, antiquo tantum submissa draconi
     effera gens hominum, ducto corruptior aevo,
     non Evam cecidisse sat est, transcenditur omni
     inventor leti lapsu, nec sufficit illud,
150 vicit inexpertum quod serpens pristinus Adam.
     Non contenta suo foedari vita parente
     affectat mortem propria virtute mereri.
     Expectasse diu non profuit. Insuper omne
     concessum veniae rapuerunt crimina tempus.
155 Iam nimium longas patientia presserit iras,
     vindictae iam tempus adest. Non fulmina caelo
     flammeus ardor aget vasto nec cedet hiatu
     quae premitur nimio succumbens terra tumultu,
     sed sordens vitiis fluctu delebitur orbis.
160 Ad chaos antiquum species mundana recurrat
     inque suas redeant undarum pondera sedes.
     Arida decedat lymphis rursusque sepultas
     terrarum facies informis contegat umor.
     Haec clades vivis carnique hic terminus esto."

waiting to see if a better intent prompted anyone to come to   135
his senses and abandon all part in the vanity of the world.
But after that world in sworn unity decided to pursue the
path to destruction on which it was already set and trium-
phantly adopted in every one of its senses the hallmark of
sin, when no one could move back from the brink or take a   140
backward step, so impetuous then was their spirit, the Cre-
ator was horrorstruck at the sight and regretted the entire
world he had brought into being. Then, deeply moved, he is
said to have thundered out these threatening words from on
high and given vent to the anger aroused in him with the fol-
lowing speech: "O savage human race, devoted to nothing   145
that is good and constrained by no law, subject only to the
ancient snake and growing more corrupt with the passing of
time, it is not enough for you that Eve has fallen—the dis-
coverer of death is outdone in your every crime—nor does   150
the victory of the serpent of old over the unschooled Adam
suffice for you. Life, not satisfied with being degraded by its
own ancestor, aspires to earn death on its own account.
Nothing has been gained by a long delay. What is more,
criminality has appropriated for itself the time I had al-
lowed for forgiveness. Already for too long patience has sup-   155
pressed my anger; now the time for punishment is at hand.
No fiery bolts will propel lightning through the vast expanse
of the sky, nor will the earth give way and gape asunder, as-
sailed by the earthquake's loud crash, but the world, defiled
by sin, will be destroyed by a flood. Let the aspect of the   160
world revert to ancient chaos and the weight of the waves
resume their former location. Let dry land give way to wa-
ters and unsightly liquid cover the face of the earth to bury
it once more. Let this bring destruction for the living and

165 Sic Pater aeternus disponens funera rerum
diluvium dextra terras vibrabat in omnes.
　　 Interea pleno vivebat iustus in orbe
unus homo et mentem solus servabat honestam.
Nullus vota Deo donis precibusque ferebat
170 hunc praeter, dignum quem summus laude Creator
nosset et exceptum vitae servare pararet.
Stemmatis hic sancti, nam claro nobilis ibat
a proavo, quem prisca fides et conscia virtus
in caelum sine morte tulit; sic celsa petenti
175 successit magno non impar pronepos actu.
Nec plus est illum salvi cum corporis usu
terrenas liquisse domus, intrasse supernas.
Denique quo priscus quondam conscenderat Enoch,
Helias curru post tempora longa secutus
180 scribitur ignitis scandens penetrasse quadrigis,
cum suspensa leves transmitteret orbita ventos
ungula vel premeret calcatas pondere nubes
vallatumque ferens sanctum non ureret ignis
et motus servans nesciret flamma calorem.
185 Hos igitur satis est caelum potuisse mereri
membrorum sub lege sitos, sed non tamen illud
segnius admirer, sancti quod tempora Noe
unius ob meritum natis nuribusque tuendis
orbis in exitio potuerunt ferre salutem.
190 　　 Est ille in caelis numero praestantior omni
angelicus sine fine chorus, qui laude perenni

the end of all flesh." With these words the eternal Father 165
prescribed death for the world and brandished with his right
hand a flood to envelop the whole earth.

At that time there lived but one just man in the entire
world, and one person alone preserved a virtuous mind. No
one made vows to God with offerings and prayers apart 170
from him. The supreme Creator knew him to be deserving
of honor and was preparing to take him into his care and
keep him alive. He was of sanctified ancestry, for he was
nobly descended from a distinguished great-grandfather,
whom traditional faith and regard for virtue carried to
heaven without experiencing death; the great-grandson by 175
his glorious deeds was no unworthy successor to a man who
ascended on high in this way. Nor is his a greater deed, in
quitting the terrestrial abode and entering the celestial with
body still intact. Indeed Elijah is described as following by
chariot a long time later where ancient Enoch had once as-
cended, breaking through to heaven borne by a fiery four- 180
horse team, as his path through the air navigated the light
breezes and the horses' hooves trampled underfoot the
clouds. That fire bore the holy man upward but failed to
burn him—such was his protection—and its flames, as they
continued to carry him forward, were devoid of heat. And 185
so, though it is noteworthy that these men could earn a way
to heaven while still subject to the law of the body, I am not
any less inclined to marvel at the fact that in the times of the
holy man Noah that one man by his merit was able to pro-
tect his sons and daughters-in-law and to secure salvation in
the face of the world's destruction.

In heaven there exists that everlasting choir of angels, 190
exceeding all number, that acclaims and extols God with

conclamat celebratque Deum famulantia suetus
ferre ministeria et iussis parere supernis.
Hi nunc, quod rectum mortalia corda precantur,
195 concipitur dignis sancto quod pectore votis,
quidquid larga manus collectis sparsit egenis,
excipiunt sanctoque ferunt super astra volatu.
Quin etiam iustos, fragilis dum vita fatigat,
tutantur mundique inter discrimina servant.
200 Sed tamen in cunctis praecellit clarior ille,
maxima quaeque Dei quo dispensante ministro
res geritur summisque parat mysteria causis.
Hic dominum caeli venturum corpore sumpto
virginis intactam iussus praedixit in alvum
205 sacraque dotali complevit viscera verbo.
Hic et Baptistae praecurrens nuntius ortum,
desperata diu dum ferret germina patri,
inter sacra virum conterruit et dubitantes
protinus ingrato restrinxit in ore loquellas,
210 donec praedicto fecundam redderet ortu
prolis anum, multos sterilis quae tenta per annos
fudit diffidens effeta puerpera fetum.
  Hic rerum sollers summusque archangelus alto
aera per liquidum levibus circumdatus auris
215 vibratasque movens ignito in corpore pinnas
nulli conspectis ad terram motibus ibat
et tum forte gemens cunctorum crimina Noe
inflexis stratus genibus cum supplice planctu
mundanis veniam mundo nolente petebat,
220 cum subito clausis foribus tunc aliger intrat

perpetual praise, dedicated to paying him devoted service
and to obeying his high commands. In the present day they
take up the righteous prayers of mortal hearts, the virtuous   195
vows conceived in pious breasts, and all that generous giving
has distributed among the assembled poor, and carry them
in devoted flight beyond the stars. And further, they protect
the just when the frailty of life oppresses them and preserve
them among the perils of the world. But yet there is one   200
that stands out among them all, who serves as God's agent
for all his most important actions and for the divine myster-
ies those actions impart in affairs of greatest moment. He it
was who was bidden to prophesy that the lord of heaven
would take on bodily form and enter the unsullied belly of a
virgin, and who with his words as wedding gift brought full-   205
ness to her holy womb. He too as a messenger presaged the
birth of the Baptist, when he brought to a father long aban-
doned hope of offspring. He filled that man with fear while
he was performing his sacred office, and when the priest ex-
pressed his doubts in ungrateful speech, immediately ren-
dered him silent, to remain so until the birth of the pre-   210
dicted child showed the priest's aged wife to be fertile; a
woman who remained barren for many years, worn with age,
against expectation in labor gave birth to a baby.

This archangel, who was supremely skilled and of the
first rank in heaven, passed to earth through the clear air
enveloped in gentle breezes, the wings beating on his body   215
of fire, his movements observed by no one. It happened
at that time that Noah, grief-stricken at the crimes of all
humankind, was begging on bended knee with urgent la-
ment for pardon for the inhabitants of the world, though
the world wanted none of it, when suddenly then that   220

conspicuus claro resplendens nuntius ore.
Horrescit visu tanto perterritus heros
mortalisque oculus personam ferre supernam
vix valet et pavidi detorquent lumina vultus.
225   Ille salutiferis primum mulcere timentem
aggrediens verbis caeli mandata ferebat:
"Pax tibi, iuste virum, pacem tibi missus ab alto
imprecor, ut pulso capias mea dicta pavore.
Haec mandat summus terrae pelagique creator.
230 Insperata quidem cunctis sententia leti
imminet; hanc solus sed qui transire mereris
et praescire potes. Nam te calcata voluptas
iam pridem rectum toto discrevit ab orbe.
Unica sed quoniam saevum depellere letum
235 vita tibi poterit, tantos evadere casus
qualiter incipias, paucis ex ordine fabor.
Finis erit rerum permissis undique lymphis
atque relaxata vastabitur orbis abysso.
Nunc age, congestis crescat fortissima lignis
240 machina, quae surgens fluctus superenatet omnes.
Tercentum cubitos per longum ducta tenebit,
bis quinis lato claudatur bisque vicenis,
in triginta illi constabit culminis altum;
per medium pariter longo cenacula tractu
245 edita suspensis domibus tabulata levabunt,
ut generis proprii servans consortia mansor
componat partis discreta cubilia cellis.

resplendent winged messenger, clear to view, with radiant countenance, entered before him, though the doors were all shut. At such a sight the heroic man was terrified, and a tremor passed through his body; his mortal eyes could scarcely endure the sight of the heavenly figure; his face in fear averted its gaze.

The angel then conveyed the orders of heaven, first try- 225
ing to allay Noah's fears with words that promised salvation: "Peace upon you, just among men; I am sent from on high and wish only peace for you, so banish your fear and take in my words. These are the orders of the almighty creator of earth and sea. A sentence of death is hanging over everyone, 230
unsuspected though it be; only you have earned the right to survive it and to be able to know of it in advance, for by treading pleasure underfoot you have long since been set apart from the whole world as a virtuous man. Seeing that your life alone will be able to repel cruel death, I will tell you 235
briefly in detail how to set about escaping so great a disaster. With it will come the end of the world; everywhere the waters will be given free rein and the earth will be wiped out with the release of the abyss. So come then, let a craft be built of the strongest wooden construction to rise on the 240
waters and to sail over the whole flood. It is to measure three hundred cubits in length, its breadth shall be encompassed in twice-five and twice-twenty cubits, and its top shall amount to thirty cubits in height. Inside are to be decks, all of some length, that support elevated stories with 245
cabins erected in them so that their occupants may continue to keep company with their own kind and maintain their quarters separate in the rooms created for them.

Tum ne rimosi compagum forte meatus
accipiant inimicum imbrem, linire memento
250 iuncturas laterum pigrumque infunde bitumen.
    "Taliter effectam cum consummaveris aedem,
protinus ingredere ac mundum dimitte cadentem;
exclusit quem culpa frequens, includere vita
incipiat circumque fremant te sospite mortes.
255 Quin etiam lateris sociam succedere tecto
et cum coniugibus natos intrare iubebo.
Tuque secundus eris deleti germinis auctor,
ut te post primum repleatur terra parente.
Sed quia perfecto divinis viribus orbe,
260 post operis finem, post leges postque sacrata
Sabbata formari quidquam non convenit ultra,
ne penitus cessans intercidat omne creatum,
spirantum e cunctis pecorum celerumque volucrum
silvarumque feris et quae iumenta vocantur
265 vel quae per tacitos reptant labentia motus,
bina cape et tecum claustro victura reconde,
sic tamen, ut proprios teneant sua vincula sexus,
unde genus rursum tellus implenda resumat.
    "Nec timeas ne forte feros animantia motus
270 servent aut solitis praesumant rictibus iras.
Foedus erit totis quae discordantia profert
per varios natura modos, et pace fideli
parebit iussis quidquid concluseris illic.

Further, so that the series of joints not split open and take in
water dangerously, take care to coat the joins in the hull and   250
smear them thickly with glutinous pitch.

"When you have completed the construction according
to these precepts, immediately go on board and leave be-
hind you the failing world; its mass wickedness has set you
apart, now let life begin to take you in as its own; let deaths
rage around you, while you remain unscathed. Further, I bid   255
you have the partner of your side, your wife, come under the
protection of your roof and your sons enter there too along
with their spouses. You will be the second author of the
doomed human race in that the earth will be repopulated
with you as parent, succeeding the first author Adam. But
since the world was brought to completion by God's power,
after the end of his labors, after the establishment of his   260
laws, and the sanctification of the Sabbath, nothing more
can properly be created afresh. So, lest all creation fail en-
tirely and collapse, take two of all domesticated creatures
and swift-winged birds that live and breathe, two of all wild
animals and of beasts of burden, as they are called, and two   265
of all the reptiles that silently slither along, and shut them
up with you within the hold to save their lives. But do this in
such a way that each sex is subject to the impulses proper to
it, so that in the earth that must be replenished breeding
will once again resume.

"Have no fear either that these animals will persist in
their savage emotions or with their accustomed snarls act   270
out their anger. There will be a pact between all creatures
whom nature makes in various ways in conflict with each
other, and every animal you enclose there will faithfully give
heed to your commands and keep the peace. Only one thing

Serpentis tantum semper figmenta caveto.
275 Vertice submisso blandum licet ille trisulcis
finxerit abscondens per dulcia sibila linguis
immortale odium, numquam tu credulus illi,
quem nimis expertus vitandum praemonet Adam.
Hostis namque semel voluit quicumque nocere,
280 hic semper suspectus erit penitusque cavendum est,
ne iam mentito coniungat foedera prudens.
Tu post exemplum iussis servire memento."
    Haec fatus vacuum levibus secat aera pinnis
mortalem fugiens aciem caeloque relatus
285 heroem trepidum mandata lege reliquit.
Ipse tamen tali manibus cum voce levatis:
"Quisquis," ait, "nobis tantam spondere salutem
seu missus seu sponte tua super aethere celso
venisti et placidum sacrasti foedere pactum,
290 sis fautor firmentque tuas promissa loquellas
auxiliumque tuum conatibus insere nostris,
ut tenuis tantam valeat manus edere molem."
His breviter dictis vitae spem corde reponit
aggrediturque celer sacri praecepta laboris.
295   Quis tantus capiat sensus, quis denique sermo
explicet advectis fuerit quae copia lignis!
Nudati colles, spoliatae robore silvae,
mons ut quisque fuit famulo placuere paratu:
Pelion immensas committit vertice quercus,
300 insuper exponit multa virtute recisum
Ossa nemus Pindoque abies subducitur alta.
Atlans ipse novas ictu resonante secures

more: be constantly on guard against the deceitfulness of the serpent. Though with lowered head it pretends to be friendly, concealing its everlasting hatred with coaxing hisses from its three-forked tongue, never put any trust in it; Adam, from bitter experience, counsels you to shun it. For any enemy who has once intended harm will always be an object of suspicion, and great care must be taken to prudently avoid entering into an alliance with an already proven deceiver. After this cautionary tale be sure to follow my directions."

With these words the angel, quitting mortal sight, parted the empty air on nimble wings and was carried up again to heaven, leaving the hero Noah behind, apprehensive at the mandate he had been given. Yet with hands upraised he spoke as follows: "Whoever you are who have come to promise such wonderful salvation to me and have sealed with a covenant this sacred pact of peace, whether you were sent by another or come of your own accord as an emissary from high heaven, show favor to me; let the events you have promised affirm the truth of your words, lend your aid to my endeavors, so that my feeble hand can build so vast a structure." With these few words he laid up hope in his heart for life and swiftly set about the sacred task as instructed.

What mind has the power to conceive, what speech to express the abundance of timber that was brought to that place! Hills were laid bare, forests stripped of their trees, every single mountain courted favor by offering up its materials: Pelion furnished immense oaks from its summit, Ossa contributed a whole forest felled with great vigor, while from Pindus lofty stands of fir trees were transported away. Atlas itself felt unfamiliar ax strokes, echoing with the

sensit et annosas dedit ad navalia pinus.
Invictum tunc surgit opus, contexta levatur
305   porrectis trabibus praecelsi culminis aedes.
      Haec inter discors varii sententia vulgi.
Nam multi lymphis obstacula tanta parantem
irrisere virum, moles quod clausa moveri
fluminibusque dari nequeat, quam forte vel ampli
310   Euphrates Nilusque queant vix claudere ripis.
Humani generis quid mens incredula reris
mortalem non posse manum coniungere ponto
aedem longinquam? Pontus namque obvius ultro
curret et adductum tanget stans fabrica litus.
315   Ast alios celsam compacto robore massam,
ignaros quamquam cladis causaeque latentis,
mirari novitas et formidare coegit.
      Haut aliter studium iam tunc diviserat omnes,
quam nunc mundus habet. Sunt qui compuncta fideli
320   corda dicant operi rebusque instare supremum
discrimen norunt, corpus quo concidat omne
bacchatamque diu consumant saecula carnem.
Effugiet tunc ille malum quicumque paratus
construat ut validam praeduri tegminis arcam.
325   Per lignum vitale crucis servatus ab undis
tunc cernet quanto contempserit otia fructu.
      Haut procul attentum contemplans hunc operantem
nonne piger quisquam lucri taedensque laboris
insanire putet, cura quod solus inani

blows, to provide for the shipbuilding long-lived pines.
Then the invincible structure began to grow, and the edifice,   305
built of long timber beams, surged up to a towering height.

While this was happening, a variety of people's opinions
were at odds. Many mocked Noah for building so large a de-
fense against the waters, a massive enclosed structure that
could neither be moved nor launched on any rivers and that
even the Euphrates and Nile in full flood could hardly en-   310
compass within their banks. Oh why, human mind, are you
skeptical, why do you doubt that a mortal hand can bring
that edifice, however far away it may be, into contact with
the sea? In reality, in fact, the sea will spontaneously hurry
to meet it, and while still stationary its timbers will touch
the shore that has advanced toward them. For others, how-   315
ever, although they were ignorant of the disaster to come,
and the reason for the craft's building was concealed from
them, its strangeness inspired wonder and fear at its tower-
ing bulk and solid construction.

Strong feelings had already caused division among every-
one then, just as is the case in the present-day world. There
are some now who dedicate their devout hearts to acts of   320
faith in full knowledge that an ultimate peril threatens the
world, in which every body will fail and the ages will bring to
an end the long riot of the flesh. At that time all who build
themselves a strong ark as impenetrable protection will es-
cape such suffering. Preserved from the waters by the life-   325
giving wood of the cross, they will then see how much they
profited by scorning idleness.

Would not anyone who was remiss in pursuing his own
gain and impatient of toil, when he saw at no great distance
this man so hard at work, think him mad because he alone

330 aestuet et rebus nolit pereuntibus uti?
Sic epulans parcum, sic largum quisquis avarus,
sic nudum raptor, sic castum ridet adulter,
sic circumscribens illuso simplice gaudet.
Desipuisse dolet dives, cum congregat aurum,
335 spargentem nummos ultroque in paupere censu
consumptis opibus miserum re speque beatum.
    Inde repentinum Iudex cum cerneret orbi
adventare diem: "Finis sic protinus," inquit,
"imminet, ut iusti quondam sub tempore Noe,
340 diluvium varios mundi cum repperit actus
et carnem consumpsit aquis opifexque salutis
evasit parto diffusa pericula claustro."
Haec evangelicis sunt inclamata figuris.
    Providus interea consummat conditor arcam.
345 Tum iussae accurrunt volucres, tum bestia quaeque
consuetum linquens silvoso tegmine lustrum
deposita feritate venit seseque tenendam
ingerit occurrens et libertate relicta
includi gaudet. Tantum secreta futuri
350 vis valet. Occultus brutis in sensibus ardet
terror et expectans agitat formidine vita.
Ast homines, quos sors certi discriminis urget,
vicina nec morte pavent. Satis undique constat
vitali indicio praecedere saepe timorem.

was obsessed with unprofitable cares and unready to enjoy 330
the transient material world? In the same way the gourmand
mocks the frugal, all misers the generous, the thief the de-
spoiled, and the adulterer the chaste; in the same way the
cheat rejoices at tricking the innocent. The rich man, as he
amasses his gold, deplores the folly of the person who gives 335
his money away and spontaneously exhausts his wealth to
become poor, though that person, however materially im-
poverished, is rich in expectation.

When the Judge sees the last day for the world is immedi-
ately approaching, he will say, "The end is close at hand, as in
the past in the time of Noah the just, when a flood overtook 340
the various activities of the world and consumed all flesh in
the waters, with only the author of salvation escaping the
widespread disaster in the stronghold he had secured." This
message the gospels proclaim in figural language.

Meanwhile its farsighted architect completed the con-
struction of the ark. Then on command birds flocked to- 345
ward it, and animals of every kind, leaving their customary
haunts in the woodland cover and abandoning their fierce
nature, added their numbers; hastening forward, they pre-
sented themselves for enclosure and rejoiced to abandon
their freedom for caging. So powerful was the unseen force
of what was to come. In the senses of brute beasts invisible 350
terror flared up; in apprehension for the future their lives
were prey to fear. But humans, when the risk of certain dan-
ger threatened them, felt no fear, though death was already
at hand. Yet fear, as is widely established, often provides a
saving premonitory sign.

355 Securos laetosque reos tellure Gomorrae
iam prope sub flammis sententia dicta videbat.
Ninivae contra populis terrore salubri
praevaluit pro pace metus. Nam venerat istic
iussus multum ille et terris iactatus et alto,
360 qui clamaturus tantae discrimina plebi
diluvium timuit mundo constante propheta.
Hauserat hunc valido pervadens belua rictu
immersumque mari ventris concluserat arca.
Degluttire virum faucesque implere capaces
365 ardenti monstro cum sit permissa potestas,
non licuit mordere tamen; nil dentibus actum.
Intravit cupidum deludens praeda vorantem
invasusque cibus ieiuna vixit in alvo,
dum tres luce dies una sub nocte prophetae
370 sol ageret litusque novum vacuanda viderent
et castigatum vomerent ergastula pastum.
　　Ut monstro exutus vates caelumque recepit
contingens terras, magnam tunc percitus urbem
terribili cum voce petens: "Quid criminis," inquit,
375 "ardetis flammis? Restinguent omnia poenae.
Iamque venit finis; lentum est hoc dicere, venit."
Non plus fatus erat, totus coniurat in omne
lamentum populus: procurrunt undique fletus,
pectora tunduntur, caelum suspiria pulsant.
380 Mollibus abiectis cilicum dant tegmina saetae
inque cibos cinerem lacrimasque in pocula fundunt.

The sentence passed on the guilty inhabitants of the land   355
of Gomorrah saw them still happy and unconcerned when
the flames were almost upon them. By comparison, because
of a salutary forewarning, fear overcame passivity for the
people of Nineveh. For a man had journeyed there, as or-
dered, much buffeted by land and sea, a prophet to proclaim   360
to that mighty people the peril they were in; he feared a
flood, though the rest of the world was secure. A creature
had seized and engulfed him with its powerful jaws; the ark
of its belly had closed around him and submerged him in the
sea. Although the predatory monster was granted the power
to swallow that man and fill its ample maw, yet it could not   365
sink its teeth in him, it could not bite. He entered the greedy
creature that devoured him as its prey, but only to deceive;
though taken in as a meal, he lived on in a stomach that re-
mained hungry, until the sun traversed three days with its
light—but for the prophet one single night—when his   370
prison, soon to be emptied, caught sight of a coastline and
vomited up its chastened would-be dinner.

When the prophet was expelled from the monster and
regained daylight once more, setting foot on dry land, he
hurried straight to that mighty city and with fearful urgency
asked: "Why are you on fire with the flames of wickedness?   375
Your punishment will extinguish everything. The end is al-
ready at hand; or rather, for these words are not urgent
enough, it is already here." He said nothing more; the whole
populace joined together in every expression of grief: on all
sides tears were shed and breasts beaten, their sighs reached
up to strike the heavens. Throwing off their fine garments,   380
they clothed themselves in rough goat-hair shirts, mixed
ashes with their meals, and shed tears into their cups. Their

Ipse etiam, dignus tali qui tempore princeps
ante aciem flentum portet vexilla salutis
atque, novum dictu, metuens discrimina vincat,
385 proicit hic sceptrum, linquit sublime tribunal,
pallia blattarum spreto diffibulat auro,
serica despiciens atque aspera tegmina sumens.
At pius ex alto contemplans talia Rector
exertas revocat sedatis motibus iras
390 vibratumque tenens restinxit missile fulmen.
    Temporibus propriis iustus sic conditor arcae
securo solus timuisse pericula mundo
gaudebit, finem cunctis, sibi ferre salutem
diversam cernens meriti discrimine sortem.
395   Ergo ubi silvestres sexu collegit utroque
inclusitque feras, pecudum tunc eligit illa
sumere, quae pastu licitum vel munda vocantur.
Hinc tantum septena dedit viventia claustro,
ut ternis paribus servato semine salvis
400 septima quae fuerint sacris quandoque litentur.
Et iam vitalis concluserat omnia carcer.
Tunc iustum cunctosque suos natosque nurusque
accipit expectans claustrum vitaeque reponit.
Nam servos nondum dederat natura vocari
405 nec dominos famulis discernere noverat ordo.
Primus enim maculam servili nomine sensit
huius natorum medius, qui forte cachinno
distectum petiit misero spectamine patrem
materiamque sui risit deformior ortus
410 et plus iam turpis nudato simplice nequam.

ruler too, a man well fitted to carry the standard of salvation
at such a time at the head of the ranks of the grieving, and,
strange to relate, by his fear to overcome danger, threw away 385
his scepter, quit his lofty throne, and unpinned his purple
cloak, scorning the finery of gold; silk he despised, he
adopted instead coarse clothing. Then the merciful Lord,
observing all this from on high, his emotions pacified, re-
called his unsheathed anger and extinguished the lightning 390
bolt he was brandishing, restraining it from its course.

In his own day the righteous builder of the ark will like-
wise rejoice that while the rest of the world was uncon-
cerned, he alone feared the coming dangers, seeing that a
different fate was bringing destruction to everyone else, but
to himself salvation, according to distinction in merit.

And so, when he had collected together and enclosed in 395
the ark wild animals of both sexes, Noah then selected for
inclusion those livestock that are called permissible to eat
or clean. Of these he enclosed only seven living specimens,
so that three pairs should survive to preserve the bloodline,
but the seventh was to be offered as sacrifice in a future rite. 400
And now the life-giving prison had already taken all the ani-
mals in, when its eager confines received that righteous man
with all his sons and daughters-in-law and made them its
cargo, destined for life. For as yet nature had not given any-
one the name of slave, and no hierarchy was able to distin- 405
guish masters from servants. The first to feel the stigma of
being called a slave was Noah's middle son, who greeted the
pitiable sight of his unclothed father with ill-fated laughter;
he mocked the source of his own birth, though he was the
more unsightly, and in his wickedness he was more disgrace- 410
ful than the naked innocent, his father. But after saintly

Quod postquam sanctus potuit cognoscere Noe,
natum germanis famulum dedit. Inde repertum
tale iugum; cuncti nam semine nascimur uno.
Servitii certe causam fecisse reatus
415 cernitur et liber peccans fit crimine servus;
si rursum nexu famulus stringatur honestus,
natales faciens sibimet iam nobilis hic est.
    Nuntius interea, dudum qui missus ab alto
detulerat iusto caelestis munera verbi,
420 protinus ut clausum vidit rebusque paratis
expectare diem, rursus descendere caelo
festinans laxos firmavit cardine postes
inclusitque viros atque ostia fortia traxit
confestimque levans supero se rettulit axi.
425   Aevo sexcentos senior transcenderat annos
lunaque bis plenos addebat menstrua cursus,
septimus et decimus qui post illuxerit orbi,
ultimus ille dies iam nunc dabit omnia leto.
Ilicet obtegitur caelum nimiisque tenebris
430 victa repelluntur fuscati lumina solis.
Insanas hominum mentes vix tangere terror
coeperat, insuetus mox profluus aethere nimbus
et valido primum similis demittitur imbri.
Arida terrarum pariter maduere per orbem,
435 una fuit toto facies et nubila caelo.
Aegyptus tunc ipsa novas expavit ad undas
alsit et infusus Garamans dudumque calentes
umida Massylas tetigerunt frigora Syrtes.
Nec longum pluviae species, non denique guttae
440 stillant, sed rupto funduntur flumina caelo.

Noah learned the truth, he handed his son over to his brothers to be their servant. That was the origin of the servile bond, for we all are derived from the one seed. Certainly wrongdoing is observed to be the cause of slavery, and a free 415
man who sins becomes a slave by reason of that wrong; if, however, a servant is virtuous, though constrained by his servitude, he makes his own conditions of birth and becomes ennobled.

Then the messenger who had been sent previously to bring the gift of heaven's word to that righteous man hurried to descend from heaven once more, as soon as he saw 420
Noah was inside and was only awaiting the day, all preparations made; he secured the open door on its hinges, shut in the men, and pulled closed the sturdy portals, then swiftly rising aloft betook himself to heaven on high.

Reverent Noah had surpassed six hundred years in age, to 425
which the moon added two full monthly courses; the seventeenth day to dawn thereafter on the world was to be its last and then already would consign all things to death. Straightaway the sky became overcast, and the light of the sun was 430
obscured and suppressed, overwhelmed by great darkness. Terror had scarcely begun to affect men's deluded minds, when suddenly a cloudburst of unusual force issued from heaven, falling at first like a violent rainstorm. Throughout the world dry land became universally sodden, while the 435
whole sky presented a single appearance, covered in cloud. Egypt then shuddered with fear at these strange new waters, and the Garamantes grew chill under the flood; the cold and the wet reached the Massylian Syrtes, so long burning hot. The appearance of rain did not last long; in fact, there were no pattering raindrops, but rather the sky burst open and 440

Non aliter Tanais, nivibus cum pascitur, albus
Riphaeo de monte ruens illiditur amni
praecipitatque simul, longo quod tramite ducat.
    Undarum tali quatitur certamine tellus,
445 atque locum fecit compressus fluctibus aer.
Nec tamen hic lymphas tantum fudere superna,
terrestres etiam consurgit mundus in iras.
Rumpitur omne solum, crebros dant arva meatus,
prosiliunt fontes ignotaque flumina manant.
450 Vergitur in sursum mutato pondere nimbus;
inde cadens caelis, hinc terris undique surgens
occurrit mox unda sibi iunctoque furore
coniurant elementa neci. Transcenditur omnis
riparum limes fluviis atque obice rupta
455 saevit laxatis discurrens umor habenis.
    Sed cum diffusae spatium concludere terrae
omnia certarent mundumque implere capacem,
suspendi forsan potuit sententia leti
atque mora maiore trahi, quo tardius omnem
460 concedens spatium rapiat sors ultima carnem,
oceanus, vertex rerum, ni fervidus uno
litore, quo tantum terras atque aequora cingit,
exiret rumpensque fidem perfunderet arva.
Dissipat aeternas leges et sede relicta
465 regna aliena petens naturae foedera turbat.
    Ut diros primum pelagi sensere furores
illustres fluvii, magnos quos inclita cursu
fama refert, motusque novos stupuere parumper,

rivers of water poured down. In the same way the Don, when fed by snows, pours in a white torrent down from the Riphaean range, comes crashing and boiling down, and sweeps away whatever it picks up in its long career.

The whole earth was shaken by such a collision of waters; the air gave place, constrained by the flood. Not only did the heavens pour down their waters, but the world rose up in earthborn anger too. The land everywhere developed fissures, fields frequently became streams of water, springs burst out of the ground, and rivers began to flow where previously unknown. Clouds of moisture moved upward, defying their weight, waters both fell from the skies and rose everywhere from the earth, soon meeting together as one, and the elements in their common frenzy joined in a deadly alliance. Every riverbank was overtopped by the current; the flood ran amok, bursting through all barriers and throwing off all restraint in the inundation.

But although all this water was striving to encompass the wide extent of the earth and to fill the spacious world, the sentence of death could perhaps have been postponed and delayed longer in its advance so that the ultimate fate would allow more time and carry off all flesh more slowly, if not for the fact that the turbulent ocean, an elemental force, was exceeding the confines of the single shore which alone kept land and water apart and was breaking faith by swamping the earth. It was transgressing eternal laws and, in leaving its proper home and invading another's realm, was throwing into disarray the compact of nature.

When the famed rivers whom glorious report celebrates for the size of their stream first felt the sea's cruel rage, for a while they were astounded at these new forces; then they

ut credas sapuisse fugam, sic versa retrorsum
470 per terras spargunt sublata volumina ponto.
Insequitur tamen oceanus refugisque fluentis
imminet et salsis impellit molibus amnes.
   Tum maior strepitu tanto mortalibus aegris
fit metus, ascendunt turres et celsa domorum
475 culmina praesentemque iuvat vel tempore parvo
sic differre necem. Multos, dum scandere temptant,
crescens unda trahit, quosdam montana petentes
consequitur letoque fugam deprendit inanem.
Ast alii longo iactantes membra natatu
480 defessi expirant animas, aut pondere nimbi
obruta flumineas commixta per aequora lymphas
in quocumque bibunt morientia corpora monte.
Aedibus impulsis alii periere ruina
inque undas venere simul dominique domusque.
485 It fragor in caelum sonitu collectus ab omni
quadrupedumque greges humana in morte cadentum
augent confusos permixta voce tumultus.
   Haec inter miseri ferventia funera mundi
praegravis insanis pulsatur motibus arca
490 compagesque tremunt, stridens iunctura laborat.
Non tamen obstructam penetrat vis improba, quamquam
verberet et solidam fluctu feriente fatiget.
Non aliter crebras Ecclesia vera procellas
sustinet et saevis sic nunc vexatur ab undis.
495 Hinc gentilis agit tumidos sine more furores,

reversed their direction and scattered their sea-driven bil- 470
lows over the land—you might imagine they were intending
to flee. Yet the ocean pressed hard upon them: hot on the
heels of the retreating streams, it drove forward the rivers
with the weight of its salt waters.

Then the great din increased the fear felt by corrupt hu-
manity: they mounted up on towers and lofty roofs of dwell-
ings, pleased to postpone imminent death even for a brief 475
period of time. Many the mounting wave dragged under as
they strove to climb upward, some it overtook as they made
for mountain heights and put a halt to their unavailing flight
with death. Again others grew weary from the prolonged
exercise of their limbs in swimming and gave up the ghost; 480
on every mountaintop dying bodies, succumbing to the
violence of the rainstorm, swallowed a mixture of sea and
river water combined. Still others, when their houses were
knocked down, perished in the destruction; master and
mansion simultaneously falling under the waves. From every 485
side the din gathered in force and resounded with a roar to
heaven; herds of animals, falling to earth among the dying
humans, added their voices and increased the hubbub and
confusion.

Meanwhile the laden ark, amid the seething destruction
of the doomed world, was buffeted by the raging forces of
the elements; its structure shook, and the joints creaked un- 490
der the strain. But the violent assault still did not breach the
ark's defenses, although it pounded the resilient structure
and subjected it to a barrage of waves. In no different way
the true Church endures frequent tempests and is even now
harassed by equally violent waves. On one side the pagan 495
swells up with unparalleled fury, on another the Jew rages

hinc Iudaea fremit rabidoque illiditur ore,
provocat inde furens heresum vesana Charybdis.
Turgida Graiorum sapientia philosophorum
inter se tumidos gaudet committere fluctus.
500 Obloquiis vanos sufflant mendacia ventos,
sed clausam vacuo pulsant impune latratu.
  Iam medium crescens arcae contexerat unda
commovitque cavam suspendens undique molem
et melius tutam facili portante natatu,
505 quoque vocant undae, sequitur iam mobile pondus.
Cedamus mundo, dum ducimur; omne resistens,
si flecti nescit, metuat vel pondere frangi.
Sed sic cedamus, fluxum ne sentiat intus
peccatumve trahat mens impenetrabilis ullum.
510   Navigat interea claustro commissus eunti
fons vitae servatque furens super omnia pontus
orbis depositum, fido quod tegmine promat,
cum pax terrarum reddi sibi debita poscet.
  Ergo ibant undae, tellus subducitur omnis,
515 collibus impositae vicerunt edita lymphae.
Delituit tectus ponto tum piniger Othrys,
Parnasi vertex cautem non protulit altam,
ipsa cupressiferi latuerunt saxa Lycaei,
subductae rupes, aequatae fluctibus, Alpes.
520 Omnibus exclusis totus iam denique mundus
axis et unda fuit; nam cunctis morte subactis

and fiercely gnashes his jaws, or heresy, in its mad passion
a Charybdis-like whirlpool, launches its challenge. The in-
flated wisdom of Greek philosophers takes pleasure in
whipping up swelling billows of mutual rivalry. Such fictions   500
inflate into gales of empty abuse, but for those enclosed in
the ark their attacks cause no harm with their fatuous bay-
ing.

Now the rising water had covered the lower half of the
ark and set the hollow craft in motion, bearing it up on every
side. It was all the more secure because of the ready buoy-
ancy that kept it afloat; wherever the waters summoned it,   505
the now freely moving hulk followed. We too should yield to
the world as it carries us along; everything that resists, if it is
incapable of bending, must fear being shattered by its own
weight. But we should yield in such a way that the mind, re-
maining inviolate, experiences no inner weakness and incurs
no sin.

Meanwhile the source of new life sailed on, consigned to   510
that floating hull, and the sea in its universal rage yet pre-
served the pledge of the world's future in its keeping, with
the intent to produce it once more from that secure custo-
dianship when peace returned to the earth and demanded
what was due to it repaid.

And so the waves advanced, all land was submerged, and   515
the depth of the waters overtopped the mountain peaks.
Pine-clad Othrys disappeared under the sea, the summit of
Parnassus no longer showed its beetling crags, even the
rocky face of Lycaeus with its cypress trees was invisible,
and the Alpine peaks shrank to be level with the waves.
With everything submerged, the whole world was now just   520
sky and sea. All land creatures had succumbed to death; sea

regnabant pelagi silvoso in gurgite monstra,
et iam vicinum pulsabant umida caelum;
iamque quater denis manabat noctibus imber
525 compleratque necem, nec iam quod tolleret ultra
mors habuit pressitque natantia funera pontus.
  Frenantur tandem pluviae, resplenduit aether,
redditur et caelis vultus. Sol ipse reductus,
sed non inventis, quis reddat lumina, terris,
530 tantum luxit aquis. Tristis videt aequora fulgor
quamque breves radios admotas frangit in undas,
tam consumendis fervens ac proximus instat.
Nec minus et patuli terrae clauduntur hiatus
quaeque prius vomuit letali ex ore fluenta,
535 obicibus propriis constricta resorbet abyssus.
Nec tamen ut venit, breviter sic lympha recedit;
siccant non pauci, longo sed tempore, menses,
quod pauci fudere dies. Iam ducta natatu
Armeniae celsis instabat montibus arca
540 et nondum nudis fundo consedit in arvis.
  Ut stabilem sensit senior motuque carentem
nec fluitare natans ventosa per aequora lignum,
credidit abductis nituisse liquoribus orbem.
Tum reserat summam sublimi a fronte fenestram,
545 emissa refluos exploret ut alite fluctus.
Illa volans longo diverberat aera plausu
atque quatit vacuas pinnarum motibus auras,

monsters reigned alone in the underwater forests, and indeed the waters were now striking in close proximity the heavens; for forty nights now the rains had been pouring down and had taken in full their deadly toll; death had nothing further to prey on—the sea overwhelmed the floating corpses.

At last the rainfall was curbed, the heavens shone bright again, and the sky assumed once more its proper appearance. The sun itself made its return, only to find no land on which to bestow its light; it shone on water alone. In sorrow its beams looked out over the deep; the shorter its rays were, intercepted as they were by the nearby waves, the more intense and immediate was the force it exerted to burn those waters off. The fissures too that had opened in the earth closed up again, and the abyss reabsorbed the torrents that it had previously with deadly effect spewed from its mouth, confining them behind their proper barriers. But the waters did not recede as quickly as they had come; it took no small number of months, an extended period of time, to dry up what a few days had shed. But now the ark, borne along by the flood, made contact with the high mountain peaks of Armenia and settled with its hull on the not yet exposed land.

When the patriarch realized that the ark was solidly grounded and no longer in motion and that its floating timbers were not still adrift on the windswept seas, he believed that the waters had retreated and the world shone forth once more. Then he opened the topmost window in the lofty flank of the ark to send out a bird to explore the waves' retreat. For a long time in its flight it rhythmically cleaved the air and agitated the vacant breezes with the motion of

cumque diu fessis undas perstringeret alis
nec locus optatam requiem concederet ullus,
550 consuetum repetit prospecto ex aequore claustrum.
Exceptam senior manibus tum colligit intus
advertens nullas patuisse per umida terras.
　Interea magna pontus se mole movendo
in chaos antiquum linquens mundana redibat.
555 Excelsi tandem proferre cacumina primum
incipiunt, post quos tenues crebrescere montes.
At vero ut pelagus cinxerunt litora priscum
oceanusque sacer notas collectus in oras
contentus solito labentia flumina tractu
560 sorbuit et cunctis distrinxit frena fluentis
torrentesque suae clauserunt undique fossae,
libera subductis nituerunt arida lymphis.
　Tunc interposito producens tempore corvum
scire cupit senior vacuumque interrogat orbem.
565 Ales ut extensis nitidum petit aera pinnis,
aspiciens plenis stipata cadavera terris,
carnibus incumbens et mox oblita reverti
rectorem placidum communi in sede reliquit.
Sic nescis, Iudaee, fidem servare magistro,
570 sic carnem dimissus amas, sic gratia numquam
custodi vitae Dominoque rependitur ulla.
Mente vaga sic laxus abis, sic foedera legis
rupisti et primum violasti, perfide, pactum.

its wings. But when on wearied wings it continued for a long time to scour the waters, but no location offered the respite it was seeking, then after scouting the sea it returned again   550
to its familiar confines. The patriarch caught it with his hands and brought it inside the ark, realizing that no land was yet visible in the swamped earth.

Meanwhile the vast bulk of the sea was on the move, quitting the natural world and reverting to primordial chaos. First lofty mountains at last began to reveal their summits,   555
then afterward numerous lower ones began to appear. When coastlines encircled the sea as before and the hallowed ocean was contained, withdrawing to its familiar shores, it absorbed the rivers that now flowed in their customary course, imposing curbs on every stream; on every   560
side trenches closed over underground torrents, and dry land, freed by the retreat of the waters, shone bright and clear.

Then the patriarch, eager to gain knowledge and find out about the deserted world, after a period of time had elapsed brought out a raven. When the bird stretched its wings and   565
flew off into the bright sky, it caught sight of bodies lying thickly packed on the earth, and alighting on the carrion, soon forgetful of returning, abandoned its gentle overseer in his shared refuge. In the same way, Jew, you too are incapable of keeping faith with your master, in banishment you   570
love the flesh, and you never give any thanks to the Lord and the protector of your life. In the same way too with vagrant spirit when released you flee away; you have broken the covenant of the law and in your treachery transgressed that first agreement.

Temporis ut spatio senior collegit inertem
575 iam potuisse satis corvum se reddere claustris,
ignarus tardi reditus causaeque morandi,
ne fors innexis fessum consumpserit alis
iunxerit et cunctis pereuntibus unda recurrens,
protinus albentem mittit de sede columbam.
580 Illa memor iussi rapido petit arva volatu
paciferaeque videns ramum viridantis olivae
decerpit mitique refert ad condita rostro.
Tali legatus firmavit foedera simplex
indicio purumque pius sic comperit orbem.
585 Integer emensum vertebat circinus annum,
quo felix claustrum spirantia cuncta tenebat.
Tum pater ablatis obducta repagula serris
pandit et inclusis desuetum reddere solem
incipit, effeto redeant ut semina mundo.
590 Ante tamen iustus iubeat quam sparsa vagari,
singula de septem, quae dudum claudere munda
curavit, natis pariter nuribusque vocatis,
caespite constructa disponens immolat ara
accendens sanctos his primum altaribus ignes.
595 Plurima dum magnis adolentur corpora flammis
et numerosa levat praepinguem victima fumum,
suavis odor laetum tetigit trans aethera caelum
primaque purgati suscepta est hostia mundi.

The patriarch after a while realized that the recalcitrant raven had had enough time to be able to return to its pen, 575 and in ignorance of the reason for its tardy return and delay—perhaps misfortune had overcome it in its weariness as its wings gave out, and the retreating water had added the bird's body to all the others that had perished—he immediately sent out a white dove from the ark. Mindful of its instructions, it flew rapidly toward land and, seeing a branch of green olive, symbol of peace, it plucked it and carried it back gently in its beak to the hold of the vessel. With that evidence the humble envoy confirmed the fulfillment of the pact, and thus righteous Noah discovered that the world had been made pure.

An entire circuit of a year had measured out its course, 585 during which that happy imprisonment embraced all living things. Then father Noah threw open the door bolts that had been drawn shut and removed the bars; he began to let in the sunlight, an unfamiliar sight, to the animals that had been shut in, so that a breeding stock would return to the played-out earth. But before that righteous man bid them 590 disperse and roam the earth, he set aside one of the seven animals from each of the clean species that he had taken care originally to enclose in the ark, and in the presence of his sons and daughters-in-law had the animals sacrificed on an altar constructed of sod, the first time a sacred fire had been kindled on altars like these. As the many carcasses 595 were being consumed by the towering flames and the large number of victims was sending up the richest of savors, a sweet scent passed through the air to reach up to heaven, and the first sacrifice of the purified world received acceptance.

Tunc igni permixta sacro vox intonat ista:
600 "Hactenus infectus contagia traxerit orbis;
sufficiat regnasse nefas. Mundata lavando
perpetuo niteat tellus vultusque reductos
contineant elementa suos; non amplius ullis
perturbata malis moles mundana fatiscat.
605 Vos quoque, quos leti salvavit tempore vita
intactosque tenens casu defendit ab omni,
ducite securum servatis legibus aevum.
Vosque caput generis fecundo semine prolem
spargite, diffusum late quae compleat orbem,
610 deletum instauret numerum dominetur et orbi.
Fertile quin etiam reddant animantia germen,
quod tamen inflexum famulabitur ordine prisco.
Insuper et terris ex hoc iam non erit ultra
diluvium regnans carnem quod conterat omnem.
615 Unum quod fuerit, signo monstrabitur uno
nec similem repetita necem peccata videbunt
et, si crimen erit, terror non deforet alter."
Sic unum Genitor iurans baptisma sacrabat,
ut semel ablutum lymphis purgantibus orbem,
620 sic sperare reos lavacrum non posse secundum.
Vix tribus exactis caeli iam partibus ibat
pronus in occasum radius, cum forte remotam
axe sub eoo iussus contingere nubem
protulit excussum madefacto ex aethere signum
625 arcus et emicuit, quem nunc "Thaumantida" Graio,
"Irim" Romuleo vocitant sermone poetae.
Pendulus obliquum solem cum senserit umor,
ancipites vario mittit splendore colores,

Then in the midst of that sacred fire this voice thundered out: "Let the pollution the infected world has contracted 600 last only till now; let this be an end to the reign of crime. Let the earth shine brightly forever, now that it is washed clean by the flood, and the elements retain the natural appearance they have regained; never again may the fabric of the world be prey to evil and succumb. You too, whom life spared in a 605 time of death and whom it kept safe, protected from every mischance, live now a carefree existence in observance of the laws. You are the font of the human race; be fertile and from your seed disperse your offspring far and wide to fill the earth's broad expanse, to renew the exterminated popu- 610 lation, and to have dominion over the world. Let animals too produce again a fertile stock that still will bow in sub- mission and be your servants as before. Moreover, from now on no flood will rule over the earth to destroy all flesh. A 615 single portent will show that this was a unique event; if sins recur, they will not experience a like destruction, but there will a different cause for fear, should criminality arise." In this way the Father sanctified a single baptism, taking an oath that just as the world had been washed clean by purify- ing waters just one time, so sinners could not hope for a 620 second cleansing.

The sun's rays had now just crossed three-quarters of the sky and were heading toward setting, when, bidden to strike a distant cloud in the eastern heavens, they brought forth a sign wrung from the damp air: a rainbow shone forth, which 625 poets in the Greek language call "Thaumantis," in the Ro- man, "Iris." When the suspended moisture is struck by the sun at an angle, it creates indeterminate colors of various

nec numerare queas sic mixtos lumine visus.
630 Inludunt dubii diversis vultibus orbes
sapphirusque virens, maculosus, caerulus, albus.
Purpureum de nube trahit, de sole coruscum,
de caelo nitidum, de terra sumitur atrum,
et tamen abiunctis quae constant haec elementis,
635 sic diversa putas, ut concordantia cernas.
Hanc formam signo trepidis mortalibus arcus
praestitit esse Deus promittens nube serenum
nullaque iam terris debere pericula caelum.
    Nunc quicumque cupis veram servare salutem,
640 illud suspicies signum quod signa figurant.
Namque dator vitae praemisit talia Christus
et geminata dedit substantia Salvatorem.
In terris sumptae nitida de virgine carni
naturalis inest patrio de germine fulgor;
645 et medius quidam mediator in aethere celso
munere multimodo varius, sed fulgidus omni,
vitalem monstrat sacrati pigneris arcum.
    Istum corde vide, quisquis baptismate lotus
ad caelum liber culpis pereuntibus exis.
650 Namque legis: "Forma vos," inquit apostolus, "ista
salvabit lavacrum, prisci cum tempore Noe
conclusas lignis animas discriberet octo."
Comparat ille datum, tu servans dilige donum,
hoc votis precibusque gerens, hoc fletibus optans,

hues; it is impossible to enumerate all that is seen, indistinct as they are in their shadings. The uncertain contours of the   630 bands confuse with their divergent features: gleaming sapphire, dappled, sky blue, and white. From the cloud it draws its rich sheen, from the sun its brilliance, from the heavens it derives its radiance, and from the earth its darker tones. But still, though these qualities owe their origin to different elements, in recognizing their diversity you may simultane-   635 ously contemplate their harmony. This image of the rainbow God granted to fearful mortals as a sign, promising a sky that was cloudless and a future in which the heavens would be responsible for no disaster to the earth.

Now all you who wish to secure true salvation, observe   640 this sign that other signs serve to figure. For it was Christ the bestower of life who created such prefiguring; the rainbow's double nature symbolized the Savior. On earth the flesh he received from an unspotted virgin took on a natural brilliance from his paternal descent; at the same time,   645 as a kind of intermediary between both realms, he displayed in the lofty heavens a sacred pledge, the life-giving rainbow, for many are his gifts, multihued and resplendent every one.

All you who emerge from the cleansing of baptism free to journey to heaven with your sins purged, keep this image before you in your heart. For you read in the words   650 of the apostle: "In accordance with this figure baptism will save you, since in the time of ancient Noah it set apart eight souls in their enclosure of wood." He won for himself that gift, you must lovingly preserve it, seeking with your vows and prayers and longing with your tears for this boon,

655 ne redeant peccata tibi, ne mersa leventur,
mortua ne surgant, ne debellata rebellent,
ne post ablutum valeant discrimina crimen
et flammam timeas, quo iam non suppetit unda.

that your sins do not return, that what has been submerged 655
not rise to the surface again, that what has been slain not be
reborn, that what has been conquered not war again, that
after you have been washed free of sin your perils do not re-
gain their force and you grow fearful of the flames, since no
longer have you recourse to water.

De transitu Maris Rubri

Hactenus in terris undas potuisse canenti;
terram inter fluctus aperit nunc carminis ordo.
Illic Diluvium quos perderet ante petivit,
nunc ad diluvium pleno succensa furore
5   sponte sua current periturae milia gentis,
sed non ut dignum tanti praeconia facti
eloquium captent; divina in laude voluntas
sufficit et famulo monstrari munere votum.
Quod si quis nequeat verbis persolvere grates,
10   non minimum virtutis habet vel credere gestis,
signa per electos quae porrexere priores.
In quibus excellit longe praestantius illud
quod Pelago gestum Rubro celeberrima perfert
scriptorum series, in cuius pondere sacro
15   causarum mage pignus erat pulchramque relatu
pulchrior exuperat praemissae forma salutis,
historiis quae magna satis maiorque figuris
conceptam gravido peperit de tegmine vitam.
    Sustinuit duros externa in sede labores,
20   cum Pelusiacae serviret subdita genti,
plebs oppressa diu, densi quam pondere caeni
et laterum numeris operis mensura diurni
afflictam saevi vexabat fraude tyranni.

The Crossing of the Red Sea

My previous song was of the power water exercised over land; now the sequence of my poem exposes land among the waves. In that case the Flood first sought out whom to destroy, but now a doomed race in its thousands will of its own accord rush into the flood in the full heat of its frenzy—not that the celebration of so great a deed will receive proper expression in my song, but in the praise of God the will is enough and to show that will in a humble offering. But if someone does not have the ability to express his thanks in words, it is not the smallest of virtues to have faith at least in the events that the actions of special persons from the past have handed down as signs. Among these by far the most outstanding are the events at the Red Sea that the far-famed narrative of the scriptures records, a narrative in whose solemn gravity there was furthermore a pledge of greater things: the beauty of its form, prefiguring salvation, surpasses that of the simple record of events; though in the historical account the story is great, in its figural sense it is greater—it conceived and brought forth the promise of life from its fertile encasement.

A people long oppressed endured hard labor in a foreign country when they served in subjugation the nation of Egypt. Their daily assignment of work, with the weight of the thick clay and the required quota of bricks, was wearing them out, the victims of a cruel tyrant's mistreatment.

Invisam sibimet frendens qui crescere turbam,
25 augeri doluit famulos; nam iusserat, ut lux
vidisset quoscumque mares, mox docta necaret
omnis anus natumque premat sollertia sexum.
Sed tamen aversae fugerunt talia matres
atque interdictos detrectant perdere fetus,
30 persistente Deo plebem diffundere sanctam,
quoque magis mens caeca trahit crudelia vota,
hoc plus accrescunt tenerae primordia gentis.
    Viderat interea Genitor de sede superna
afflictamque manum placido prospexerat ore.
35 Iam sacer innocuas dederat de fomite flammas
et rubus in rubeo viridis permanserat aestu,
quo signo spinas nostrae fervescere mentis
et lucere, pium qui non consumeret, igne
devotus nosset sanctis in cordibus ardor.
40   Ilicet electi vates mandata ferebant,
depromit regi cum primus talia Moyses:
"Servitii longo lassatam pondere plebem,
oppressos cophinis umeros attritaque colla
quasque opus assiduum fecit durescere palmas
45 laxandi iam tempus adest. Dimitte precantes
tandem caelesti Domino persolvere vota
et complere datos patrio moderamine ritus."
    Ille fremens inquit: "Quae tanti causa tumultus
quisve novus populum deus exigit omine misso?
50 Scilicet hae vacuae tangunt caelestia curae,

Raging at the increase in size of the population he so hated, he fretted at the growth in numbers of slaves; accordingly he gave the order that as soon as the light of day looked upon any male children, all the old women who practiced as midwives should kill them; their diligence was to do away with that sex at birth. The mothers, however, in repulsion shunned such actions and refused to kill their forbidden offspring, while God continued to multiply the numbers of the holy people. The more the tyrant's mental blindness conceived cruel schemes, the more the first beginnings of the young nation grew.

Meanwhile the Father had kept watch from his seat above and with benign countenance viewed the suffering people. Already a sacred thornbush had produced with its kindling harmless flames: its briars had remained green among the red-hot fires. By this sign the devout fire of passion in the hearts of the holy came to know that the thorns of our spirits grow hot and glow with a fire that does not consume the pious man.

Immediately the chosen prophets carried their instructions to the king; Moses it was who first addressed him with these words: "The time has come to free a people long wearied by the weight of servitude, whose shoulders are stooped and whose necks rubbed raw by the baskets they must carry, whose hands are calloused by unremitting labor. In answer to their prayers let the people go at last to fulfill their obligations to their heavenly Lord and to perform the rites bequeathed to them according to ancestral practice."

In a rage the king replied: "What is the cause of such an uproar, what new god sends omens and lays claim to a people? I suppose these are the kind of idle concerns that sway

ut dominus dominis famulos nunc tollere priscos
vellet et ad tumidos mittat mandata rebelles.
Quis deus iste foret cui me parere necesse est,
aut sceptris celso quid formidabile regi?
55   Sed vestras nimium seducunt otia mentes,
et nisi laxatos requies concessa foveret,
nulla supervacuis tererentur tempora verbis.
Quae si castigans restringat sarcina maior,
inlicitus vetitum conari desinet ausus.
60   At vos, signifero qui talia vota ducatu
instruitis vanoque plebem subvertitis ore,
conspectus vitate meos vultumque cavete.
Ditem namque Pharon vel pollentissime cursus
testor, Nile, tuos et divae vocis Anubem,
65   cum rabidus latrat, iam non impune futurum,
si nostrum rursus repetant haec dicta tribunal.”
   Virgam forte manu gestabat legifer heros,
quo baculo nitens gressum tum dextra regebat;
excutit hanc valido proiectam comminus ictu.
70   Tum, mirum dictu, commotum serpere lignum,
non insensibiles ceu promit palmite ramos
vita movens tantum, quos praestat crescere fructus,
sed flexu reptans mutati et corporis usu
sensum animamque gerens coepit decurrere virga;
75   mox anguem formata refert. Conterritus haesit
aeternumque niger tunc palluit ore tyrannus,
sed ne confusum tali succumbere signo
cerneret assistens vultu nutante satelles,
dissimulat summo rem gestam credere iussu.

heavenly beings, for a lord now to steal other lords' slaves of long standing and to communicate instructions to insubordinate rebels. What god could he be that I should obey him? What cause for fear for a mighty king endowed with royal scepter? No, it is leisure that leads too far astray your minds; 55 if you had not received relief to cosset you and allow you ease, you would not be wasting any time in superfluous speechifying. But if as a punishment a heavier burden disciplines you, your illicit boldness will cease to attempt what is forbidden. But as for you, who as standard-bearers take the 60 lead in prompting such desires and corrupt your people with your empty speeches, keep clear of my sight and beware my countenance. For I call to witness wealthy Pharos and your streams, Nile, mightiest of rivers, I call on Anubis to witness, whose voice when fiercely baying is divine, that in the 65 future it will not go unpunished if again these representations return to my tribunal."

It so happened that the heroic lawgiver was holding in his grip a staff, the cane that his hand relied on to guide him when walking; this he flung vigorously from him to the ground before him. Then, remarkable to relate, the wood 70 began to move and crawl, not in the way that life produces insentient branches on a vine, invigorating only the fruit, which it causes to grow, but rather the staff took on sensation and life and began to slither away with a writhing motion natural to its changed physical shape; soon, that change 75 completed, it revealed itself a snake. Gripped by fear, the perpetually dark-skinned tyrant grew pale in the face, but so that a servant who was standing by with bowed head not see him discomfited and bested by such a miracle, he pretended not to believe that the action was performed on the orders

80 Nec divina volens, hominum sed facta putari
    praecipit, ut quoscumque magos vel carmina doctos,
    illicitam diris temptantes fraudibus artem,
    Aegypti longinqua darent, hos talia cogens
    murmure funereo faciat monstrare minister.
85 Undique tunc iussi concurrunt et medicatas
    armant quisque suas noto phantasmate virgas.
    Dant iactae vanas species anguesque putati
    inlusos terrent oculos fallente figura.
    Nec longum tumuere magi; consumitur omne
90 quod fecisse rati. Fictos namque arte dracones
    primus adhuc mordax absorbuit ore cerasta.
    Postquam virtutis clausit spectacula Moyses
    victorisque tenens caudam tellure levavit,
    decedit serpens ligno vultusque recedit,
95 diriguere vagi durato corpore flexus.
    Quid multis? Fit virga prior, qua deinde sacerdos
    plurima succiduo monstravit tempore signa.
       Hinc dirum frendens pharaonis conscius ardor,
    divinae incipiens per cuncta resistere dextrae
100 et, quae cognoscens, nolens tamen ipse fateri,
    protinus expulsos iussit discedere vates.
    Illi divinas pulsant cum fletibus aures,
    ut fremitus gentis tandem frenetur iniquae,
    quam gravius saevam monitus fecere superni,
105 ipsis quin etiam caelestibus arma minantem.

of the Most High. Wishing that these actions be seen not as 80
divine but human, he gave orders to the servant to gather
together all the magicians and experts in spells, practi-
tioners with their treacherous deceptions of forbidden arts,
that the length and breadth of Egypt could supply, and have
them perform similar actions with their own dismal mutter-
ing. Then, as bidden, all came running from every direction, 85
each equipping his enchanted wand with its own familiar
phantom. When thrown to the ground, these produced in-
substantial illusions; imagined to be snakes, they terrified
the onlookers, who were misled by their deceptive appear-
ance. But the magicians' pride did not last long; everything
they thought they had achieved was brought to nothing. For 90
that first snake, still capable of biting, swallowed down its
throat the fake snakes that the art of magic created. After he
had completed this show of wonder-working power, Moses
took the victorious snake by the tail and lifted it from the
ground. Then what was serpent gave way to wood, its previ-
ous aspect vanished, and its mobile coils grew rigid as the 95
body hardened. Why waste words? It became again the staff
it once was, with which in the time to come the priest of
God was to perform very many miracles.

At this the pharaoh, inflamed by knowledge of the truth
of what had happened, flared up in a terrible rage—he began
to resist God's hand in every way and to refuse to admit 100
what he knew to be true—and he immediately ordered the
two prophets be driven away. But they laid siege with tears
to the hearing of God, begging that the outbursts of that
unjust race be checked at last, for God's past instructions
had only made that people all the fiercer and even caused 105
them to threaten to take up arms against heaven itself. Then

Tum Pater accipiens gemitus lacrimasque precantum
taliter hortatu blando solatur amaros:
"Ne tantum vacuo summittite corda timori,
plebs mea, quam toto mundi de corpore sumptam
110 elegi et propria solam mihi sorte sacravi.
Iam nunc cernetis, quanto primordia vestra
prosequar auxilio saevos ac persequar hostes.
Ducam sublimem portenta per omnia dextram.
Nec volet in paucis Pharius rex cedere signis,
115 longius ut duram vincant miracula mentem.
Post haec laxatos quin et discedere coget
expelletque solo; quod nunc negat, ingeret ultro.
Ibitis ad magnas post fortia proelia sedes,
qua vocat expectans praefertilis ubere terra
120 et claras victis condetis gentibus urbes.
Vos modo promissis tantum confidite donis
et quos deposcent ingentia facta labores,
laeta ferat virtus seseque ad prospera servet."
Talibus auditis melior spes accipit illos.
125 Attollunt animos palmasque ad sidera tendunt
concipiuntque fidem votis gratesque rependunt.
   Postera lux dubios primum praemiserat ortus
et successorem depulsa nocte ferebat
insistens aurora diem; tum flumina sanguis
130 imbuit et subito maduerunt arva cruore.
Sed non hoc minimis portentum contigit undis;
fluviorum rex ipse rubet nec lumine prisco

the Father gave ear to the groans and tears of his suppliants and relieved their distress with this comforting speech: "Do not surrender your hearts so wholly to empty fear, my people, for from the whole expanse of the world it is you I have 110 chosen to be mine, and you alone I have sanctified to my care with your own special destiny. Soon now you will see the power of my aid, how I will advance your first undertakings but bring confusion to your cruel enemies. I will unfurl my hand on high to perform every kind of miracle. But the Egyptian king will not be ready to yield after only a few signs, and so it will need longer for the miracles to conquer 115 his stubborn heart. But after that you will be free; he will even go so far as to compel you to leave and will drive you from his land; what now he refuses, he will of his own accord insist on. After some fierce battles you will make your way to a glorious new abode, where a land of surpassing fertility summons and awaits you, and where you will found famous 120 cities after defeating the peoples there. All you must do is put your faith in the gifts that are promised and let cheerful fortitude endure the trials that great undertakings require, continuing until the prosperous times to come." When they heard these words, greater confidence possessed them. Their spirits were raised; they stretched out their hands to 125 the stars, expressed their faith in their prayers, and returned thanks to God.

The next light had revealed the first faint sunrise, and, hard on its heels, dawn was introducing day as successor to the banished night, when blood discolored the rivers and 130 soaked the fields with a sudden inundation. Nor was this a prodigy that affected only the smallest streams; the king of rivers itself, the Nile, grew red and without its former

Nilus agit proprium quem sumpsit fonte nitorem.
Quin magis averso ne tangat pristina Nilo,
135 sanguis in extremum certans manare canalem
carnosus, non carnis erat nec corpore fusus,
aut strages quam multa simul quo vulnere possit
lympharum damnum proprio supplere cruore.
Naribus obstructis pressi vinctoque natatu
140 interiere simul peregrini in gurgite crasso
auxeruntque suo saniem de funere pisces.
Et fortasse rear cladis mortisque futurae
sanguinis indicio iam praecessisse ruinam,
hoc ipsum ni poena foret. Nam scilicet omne
145 Aegypti spatium, vel quo patet ampla Canopus,
mox inter pingues sitiens defecerat undas,
si non Omnipotens celerem super arva medellam
spargeret et nitidos revocaret vallibus amnes.
   Tum vero ut requiem pestis subducta reduxit,
150 effertur rursus dilata morte tyrannus
et vix evasum contemnens mente flagellum
innocuam flagris persistit subdere gentem.
At quid per cunctam stilus aestuet ire superbi
perfidiam, caesi numerans periuria regni?
155 Sed tamen extorquent varium mendacia monstrum
undaque vicino vixdum purgata cruore
ranarum foedis texit cantatibus urbes.
Complentur cellae, strati, penetralia, mensae,
sustinet innumeros regalis purpura saltus,

brilliance lacked the natural clarity it derived from its source. In fact the Nile turned aside so as not to sully its tra-
ditional course, while the blood, which pressed forward to   135
flow even into the furthest channels, was like that from liv-
ing flesh, but not from it—it did not come from any living
body nor from any wounds, for no massacre, however great,
could with its own bloodshed together take the place of the
quantity of water lost. Fish, now out of their element in the
viscous current, met their end, overcome by the obstruction   140
to their breathing passages and their inability to swim, and
in so doing increased the waters' corruption with their dead
bodies. And indeed I could perhaps imagine that the de-
struction in the fatal disaster to come was presaged by the
omen of the blood, if this was not in itself a punishment. For
in fact the whole region of Egypt, even as far as the broad   145
extent of Canopus, would soon have succumbed to thirst in
the midst of the congealed waters, if the Almighty had not
dispensed a swift-acting remedy over the land and sum-
moned back the streams, clear once more, to their valleys.

But then when the pestilence was removed and peace re-
turned, the tyrant flared up once more after death was post-   150
poned, and, slighting the scourge only barely escaped, he
continued to subjugate with the whip an innocent people.
But why should my pen strive to recount all the treachery of
that proud man, enumerating the falsehoods of that doomed
kingdom? However, his deceitfulness still made necessary a   155
variety of prodigies; waters, scarcely yet purified of recent
blood, swamped the cities with the rasping croaks of
frogs. Storerooms and streets, the innermost recesses of
houses, and the very tables were filled with them; even
the royal purple must put up with the countless hopping

160 atque premens homines frendet subcumbere ranis.
Quarum mox cumulis tonitru feriente subactis
congestisque sonans muscarum nubis ad auras
exiit infecto corrumpens aera flatu,
illic, quas scinifes vocitant, quantosque volatus
165 pendula committunt levibus corpuscula ventis
pinnarumque vices peragunt stridentibus alis,
fundunt se pariter turbataque moenia complent.
Et licet immersis defigant vulnera rostris,
plus horror quam poena movet. Sed tollit et istam
170 ventus agens, cessat laxata molestia paulum
confestim cessante metu nec longius ira
sentitur quam plaga calet. Sed peste remota
succedunt aliae gravius. Consumitur omne
iumentum cunctosque greges nox abstulit una;
175 nec tantum damnosa reos portenta fatigant.
Vertitur ad carnem quae suscitet ira dolores,
insidunt penitus turgentia vulnera membris,
et sacer incubuit percussis artubus ignis.
Creditur hic etiam casu contingere languor,
180 sed morbus mentis discrimina corporis urget.
    Praeterit ille dies; tum demum luce secuta
concutitur caelum tonitru nubesque coactae
terribili splendore micant: ferit omnia fulgor
fulmen agens, totas uno sub tempore mortes
185 aethere turbato terris elementa minantur.
Ignibus inseritur praegrandis pondere grando,
non ut nube solet terris nimbosa venire,

creatures—it could subdue humans but raged at succumb- 160
ing to frogs. But soon those creatures fell victim themselves
in droves to thunderbolts, and from their heaped-up bodies
a humming cloud of flies mounted up on the breezes, pollut-
ing the air with noxious exhalations. There these insects,
which are called gnats, whose tiny bodies in great numbers 165
commit themselves to flight suspended on the light breezes
and rely on buzzing wings to play the role of feathers, rose
up in a swarm and filled the city walls, throwing everything
into confusion. And though they inflicted wounds with pen-
etrating stings, the repulsion they aroused was greater than
the pain. But when a wind arose to dispel that swarm, and 170
the discomfort it brought ebbed a little and passed away,
fear too quickly passed off and the sense of God's anger re-
mained no longer than the plague was at its height. But
when that plague was removed, other more grievous ones
followed. All the livestock then died, a single night carried
off all the flocks, but those punitive prodigies did not alone 175
assail the guilty. The divine anger that brought these suf-
ferings next turned its attack against flesh, swelling ulcers
settled deep on the body, and a holy fire took possession of
inflamed limbs. In this case too the sickness was believed to
be a chance occurrence, but that disease of the mind com- 180
pounded such bodily ills.

That day passed; then when finally first light dawned, the
sky was shaken by thunder and massed clouds let out flashes
of terrifying brilliance: lightning bolts were striking ev-
erywhere, the elements in the tumultuous heavens threat- 185
ened at that one moment universal death on earth. Along
with that fire came exceptionally heavy hail, not of the kind
that is accustomed to fall to earth from a rain cloud, but

    sed quemcumque cadens ut deprimat atque ruinam
    pondere vel solo faciat. Coniungitur ergo
190 grandineum flammis ferventibus aere frigus
    et natura neci servans assignat utrumque.
    Hic primus stragem sparsis dat mortibus imber;
    exim restantem surgit consumere fructum
    brucus et excusso confidens crure lucusta.
195   Hoc sed docta malis et iam discrimine crebro
    tamquam lene satis callosa superbia duxit.
    Insequitur velox, gravius quae vindicet, ira.
    Caecas mane novo surgens sol sparserat umbras
    et laetus iubaris splendebat fronte sereni,
200 cum surgens mediam nubes se porrigit atra
    nascentemque diem depulso lumine clausit.
    In molem nox densa coit, perit obrutus aer
    palpantesque manus densas sensere tenebras
    atque repercussus vexatur anhelitus aeger,
205 et si sopitos flando quis suscitet ignes
    aut flammas excire velit, compressa necantur
    lumina nec vibrant restrictos pondere motus.
    Quo quemcumque loco tenebrosus repperit horror,
    continuit; vidit nullum nec visus ab ullo est.
210 Squalentes pariter viventia milia credas
    infernas intrasse domos aut forte revulsa
    obice terrarum patriam sordentis abyssi
    migrasse in superos ac mundum luce fugata
    sub leges misisse suas. Tres perdidit ista
215 nocte dies dignis pendens periuria tellus.

enough to crush anyone it fell on and to wreak destruction just by its weight alone. In this way the cold of hail was com- 190 bined in the air with the burning heat of flames, and nature, preserving each quality, enlisted them to kill. These storms first caused destruction and widespread death; then grasshoppers and locusts, supported by their outstretched legs, rose up to consume what crops remained.

Though already instructed by sufferings and by frequent 195 disasters, the ruler's stubborn pride still considered this quite insignificant. But divine wrath swiftly followed up with a more severe punishment. The rising sun had already scattered the dark shadows as a new morning broke, and its welcome visage with its clear beams was spreading its radiance, when a dark cloud rose up and extended itself 200 between earth and sun, shutting out the nascent day and banishing the light. That night coalesced into a dense mass, overwhelming and suppressing the air; hands in groping their way felt the thick texture of the darkness, and breathing, because obstructed, was weak and labored. If anyone 205 wanted to reignite dormant fires by blowing or to reawaken flames, their light was smothered and extinguished, the flickering sparks quenched by the weight of the gloom. Wherever the horror of that darkness came upon anyone, there that person remained; they saw no one and were seen by no one. You might have thought that thousands had en- 210 tered still living the forbidding homes of the underworld, or that the barrier between it and earth had been torn down and the realm of the gloomy abyss had been transferred to the population above ground and had submitted the world to its laws, after banishing the light. Then, in that unbroken night, the land forfeited three whole days in condign 215

Ista haec damnati; nam cetera fulgidus orbis
continet et solitos distinguunt tempora cursus.
   Moyses interea lacrimas, ieiunia, vota
continuat precibusque frequens ac pervigil instat,
220 maioris natu fultus solamine fratris.
Instruit hos sacris simul informatque Creator,
mystica sollemnem quo pandat victima ritum.
"Cernitis ut multa desudans clade reatum
Aegyptus contrita gemat satis undique tacta,
225 sed tamen inmota perstans cervice rebellis?
Nec portanda diu praecedunt ista ruinam.
Aegrotat quodcumque tumet, nec sana superbo
causa subest, iunctum monstrat mens turgida letum.
Unus adhuc restat, qui vindicet omnia, luctus
230 postque novem decima percellat caede merentes.
   "Vos modo perpetuos sacrorum discite mores
cultibus et propriis mansura lege tenete.
Mensibus in cunctis, orbis quos circinat anni,
iste caput princepsque foret, quem nomine belli
235 gentiles vocitant, vos tantum dicite primum,
lunaque bis septem cum fecerit addita noctes,
vespere tum sero dabitis primordia sacris.
Sumite mansuetum perfecti temporis agnum,
qui careat macula et purum det corpore vellus.
240 Hoc animal festis mactabitis, huius utrumque
signabit sanguis nitido de corpore postem.
Hoc dabit indicium servandae cura salutis:

punishment for its treachery. This is what the doomed alone experienced; for the rest of the world experienced the brightness of day, and time progressed according to its normal course.

Moses meanwhile carried on with his weeping, his fasting, and petitions, persisting with repeated prayers and vigils and supported by his elder brother's help. The Creator instructed both of them in sacred practices and showed them how a mystical victim would initiate a holy rite. "You see how Egypt, laboring under multiple disasters and thoroughly beaten down, laments the consequences of its guilt; but despite being assailed in every possible way, it remains resistant, its neck unbowed. Not long must they endure these sufferings, though, for they presage a catastrophe. Everything that swells with pride is sick, there is no health for the haughty, and a mind that is arrogant points to imminent death. A single cause for grief still remains to make the punishment complete, to strike down the guilty after nine plagues with a tenth and well-deserved slaughter.

"Your role is only to learn the sacred practices established for perpetuity and preserve them in your rituals with a permanent law. Among all the months that the circuit of the year traverses, this present one will be the principal and head—pagans name it after Mars, the god of war, but you should just call it the first. After the moon has added a further fourteen nights, then late in the evening perform the first stages of the holy rite. Take a gentle lamb of an age fully formed that is without stain and on its body bears a spotless fleece. You must sacrifice this animal at your feasting and let the blood from its immaculate body mark your two doorposts. Concern for securing your safety should prompt you

cum percussor aget tacitam sine vulnere caedem,
perspiciat sacro limen maduisse cruore,
245 hoc tantum transire volens. Distantia talis
custodiet vestras sparsis a mortibus aedes."
Sic nos, Christe, tuum salvet super omnia signum
frontibus inpositum, sic sanguis denique sanctus,
tunc praemonstrati dudum qui funditur agni,
250 oribus infusus postes lustrasse tuorum
inter labentis ferventia funera mundi
credatur casuque tuos discernat ab omni,
dum non signatos percurrit funere mucro.
Tu cognosce tuam salvanda in plebe figuram,
255 ut, quocumque loco mitis mactabitur agnus
atque cibo sanctum porrexerit hostia corpus,
rite sacrum celebrent vitae promissa sequentes.
Fermento nequam duplici de corde revulso
sincerum nitidae conspergant azyma mentis.
260   Finierat Rector leges et foedera festi
paschalis mandare viris, quod protinus omnes
arripuere simul. Peragunt convivia laeti
sollemnisque novo cultu disponitur esus,
transeat ad seros quae condita forma nepotes.
265   Nox erat et mediam carpebant cuncta quietem
umbraque libratas iamiam diviserat horas,
ecce venit tacito per dira silentia motu
angelus, exerto missus qui saeviat ense.
Nec confusa datur subiti sententia leti,
270 omne malum sed sorte cadit longeque videtur

to this sign: when the avenger without leaving a wound wreaks his silent slaughter, let him see that your doorway is daubed in holy blood and pass it alone by. This distinction 245 will protect your houses from the wide reach of death." In the same way, Christ, may your symbol marked on our foreheads protect us against all dangers, and may the holy blood shed long ago in prefiguration by the lamb, when taken in our mouths, be believed to sanctify the doorposts of your 250 people in the midst of the seething mortality of the failing world, to keep them from all harm when the sword ranges wide to deal out death to those unmarked by that sign. Recognize, reader, that the salvation of that people is a figure for you, so that, wherever the gentle lamb is sacrificed and 255 as victim offers up its holy body to eat, those pursuing the promise of life should celebrate the sacred rite in proper form. Let them expel the yeast of wickedness from unfaithful hearts and knead the pure unleavened substance of the spotless mind.

The divine ruler had finished communicating to the two 260 men the laws and covenants for the paschal festival, which all the people immediately as one adopted. Joyfully they celebrated a banquet with consecrated foodstuffs, following a new ritual that established a model to be passed down to later generations.

It was nighttime and everywhere was enjoying midnight 265 repose—already the darkness had equalized the hours to come and past—when, behold, an angel came with noiseless flight in ominous silence, dispatched to wreak violence with outstretched sword. But the sentence of death was not rushed or haphazard; all the suffering happened by design— 270 the plan for the prearranged deaths marked out in advance

quem petat in tenebris praefixi funeris ordo.
Maiores natu pereunt solique leguntur
ad mortem primos luci quos edidit ortus.
Cum dominis famuli pereunt natique potentum
275 permixta cum plebe cadunt, sic vilis, ut ille
quem celsi tenuit morientem purpura fulcri.
Haec nuda tellure iacent, haec serica velant,
disparibus stratis sternuntur corpora leto.
Non quemquam mors aequa timet, non excipit ullos,
280 in vivis tantum qui discernuntur, honores.
Pauperis ad fletum nulla pietate movetur;
ditibus ut parcat, nullo corrumpitur auro.
Aegrotum sanus, longaevum iunior ante
migrat; huic soli debet confidere nemo.
285 Hoc tantum tamen est, sibimet quo mortua distent,
vivant ut meritis, qui complent tempora sorte.
Hic numquam penitus morti licet; auferat etsi
iure potestatis lutea conpage creatum,
semine mortali genitum terraeque reductum,
290 iustorum in factis leto nil ceditur ulli.
    Ergo ut percussas suboles confusa repente
aula videt, currunt flentes ad funera matres;
mors patet et mortis non paret vulnere causa.
Pectora contundunt pugnis crinesque revellunt
295 unguibus et nigras festinant scindere malas.
Nec dominos planxere diu, mox occupat omnes
luctus quamque suus, sonat unus in aethere clamor
non uno ex fletu. Coniungit voce tumultum
nulla vacans a morte domus. Tum lumine multo
300 omni curatur populosum funus in urbe.

whom to target in the darkness. Only the elder sons perished; those who were born first to the light were chosen for death. Servants perished along with their masters, and the sons of the powerful fell in common with the ordinary people; it was alike with the humble as with the one who met his death enthroned on a purple-draped high couch. Some bodies lie on the naked earth, others are shrouded in silk, but though their beds may be different, all are cut down by death. Impartial, it fears no one, makes no exception for honors, which only among the living convey status. No pity can move it in response to the tears of the poor; no gold can bribe it to spare the rich. The healthy pass away before the sick, a younger man before the old; no one should rely on such a factor alone. There is only this one way for those who are fulfilling their allotted span of life to keep mortality at a distance, to live a life of virtue. In this case death never has any license whatsoever; though, by the power granted to it, it can carry off whatever is constructed of clay, born of mortal seed and reduced once more to earth, when it comes to the actions of the just, death is granted no purchase.

And so, when the court was suddenly thrown into confusion at the sight of the stricken children, mothers ran to the dead bodies with tears in their eyes; death was evident, but no wound showed the cause of death. They beat their breasts with their fists, tore their hair with their nails, and violently scarred their dark cheeks. Nor did they long weep for their masters, but soon each was gripped by her own private grief, and a single cry rose up to the sky from the tears of many. No house was free of death; they all joined their voices to the outcry. Then at full light the whole city was thronged with people conducting funerals. Business was

275
280
285
290
295
300

Iustitium iustum cogit maerere merentes.
Et dum quis proprio servat lamenta dolori,
exequias tardant luctus inhumataque turba
dilata iacuit tantisper sorte sepulchri
305 et nisi iam tandem vacuos et honore carentes
vel nuda tellure locet vel concremet igni,
vix collecta manus quae tantos clauderet urna.
    Tum regem circum commoto murmure sistit
maesta cohors humiles depromens voce querellas:
310 "Heu nimium nostris adversa potentia rebus
Hebraeum populi, totiens cui vindice dextra
militat omne malum, totus cui denique mundus
pugnat et irato succedunt prospera caelo.
Vis quaedam secreta dei maiorque potestas
315 haec in sceptra furit gentemque ulciscitur ipsam
orbis iactura. Solos pereuntia salvant
victores elementa suos redimuntque cadendo.
En iacet Aegyptus nec iam reparabilis ultra.
Atque utinam poenas vivis damnumque per arva
320 ferret adhuc divina manus nec funere tanto
deceptam subita vacuasset caede Canopum!
Tandem parce solo causasque expelle ruinae,
dum levior strages, dum quisquam luce tenetur,
dum superest qui terga premat, qui limite trudat
325 et, nequam si forte velint ex corde morari,
non sinat eiecto depellens hospite cladem.
Permoveat noster natorum funere luctus,

rightly suspended to allow those affected to grieve. While each person continued to lament his own grief, mourning protracted the funeral rites, with a large number of bodies lying unburied because entombment was for a period of time delayed; if they had not finally laid those untended and   305 lacking status in the unmarked earth or cremated them with fire, it would have been difficult to gather together a crew to enclose in a casket so many.

Then a grieving crowd gathered round the king with a buzz of agitation, expressing with their voices their humble protestations: "Alas, the power of the Hebrew people is all   310 too hostile to our welfare; so often does every evil fight on their behalf as their champion—on their behalf the whole world enters the fray, and prosperity attends them from the anger of heaven. Some god's hidden power and some greater force is enraged against this kingdom; the collapse of the   315 world's order takes vengeance for that nation. In perishing the elements bring salvation and victory to their own people alone and redeem them by failing. See, Egypt lies prostrate, no hope any longer of revival. If only the hand of a god was still only inflicting punishment on the living and the land   320 alone was suffering harm, that it had not taken Egypt by surprise with such slaughter, to empty it of its people with a sudden massacre. At last show mercy to this land, drive out the causes of destruction, while the slaughter is still limited, while some still remain in the light, and while there survives someone to harry that people from the rear, to drive them   from our borders, and, if perhaps they wish in the malice of   325 their hearts to linger, to prevent them, and in so doing evade disaster with the expulsion of that migrant band. May our grief at our sons' death move you, and perhaps your own

permoveat te forte tuus; vel pauca superstent
pignora quae tantos tergant servata dolores
330 et detruncatae reparent dispendia gentis."
His dictis lacrimas populus dedit. Ipse superbus
frangitur ad fletum princeps victumque fatetur.

    Haec perturbata sed dum tractantur in aula,
Hebraei vatum studio monitisque supernis
335 optima quaeque sacris fingunt epulisque requiri;
vasaque sollemnis quae poscat plurima cultus,
ornamenta etiam vestesque, monilia, gemmas
ut reddenda petunt. Nec tardus commodat hospes
ditat et ignorans trepidam manus aemula plebem.

340   Quae iam digna tuis pandantur laudibus ora,
summe Pater, qui tam saevo sic uteris hoste?
Adnuit adversus, largitur munera nolens,
quae secum dimissa ferant. Nec solvere tantum
sufficit oppressos, opibus ditantur euntes
345 thesaurosque novos libertas reddita sumit.
Inter ferventes inimica in sede furores
praedatur dominum fugiens fallitque videntem,
praesentem vacuat; non tam discedere pulsos
quam laetos migrare putes. Portantur avari
350 sic pharaonis opes, quem tunc mercede soluta
servitii longum credas taxasse laborem.
Nonnumquam rectis et quae contraria prosunt
et quae laeva malus voluit mutata recurrunt
in dextrum vertente Deo solosque nocentes

grief move you too; at least let a few children survive to assuage with their preservation our great grief and to restore the losses to our mutilated nation." With these words the people burst into tears. The proud ruler himself was overcome by weeping and confessed himself beaten.

While this was going on in the demoralized court, in accordance with the urging of their prophets and instructions from on high the Hebrews pretended that they needed all the very best objects for sacred rites and feasting; they demanded there be returned to them as their due the many vessels that customary ritual required, ornaments too and clothing, necklaces and jewels. Nor were their hosts slow to agree; in their ignorance that enemy confederacy made a fearful people rich.

What mouths now can worthily voice your praise, highest Father, who treat in this way so savage a foe? An opponent grants assent, unwillingly he lavishes bounty on the Hebrews for them to carry away. It is not enough just to free the oppressed people; as they leave they are enriched with possessions, and their restored freedom acquires new stores of wealth. Among burning passions in a hostile setting the fugitive despoils his master, tricks him before his very eyes, and robs him in his presence; you would think they were not so much departing in banishment as moving happily to a new location. In this way the greedy pharaoh's wealth was carried off; thereby, you might imagine, by paying such a price he had assessed the value of the long labor of servitude. Sometimes what is contrived against the good works to their advantage, and the evil intentions of the wicked change and turn out favorably when God transforms them,

355 vis odii perimens meditata in vulnera ducit
et partos fratri laqueos incurrere cogit.
    Egressi interea trepido de rege ministri
compellunt celerare fugam coguntque volentes,
praecipitant alacres et festinantibus instant
360 pellendasque putant pulsa cum gente ruinas.
Iam prope centenum compleverat advena lustrum
in regnis, Aegypte, tuis, ex tempore quondam
quo priscus patriarcha Iacob perduxerat illic
bis sena cum prole domum carosque nepotes,
365 quo per fecundum creverunt milia patrem.
    Procedit tandem populus moxque agmine iuncto
diram linquit humum tenebris ac luctibus orbam,
nam vicina dies nondum produxerat ortus.
Haec nox festa Deo redeuntibus annua sacris,
370 haec genti sollemnis erit, quae solvitur hoste.
Primo conspicuus fulgebat in ordine ductor
legifer adiuncto praecedens agmina fratre.
Post quos belliferae disponunt arma cohortes
ducunt et validas instructo robore turmas.
375 Arma ferunt humeris, enses per cingula laevo
dependent lateri, presso tum vertice cassis
fulget et albenti certat lux ferrea lunae.
Nituntur iaculis alii clipeosque sinistris
volvunt et rapido meditantur bella rotatu.
380 Gaudet pars etiam pharetris volucresque sagittas

while the force of hatred, consuming only the guilty, inflicts 355
on them the wounds they planned for others and compels
them to fall victim to the snares set for their brother.

Meanwhile, leaving the court, the ministers of the frightened king compelled the fugitives to quicken their flight
and drove them on, willing though they were; they were fast
moving, but the ministers hurried them along; they made
haste, but the ministers kept on their heels—they thought 360
that in getting rid of that people they would rid themselves
of disasters. That people had now fulfilled almost five hundred years as strangers in your kingdom, Egypt, since the
time when the ancient patriarch Jacob had brought there
his household, his twelve sons and their cherished offspring;
from that potent ancestor their numbers had increased to 365
thousands.

Finally the people set forth and in line of march soon left
behind that cursed land, desolate in darkness and grief, for
dawn had not yet broken on the following day. This night
was to be a festival holy to God, with rites repeated every
year; this was to be sacred for the nation that was released 370
from its foe. First in marching order shone prominently
their leader and lawgiver, in company with his brother at the
front of the line. Behind them warlike companies deployed
their weapons and led out powerful squadrons in a disciplined show of strength. They carried weapons on their 375
shoulders, swords hung on their left sides by belts, and a helmet gleamed on each encased head, its metallic glitter vying
with the silver moon. Some wielded their javelins, brandished their shields on their left hands, and with rapid flourishes prepared themselves for war. Another group took de- 380
light in its quivers and made ready swift-flying arrows to deal

hostis in occursum mittendis mortibus aptat
aut si forte virum fugientia terga sequatur,
ut pinnata leves transmittant spicula ventos.
   Incedit pavidum postrema per agmina vulgus
385 non inpar numero, caelum cum pingitur astris
aestuat aut motus pelagi crispantibus undis,
litore uel quantas converrit fluctus harenas
vel quantis stillant umentia nubila guttis.
Mirantur Pharii satrapae nec credere tantum
390 se potuisse vident; placet eiecisse tot hostes.
Sed non haec acies acie salvabere ferri.
Quamlibet innumeris peditum stipere catervis,
unus pugnabit cunctis pro milibus Auctor.
At populus lento moderatus tramite gressum
395 arreptum carpebat iter, praecedere tantum
aggressis ducibus, quantum vel tarda senectus
vel rudibus reptans infantia sustinet annis,
ne praematurus fragilem contristet eundo
aetatem sexumque labor. Sic cuncta supernus
400 dispensat nutus plebique adsistit ovanti.
   Ergo ubi signatis sederunt milia castris
armatusque pedes vulgus vallavit inerme,
vespere tum primo stanti assimulata columnae
insistens puro resplenduit aethere flamma—
405 non tamen ut moto dirum micat ignis in axe
prodita cum terris caeli portenta minantur
seu morbis tristem bellisque aut cladibus annum,
sed radiis fulgens et lumine candida laeto
ostendit nitidum castris mirantibus ignem.

out death when the enemy attacked or to have the feathered missiles cleave the gentle breezes, if they happened to be pursuing fleeing soldiers from the rear.

In the rear of the column walked the fearful masses, no less in number than the stars that spangle the sky or the cresting waves that tumble on the surge of the sea, than all the sands that the billows sweep together onto shore or all the drops of rain that moisture-laden clouds let fall. The Egyptian officers were astounded and realized they could never have imagined so great a host; they were glad that they had driven out so many enemies. But, O Hebrews, this force of yours will not be saved by the force of steel. Though you are accompanied by countless numbers of foot soldiers, it will take just one to fight for all your thousands: your Creator. So the people set out upon their journey, limiting their progress to a gentle pace, their leaders striving only to advance as far as the slowness of age or the foot-dragging of infants still of tender years could sustain, lest the ill-timed hardships of the journey wear down those frail in age or sex. In this way heavenly dispensation ordained all things and stood watch over the joyful people.

And so when in their thousands they had marked out and set up their camp, with armed foot soldiers encircling the unarmed masses, at the beginning of evening a flame took up a position in the clear heavens and shone out like a vertical column—but not in the way a fire shines ominously in the restless sky when the appearance of portents from the heavens threatens the earth with a year made grievous by disease, by war, or by catastrophe; rather with its luminous beams it showed to the amazed camp a brilliant fire, radiant

410 Diffugiunt tenebrae vicinaque sidera cedunt
et latuit rutilis oppressus fulgor in astris.
Obstipuere viri primum, perterruit omnes
incussitque metum novitas, tum luminis usus
paulatim caeleste iubar commendat amori.
415   Maxima nocturnas iam pars exegerat horas
 et volvenda dies instabat sorte propinqua.
Cunctorum ante oculos per caelum visa moveri
arripuitque viam populo spectante columna.
Protinus hanc patres sancti sensere sequendam,
420 esse ducemque ducum. Laeti mox praesule tanta
abrupere moras, castris excedere certant.
Tunc, ut quaeque tribus primum sortita laborem,
ordine carpit iter, sequitur tum cetera pubes.
    Haec inter clarum rediens lux pandit olympum,
425 flammea pallescit conspecto sole columna.
Vertitur in nubem totus qui fulserat ignis,
sed species perstat tensae super aethera formae.
Tertia nocturnos deterserat hora liquores
et matutinas scandens sol vicerat umbras;
430 ecce novum dictu, caelo servata sereno
frigida ferventi iussa est opponere nubes
se radio densumque parat tenuissima tegmen.
Sic circumiectis, tellus quis ardet eoa,
aestibus ignorat genuinum turba calorem,
435 vesperis ut credas leni respergine flatum
blanda vel umentes diffundere frigora ventos.
Nec tamen hanc nubem taetro suffusa colore

with welcoming light. The darkness dispersed, nearby con-   410
stellations gave way, and the brightness of glittering stars
was quenched and no longer visible. At first people were
struck dumb—its novelty terrified and sent a thrill of fear
through everyone—but then familiarity with the light grad-
ually won them over to love the heavenly beacon.

Now the greatest portion of the nighttime hours had   415
passed, and the day in its turn was approaching in close
order. Before everyone's gaze the pillar was seen to move
through the sky and, as the people looked on, it started its
journey. Immediately the holy elders realized that it should
be followed, that as leaders they should take their lead from   420
it. Rejoicing in such a protector, with no further delay they
eagerly vied to depart from the camp. Then each tribe took
up the march in order, according to the function it first was
assigned, and after them followed the rest of the youth.

In the meantime the returning light revealed the bright-
ness of the heavens, and the pillar of flame grew pale in the   425
sight of the sun. All that had previously shone as fire turned
into a cloud, but its appearance persisted as a shape that
stretched over the sky. Now the third hour had wiped away
the moisture of night, and the sun in its rising had van-
quished the morning mists, when, strange to relate, the   430
cloud, keeping its place in an otherwise cloudless sky, set up,
as bidden, a cooling barrier to the burning rays of the sun;
though very fine itself, it provided a dense protection.
Shielded in this way from the burning heat of eastern lands,
the mass of people was unaware of the true temperature;
you might think moist winds or the breezes of evening with   435
their gentle spray were spreading a soothing chill. Yet the
shape the cloud took on was neither of somber cast and

forma dabat nec concreto sic horrida vultu,
ut terrent, validos cum promunt nubila nimbos,
440   sed qualis madidi solem cum viderit arcus,
tanta fuit pulchrae species extenta columnae.
Noctibus ignis erat lumenque accensa ferebat,
cum sol torreret, gelidi dabat umida roris.
Has alternantem ducens cum tempore sortem
445   mutavit natura vices, substantia discors
muneribus propriis concordem reddidit usum.
Si mansit, mansere viri: si mota, secuti.
Si multis etiam iussa est pendere diebus,
subdita defixo tardabant agmina vallo.

450   Ista quater denis pietas percrebruit annis,
dum vastos heremi curris, Iudaee, recessus,
vincla pedum firmante via; dum tempore tanto
non attrita suum servarent tegmina pondus
mollitieque nova prisci durantis amictus
455   sic longaeva foret, quod non damnosa vetustas;
dum sacrum populo victum candentia manna
ferrent et caeli frugem terrena viderent,
per quam sublimis praediceret ante figura
edendum ex utero purum sine semine corpus,
460   quo caperet pascenda salus de sede superna
inlabente Deo sanctis altaribus escas.
Hoc signo summus percussa rupe sacerdos
protulit inriguos populis sitientibus haustus.
Christum namque vides stabilem consistere petram,

coloring nor ominous and of close-packed appearance like clouds that terrify when they produce violent rainstorms, but rather the extended form of its beautiful column was like the moist rainbow when it has seen the sun. At night-time it was fiery and caught alight to give illumination, but when the sun was burning hot, it produced a mist of cooling dew. Nature rang the changes, alternating the circumstances with the time of day, and each contrasted substance by its distinctive properties produced identical benefits. If the pillar stayed, the people stayed in place; if it moved, they followed. And too if it was bidden to remain suspended for many days, in obedience the forces stayed where they were within a secure rampart.

That bounty lasted for forty long years, while you set your course, O Jew, through the vast remoteness of the desert, the very journey strengthening the sandals that enclosed your feet; for that whole long period your dress showed no wear and preserved its substance intact—the passage of time, though extended, caused no damage to your long-worn but hardy clothing, which retained its softness as if new. Then brilliant white manna provided your people with sanctified nourishment, and the realm of earth saw a harvest from heaven. By this food a noble symbol foretold in advance that a body was to be consumed that came pure without seed from the womb, and by it salvation would draw sustenance from the celestial abode, as God descended upon the sacred altars. In accordance with this sign the highest priest brought forth a streaming draft of water for his thirsty people by striking a rock. For you see therein that Christ is a

465 percussus iaculo largas qui praebuit undas
porrexitque suis sacro de vulnere potum.
    Hebraei interea laeti ducente columna
per terras gressu, per caelum visibus ibant.
Ecce iterum Phariis insedit mentibus ira
470 et populus sine more ferox his vocibus armat
tandem postremos vicina morte furores:
"O nimium stultis inludens mentibus error
praestigiaeque satis nebulosa in fraude peractae!
Nonne pudet famulam nullo certamine gentem
475 sic inpune rapi? quo numine praesule tanto
deseruit vacuas discedens accola terras?
Rura vacant, coeptis desistunt oppida muris,
non solitum consurgit opus, non cultor in agris
exercet validos attrito dente ligones.
480 Torpidus exactor siluit nulloque tumultu
fervida consuetos repetunt suspendia census.
Quin potius sumptis exercitus inruat armis
imbellemque manum profugosque reducat alumnos.
Quos si servilis tantum succenderit ausus
485 ut telis certare velint, mox occidat omnis
confusa cum plebe manus. Ferventibus armis
permixtae pereant confosso pectore matres,
uberibus iunctos configant spicula natos.
Prolem quisque suam cernens ante ora cadentem
490 oblatis optet iugulis succurrere mortem.
Orbatum nostros faciat libare dolores
ultima sors populum: sic vivens omnia perdat,
tum pereat. Densa campi sub strage latentes

firm-founded rock, who brought forth abundant waters 465
when struck by a spear and offered a drink to his people
from his holy wound.

Meanwhile the Hebrew people, as the pillar led the way,
journeyed happily on foot over land, while fixing their gaze
on the heavens. But, see, once more anger took possession
of the Egyptians' minds and that people of unequaled feroc- 470
ity, as death drew near, finally steeled itself with these words
to a last frenzy: "Oh delusion, making mockery of our too-
foolish minds, and trickery contrived with quite fantastical
deceit! Is it not shameful that a servile race is snatched from
us scot-free in this way, without a fight? What god's protec- 475
tion is so great that a land's inhabitants have departed and
left it desolate? The countryside is empty, city building has
come to a halt, walls only half-completed, no construction
rises up in the usual way, in the fields no farmer wields sturdy
mattocks with their worn-down blades. Taskmasters have 480
grown silent and idle, and the din of violent tortures extort-
ing the customary quotas has ceased. Instead let our army
take up its weapons and march to bring back this unwarlike
band of fugitive dependents. But if their servile boldness
has so inflamed them that they want to challenge us to arms, 485
let their whole force perish, armed and unarmed alike. Let
mothers, caught up in the turmoil of war, perish pierced
through the chest, and spearpoints transfix their children
cradled at their breasts. Let them all, seeing their children
falling before their eyes, voluntarily offer their throats and 490
go to meet death. Let their last hours give that people in
their desolation a taste of our grief: let them lose everything
while living, and then die. And let the ground be invisible
under the thick pile of corpses and expose their bodies

tristi committant inhumata cadavera caelo.
495 Inde ubi iam totos satiaverit ense furores,
thesauros revocet fugientes dextera victrix."
Talibus excitas acuebant flatibus iras
inridente Deo, solus qui dispicit omnem
conatum rigido meditantem vana tumore
500 consiliumque ducum cassato dissipat actu.
    Ergo bella rogant. Fervens rapit arma iuventus,
spumantes ducuntur equi phalerisque potentes
suspendunt alacres splendentia frena iugales.
Pugnax pompa nitet, subiectos curribus axes
505 aurato temone trahunt. Tum cetera pubes
induitur chalybe aut fulvo circumdatur aere.
Hi loricarum vasto sub tegmine gaudent,
intexit creber sibimet quas circulus haerens,
atque catenosi crepitant per corpora panni.
510 Ast aliis tenui concurrens lammina ferro,
qua se succiduas iunctim scandente per oras
flectitur, adsuti cratis compacta metalli
horrentes habitus diversa fecerat arte.
Et tamen ardentum cuncta inter tela virorum
515 terribilis plus forma fuit. Quis namque furentes
spectet, quos laetos vix possit cernere vultus?
Inclusae galeis facies et ferrea vestis
cinxerat iratas armorum luce tenebras.
Progreditur collecta manus; rex ipse frementes
520 curru cogit equos, telis tamen undique saeptus
delituit, densam reddunt hastilia silvam.

unburied to the unforgiving heavens. Only when it has   495
slaked all its passion with the sword should our victorious
hand reclaim the fugitive wealth." With such bluster they
roused and intensified their anger, only to be mocked by
God, who alone scorns every undertaking that with over-
bearing arrogance conceives empty ambitions and who con-   500
founds the planning of rulers, bringing it to nothing.

Accordingly they demanded war. The soldiery in a frenzy
snatched up their weapons, and war horses, foaming at the
mouth, were paraded forward, swift teams reveling in their
finery with glittering bridles draped over their necks. The
procession, primed for war, was a brilliant sight, as with
gilded yoke beams they advanced the axle-borne chariots.   505
Then followed the rest of the young men, dressed in steel or
swathed in tawny bronze. Some rejoiced in the enveloping
protection of breastplates woven from numerous interlock-
ing rings, chainmail that rattled on their bodies as they
moved. Others wore thin iron plates joined together at the   510
points where the successive edges of the plates provided
flexibility. Though its manufacture was different, the dense
corselet of interlinked metal made for a terrible appearance.
But yet amid all these weapons still more terrible was the   515
appearance of the impassioned soldiers themselves. For
who could bear to look at them in their frenzy, when their
countenances, even when happy, were difficult to look on.
Their faces were enclosed in helmets, and their coats of iron
set off their dark and angry features against the brilliance of
their weaponry. The forces massed together and advanced;
the king himself drove forward his chariot's snorting team,   520
only to disappear from view, encircled by weapons on every
side, with a dense forest of spears around him. The earth

Concutitur pulsata rotis et pondere tellus,
angustavit humum latam stipata iuventus
conclusitque vias. Quidquid virtutis habere
525 Aegyptus potuit, totum mors proxima ducit.
    Iunxerat interea, ponto qua Magdalus instat,
Hebraeus populus rubranti castra profundo
evasos credens securis mentibus hostes.
Dum resident fixoque parant requiescere vallo,
530 cernunt pulvereas in caelum surgere nubes.
Cunctatis primum mox agmina saeva patescunt,
non tamen infensas patitur committere partes
sole sub occiduo vicinus proelia vesper.
    Distulit in lucem vallatus bella tyrannus,
535 et fors ardentes nondum compesceret iras
nec servare furor potuisset foedera nocti
auroramque velit motis praecedere signis,
flammea ni retro subsistens forte columna
obiectu medio gentes discerneret ambas.
540 Contemplans rex ipse tamen mirabile lumen
sic ignem metuit, quod sensu fervidus ardet.
Paulatimque mori non profuit; itur ad unam,
quae claudat cunctas pelago pandente, ruinam.
    Plebs trepidat conclusa loco finemque sequenti
545 expectat pavefacta die, non tela nec ullas
bellorum molita vices, sed voce levata
vatibus insistens: "O terque quaterque beati,
Aegyptus quos morte tulit tellure vel ampla
urnam defunctis suprema sorte paravit!
550 Digni qui tantos nequeant sentire dolores

shook under the impact of the heavy chariot wheels, and the massed ranks of soldiery made a broad plain seem small, blocking all passageways through. Imminent death was enticing onward all the might that Egypt could muster. 525

Meanwhile the Hebrew people had set up camp by the sea in a place called Magdal, close by its red waters, confidently believing that they had escaped the enemy. But as they were settling down and preparing to take their rest behind a secure rampart, they saw clouds of dust mounting to 530 the sky. Hesitating at first, they soon saw clearly the fierce enemy columns; the approach of evening, however, and the setting sun forbade the hostile parties to engage in battle.

That tyrant in his fortified camp put off warfare till the morning. Perhaps he would have no longer controlled his 535 burning rage, unable in his frenzy to respect the night and keep its truce, but instead would have deployed his standards in advance of dawn, if the fiery column, taking up a position behind, had not separated the two nations with an intervening barrier. Yet the king, in observing that remark- 540 able light, both feared its fire, and himself was passionately aflame in his senses. Nothing was to be gained by meeting death piecemeal; they were on their way to one single catastrophe that would subsume each individual disaster with the parting of the sea.

The Hebrew people were terrified to find themselves cut off and fearfully expected to meet their end the next 545 day. They wielded no weapons, however, made no warlike preparations, but with raised voices assailed their prophet-leaders: "Oh thrice and four-times happy are those whom Egypt received in death, to provide burial for their bodies at the last in its wide earth. They had the good fortune to 550

nec stragem prolis vel pignora capta videre.
Alitibus nos esca dati nec sede sepulchri
condita deserto solvemur corpora vasto.”
Talia voce viri; respondit luctibus omne
555   vulgus et accenso persultat turba tumultu.
    Tum sancti coepere duces promissa referre
solarique metum fletusque abstergere dictis.
“Quaesumus, ingratos deponite mente timores
experti multum, nec desperanda putetis
560   quae tantis spondent caelestia munera signis.
Infidisne potest elabi cordibus umquam
Aegyptus tot caesa malis interque flagella,
succumbens quae sensit humus, vos cunctaque vestra
afflicti regno salvos vixisse sub hostis?
565   Quid de transactis dicatur? Nempe videtis
ut mediatricis curet tutela columnae,
ne quid ab adversa liceat nos fraude vereri.
Quin magis erectas firma spe tollite mentes.
Ultima namque dies defixa est crastina genti,
570   quae nunc bella crepans sumptis confidit in armis.
Non sic pugna foret: nec telis tela feretis
obvia nec vestro vobis sudore triumphus
hac vice proveniet; caeli pugnabitur ira,
qua vobis placido peragentur proelia nutu.”
575   Talibus intenti vates deiecta levabant
corda virum, sancta sedantes voce timorem.
    At pontum validus ferventi flamine ventus
urebat tota consumens nocte profundum,

escape sharing our great suffering and seeing family slaughtered and children taken into captivity. We are doomed to be food for birds, and our bodies, with no tomb to house them, will decompose in this vast desert." Such were the words of the menfolk; but the whole throng responded to the grief and as one burst out in a passionate outcry.　555

Then the saintly leaders began to remind them of promises, to console their fears, and to wipe away with a speech their tears. "After all you have experienced, put from your minds, we beg, these ungrateful fears, and do not despair of　560 the promises heavenly bounty made to you with so many signs. Can your faithless hearts ever forget that Egypt was scourged by so many plagues, but that among those blows that the afflicted land endured you and all your property lived safe and sound in the realm of your chastened foe? But　565 why dwell on past events? Surely you see how the protection provided by an interposed column ensures that we need fear nothing from our enemy's hostile intent. No, rather be strong in hope, bolster your spirits, raising them up high. For tomorrow is appointed as the last day for that nation that now is agog for war, fully confident in the weaponry it　570 has mustered. That will not be the kind of battle it will be: you will not match weapons with weapons, nor will your triumph on this occasion depend on the sweat of your brow; the wrath of heaven will take up arms for you and will bring the battle to completion by God's benevolent ordinance." With these words the devoted prophets raised the people's　575 hearts from their dejection, laying to rest their fears with this saintly speech.

All night a strong, scorching wind was blowing, burning up the sea and consuming its depths, as the Father, acting

contra naturam Genitor dum fulminat undas,
580 ardet et afflatus percusso in gurgite fluctus.
Iam matutinum pervenerat horrida tempus
vix acies primosque nitens aurora rubores
spargebat mundo, taetris cum protinus omnes
erumpunt castris, fremit undique mota iuventus.
585 At pavidae plebis postquam pervenit ad aures
clangentisque tubae percussit pectora terror,
arripiunt carpuntque viam qua proxima ponti
litora sollicitant rubro nudata liquore.
    Ut summas pelagi populus pervenit ad oras,
590 cessit confestim ducti reverentia fluctus
expanditque viam, cui terram clauserat hostis.
Machina, pendentis struxit quam scaena liquoris,
frenatas celso suspenderat aere lymphas.
Aggreditur medium fugiens vincensque sequentes
595 gens electa Dei, figens vestigia terris
in regione maris. Calcantur saxa profundi,
conterit et nudum percurrens orbita limum;
torridus aspectum scissis sol inserit undis
ignotamque novo contingit lumine terram.
600 Longior et radius spatium descendere tantum
certavit fessumque iubar vix impulit imis.
    Credidit exclusos primum fluctuque repulsos
inque fugam versos Pharius dare terga tyrannus.
Praecipitare moras tali iubet agmina verbo:
605 "Ecce iterum fugitiva cohors pendentia bella
deserit auxilioque pedum confisa recedit.
Vos armis premite et clausis insistite tantum,
cetera pontus aget." Vix haec perdixerat, illi

counter to nature, hurled his bolt at the waters, and with its   580
impact on the flood the waves caught fire in the blast. Now
jagged shafts of sunlight had only just advanced to morning,
and bright dawn was spreading its first flush over the world,
when the whole soldiery immediately burst out from their
squalid camp, raising a universal roar as they moved for-
ward. But after the blare of trumpets reached the apprehen-   585
sive Israelites' hearing and struck terror in their hearts, they
quickly took up their march to where the nearby shoreline
of the sea, emptied of its red waters, summoned them.

When that people came right to the edge of the sea, in   590
obeisance the waves swiftly withdrew to make way, opening
up a sea path in place of the land route the enemy had
blocked off. The edifice that the wall of suspended water
had created held in check the waves poised high in the air.
Through its midst the chosen people of God advanced in
their flight; vanquishing their pursuers, they set foot on land   595
in the realm of the sea. They trod on the rocky seabed, and
their movement left a track scoured in the exposed mud,
while the burning sun penetrated with its gaze the parted
waves and shed on a strange land its unfamiliar light. Its rays   600
lengthened as they strove to descend so deep, and its ex-
hausted beams barely made it to the bottom.

The Egyptian tyrant first thought that, blocked off and
driven back by the waves, they had turned tail and fled.
With the following words he ordered his troops to brook no
delay: "Look, once more that refugee band shuns imminent   605
war and retreats, their only recourse to take to their heels.
They are trapped; just keep at them with your weapons and
maintain the pressure, the sea will take care of the rest."
Scarcely were these words out of his mouth, when his men

prosiliunt cursuque ruunt attingere litus.
610   Ut venere, vident arentis vasta profundi
insolitam praebere viam pansoque recessu
ceu trepidas fugisse piis calcantibus undas;
hos quoque per siccum tutos descendere callem,
securos pelagi atque sui, non arma nec ipsum
615   formidare satis patientem vincula pontum.
    Substitit ad modicum restrictis motibus agmen
frenaque suspensos tenuerunt ducta iugales.
Atque aliquis, cui vel tenuem permota calorem
tunc scintilla dabat cordi, sic forte locutus:
620   "Quis deus a prisco detorquet cardine mundum
lege nova mutatque vices et condita turbat?
Nam si servatur rebus natura creatis,
monstriferae quae causa viae? Quid denique restat,
si mare transitur gressu, nisi navibus arva
625   sulcentur caelumque suo decurrat ab axe,
in superos inferna levent, plaga fervida caeli
algeat, adflatam succendat scorpius ursam,
haec nisi confusus rerum subverterit ordo.
Non duce me quisquam siccum descenderit aequor;
630   sit suspecta mihi quae semita dirigit hostem.
Nam si bella velit librans aequalia numen,
obice servata fugitivum clauserat agmen.
Nunc abeant tantumque vagos sua monstra sequantur.
Nec satis amplectar, scissum circumvenit alte

surged forward and pell-mell charged up to the shore. When 610
they came there, they saw that the vast expanse of the dried-
up sea was furnishing an unaccustomed pathway and had
laid bare its depths, as if its waters had fled in fear before the
tread of the holy. They saw too that the Hebrew people were
moving safely downward along a dry track, unconcerned for
the sea or themselves, and that they had no fear of weapons
or of the waters, which readily submitted to be put in chains. 615

For a moment the column came to a halt; reins were
drawn in, and the horses pulled up in their stride. Then a
person, in whose heart a spark kindled to ignite some slight
flash of understanding, spoke as follows: "What god is di- 620
verting the world from its ancient axis with a new dispensa-
tion, changing its laws, and throwing into confusion what is
established? For if the nature of creation is preserved, what
is the reason for this unnatural pathway? What after all re-
mains, if the sea is crossed by foot, but for fields to be
plowed by ships, the heavens to abandon their revolution, 625
the underworld mount to the living above, the torrid zone
of the sky grow cold, the scorpion inflame the bear with its
breath, and in sum the world order be overwhelmed and
throw everything into confusion. I will not lead anyone
down into the dry seabed; let me retain my distrust of the 630
path that the enemy is taking. For if some divinity wanted to
balance equally the odds of war, he would have retained that
barrier and blocked off the fugitive host. Leave them now,
let them go, with only their freaks of nature for company
on their wanderings. I have no intention of experiencing
what the sea encloses between those high screens of water,

635 quod pelagus nudo celans discrimina fundo.”
Excipit haec ardens cum seditione tumultus
instantisque latens urget sententia leti.
    Vicerat aequoream pedibus plebs inclita vallem,
gurgitis et vacui conexa volumina linquens
640 post baratrum superas scandebat litore terras.
Effertur nigri dux agminis et pharaonem
ira subit proprio vocitatum nomine Cencren.
Arripiunt pariter reserati concava ponti
invaduntque viam. Quid non furor audeat amens?
645 Hinc equitum pars agmen agit, pars inde citatis
ire iubet stimulis rapidas super arva quadrigas.
Ut medium venit frendens equitatus in aequor
accusatque moras tam lati gurgitis ardens
ira virum, tremit artato pars altera mundo.
650 Tum per sublimem splendenti nube columnam
de caelo vox missa tonat verbique superni
interpres sanctum compellans nomine Moysen:
“Venit,” ait, “tempus, mea quo mandata probentur.
Aegypto iam finis erit, iam clade suprema
655 tot castigatam vicibus sententia gentem
puniet expugnans: ensis succede flagellis.
Tu modo divisum virga iam percute fluctum
atque reducta suos assumant aequora vultus.”
    Ille genu fixo siccati marginis oras
660 et litus, cui fluctus abest, mox iussus ut adsit,
percutit insigni credens mysteria ligno.
Hinc subitus crepitare fragor, tonat undique circum

what dangers it conceals in the exposed seabed." A violent   635
and rebellious outcry greeted these words; unobserved, a
sentence of imminent death was driving them on.

The illustrious Hebrew people had successfully traveled
on foot through the valley of waters and, leaving behind
them the wall of waves suspended over the empty gulf,
climbed from the abyss by the shore to higher land. At this   640
the commander of the dusky army was beside himself; the
pharaoh, who went by the name of Cencres, was possessed
by rage. His troops, charging forward with one accord,
surged into the hollow valley opened up in the sea. What
would that mad frenzy not dare? Some advanced in columns   645
of cavalry, others spurred their chariots with whips to speed
over the ground. While the impassioned horsemen reached
the middle of the sea and in their burning anger complained
of the delay caused by the broad expanse of the waters, a
second group feared the narrow confines of the world they
found themselves in. At that moment a voice sent from   650
heaven thundered out in a column of shimmering cloud
high in the sky and addressed the holy man Moses by name,
communicating the words of the Most High. "The time has
come," it said, "when my commands will be vindicated. Now
the end of Egypt is at hand, now my sentence will vanquish
a nation already chastised so many times and punish it with   655
a final disaster: scourge, give place to sword. You, Moses,
only strike the parted waves with your staff; let the waters
return, assuming their wonted appearance."

Moses then knelt down and, putting his faith in wood's
special mystery, struck the shore at the dry water's edge for   660
the waves that were missing before to immediately return
there at his bidding. At that there was a sudden crashing

lympha ruens primumque illic committitur unda,
qua monstrabat iter Phario sors ultima regi.
665 Postquam clausa via est fluctusque repellit euntem,
paenitet intrati iam gurgitis et fuga serum
molitur reditum. Trepidae dant terga cohortes
armaque proiciunt; pontus fugientibus instat
occurritque sequens, perit undique circumiectus
670 decurrentis aquae laxatis murus habenis.
Ille ferus semper, iam mitis morte sub ipsa:
"Non haec humanis cedit victoria bellis;
expugnamur," ait, "caeloque evertimur hoste.
Effuge quisque potes victusque evade satelles,
675 nec iam tela deo conatibus ingere cassis."
O si compunctas humana superbia mentes
ante obitum mutare velit! Quid denique prodest
tunc finem posuisse malis, cum terminus urget,
praesentis vitae spatium dum ceditur aevo?
680 "Confitearis!" ait "Sanus" scriptura "valensque."
Si tunc peccatum quisquam dimittere vovit
cum peccare nequit, luxu dimittitur ipse.
Ergo exaltatis pendens sustollitur undis
mox mergenda phalanx. Lympharum monte levata
685 pondere telorum premitur, fundoque tenaci
indutum revehunt morientia corpora ferrum.
Pars exarmatis cum primum libera membris
implicuit nantes miseris complexibus artus,

sound, and on every side water came rushing and thunder-ing all around, as the waves first massed where his final des-tiny was revealing to the royal pharaoh the road he was to follow.

After his path was blocked and the waves prevented his passage, he regretted then having entered the sea and too late strove to take to his heels in retreat. His troops mean-while turned tail in panic, throwing away their weapons, but the sea pressed them hard in their flight, pursuing and over-taking them, while on every side, all around them, the wall of water collapsed in floods as the restraints were released. Pharaoh himself, always fierce, now softened at the moment of death, said, "No human warfare gained this victory; heaven is the enemy by whom we have been overwhelmed and defeated. The day is lost, my servants, all who can es-cape, do so, flee away, and no longer waste your efforts in hurling weapons against a god." Oh, if only human pride would feel repentance in its heart and seek to change before death! How does it profit to put a stop to wickedness, when the end is nigh and the course of life on earth is succumbing to old age? "Confess!" say the scriptures, "Be strong and sound." If someone vows to cast aside sinfulness when he can no longer sin, he himself will be cast aside for his cor-rupt life.

So that army, destined soon to be drowned, was held sus-pended on the cresting waves. Borne up on the mountain-ous waters, they were weighed down by the heaviness of their weapons, and the iron armor they were wearing carried their dying bodies down to the clinging seabed. Some, as soon as they had freed their limbs from armor, clung to other swimmers' bodies in a doomed embrace, only to

auxilio decepta perit pariterque tenentes
690   alterno sub fasce ruunt nexique necantur.
Ast alii, lassata diu dum brachia iactant,
incurrunt enses iaculisque natantibus haerent,
concolor et rubro miscetur sanguine pontus.
Quin et conspicuus princeps Memphitidis aulae,
695   candentes ducens nigro rectore iugales,
inspector cladis propriae gentisque superstes
ultimus ingressis per currum naufragat undis.
    Bella vacant pugnante salo vincitque quietus
Israhel solo peragens certamina visu.
700   Tum vallis completa perit fluctuque reverso
ducitur extentum planati gurgitis aequor.
Litore iactantur tum taetra cadavera toto
exposuitque suum pelagus super arva triumphum.
    Inclitus egregium sollemni carmine ductor
705   describit factum, toto quod psallitur orbe,
cum purgata sacris deletur culpa fluentis
emittitque novam parientis lympha lavacri
prolem post veteres, quos edidit Eva, reatus.
De qua sermonem praemisso carmine sumpsit,
710   luctificos replicat tenuis dum pagina lapsus.
Si quid triste fuit, dictum est quod paupere versu,
terserit hic sacri memorabilis unda triumphi,
gaudia quo resonant, crimen quo tollitur omne
per lavacrum vivitque novus pereunte veterno;
715   quo bona consurgunt, quo noxia facta necantur,
Israhel verus sacris quo tingitur undis;

perish unrescued, for by holding on to each other the cou- 690
ples sank under the doubled burden and died entwined.
Others swam for a long time, flailing their arms till they be-
came weary, only to be struck by swords or impaled by float-
ing spears; the sea mingled with the blood, both equally red
in color. Plain for all to see was the ruler of the Egyptian
palace, urging on his snow-white team and its dark-skinned 695
driver; spectator of his own disaster and last survivor of his
nation, he plunged into the waters to be shipwrecked on a
chariot.

No need for warfare, the sea fought the battle and Israel
was victorious without raising a finger, prosecuting the con-
flict only by watching it. Then the dry valley filled up and 700
disappeared; the waves returned, and the level surface of
the waters stretched into the distance. Then foul corpses
were thrown up all along the shore, and the sea revealed its
triumph on dry land.

The famous leader of the Hebrews described that glori-
ous event in a celebratory hymn which is sung throughout 705
the world, when sin was wiped clean away by the sacred
wave, and the waters of regenerative baptism gave birth to a
new race after the ancient crimes Eve had committed. My
slender page took up the subject of Eve in the previous
poem, when it told of her grievous fall. But the memorable 710
wave of the holy triumph has wiped away all the grief that
my poor verse then recounted, whereby joyfulness rings out
loud, all sin is purged by that cleansing, and a new man
comes into being as the old one perishes; by that act good 715
deeds flourish, wrongdoing is done away with, and the true
Israel is washed in those sacred waters; because of it too a

consona quo celebrat persultans turba tropaeum,
quo praecurrentes complentur dona figurae
quas pius explicuit per quinque volumina vates.
720 Nosque tubam stipula sequimur numerumque tenentes
hoc tenui cumbae ponemus litore portum.

harmonious chorus sings in exultation a triumphant song, and prefigurations of God's bounty that the holy prophet unfolded in five books achieve consummation. With my   720
reed pipe I take my lead from his clarion and, keeping the same number of books, I will bring my slender bark to harbor here ashore.

IN CONSOLATORY PRAISE OF CHASTITY

Prologus Alcimi Aviti episcopi
ad Apollinarem episcopum

Domino sancto beatissimo et piissimo germano Apollinari episcopo Alcimus Avitus frater in Christo.

Post consummationem libellorum, quos non sic ut voluerat, edidit dispositio mea, sed tua sodaliumque quorumpiam festinatio affectuosa quidem, sed inconsulta praeripuit, cogis insuper tibi specialius dari versus illos, quos ad venerabilem Fuscinam sororem nostram de consolatoria castitatis laude conscripsi. Quos tamen cum ego post denuntiatum poematis finem epigramma rectius dicerem, tu primum libri nomine vocitasti, hoc scilicet vocabulum prolixitati eius adserens convenire. Quapropter habe me etiam in hac parte famulantem iudicio, immo potius affectui tuo, quoniam profecto iniquum est, ut, cui parui in maioribus, in exiguis contradicam. Meminerit autem pietas tua hunc ipsum, quem sic vocas, libellum vel de religione parentum communium vel de virginibus nostrae familiae familiarius disputantem illis tantummodo legendum dare, quos re vera nobis aut vinculum propinquitatis aut propositum religionis adnectit. Potes enim ex materiae qualitate metiri, quod germanae sanctimoniali secreta meditatione compositum vix vel tibi crebra victus iussione confiteor, quando aut qualiter

Prologue of Bishop Alcimus Avitus
to Bishop Apollinaris

Alcimus Avitus, his brother in Christ, to his holy lord and most blessed and pious brother, Bishop Apollinaris.

After the completion of the books which, in affectionate if ill-considered haste, you and some of your friends purloined from me so that I could not arrange for their publication as I wished, you are forcing me in addition to make a particular gift to you of those verses that I wrote to our revered sister Fuscina on the praise of chastity, in consolation. After giving notice of the completion of that poem, I would more properly have termed it an epigram, but you have given it the name of a book, no doubt maintaining that this title suits better its wordiness. Accordingly, in this matter too count me obedient to your judgment, or rather to your affectionate disposition, for certainly it is entirely improper to contradict in small things one to whom I have deferred in greater. May your holiness bear in mind, however, that this little book, as you call it, which treats intimately of the devotion of our common kinsfolk and the virgins of our immediate family, should be given to read only to those whom family ties or a shared religious profession truly binds to us. You will be able to judge from the nature of the subject matter when and how I would want a work written in secret for my holy sister coming into the hand of strangers, when I confess its existence only reluctantly and after much urging

venire in extraneorum manus velim. Sane a faciendis versi-
bus pedibusque iungendis pedem de cetero relaturus, nisi
forte evidentis causae ratio extorserit alicuius epigrammatis
necessitatem, cuius tamen tantam exiguitatem fore pol-
liceor, ut ei aliud nomen assumere nec ipse praesumas. De-
cet enim dudum professionem, nunc etiam aetatem nos-
tram, si quid scriptitandum est, graviori potius stilo operam
ac tempus insumere nec in eo inmorari, quod paucis
intellegentibus mensuram syllabarum servando canat, sed
quod legentibus multis mensurata fidei adstructione deser-
viat.

even to you. Certainly in the future I intend to step back from writing verse and joining up metrical feet, unless motivated by some clear reason that unavoidably compels the composition of an epigram, but, if that is the case, I can promise that such will be its shortness that not even you would presume to propose another name for it. For it has long befitted my calling, and now too my age, to devote my efforts and time, if something must be written, to a weightier style and not occupy myself with poetry that by preserving the proper measure of syllables appeals to a few cognoscenti, but rather compose something for a large number of readers that serves the purpose of well-measured instruction in the faith.

Suscipe complectens, Christo dignissima virgo,
Alcimus ista tibi quae mittit munera frater
inque levi calamo causarum respice pondus
et tenuis fortem commendet cantus amorem.
5   Nam quotiens sanctum compleveris ordine cursum
alternos recinens dulci modulamine psalmos,
quos vivens in corde chelys virtute canora
interiore sono castis concentibus aptat,
tunc licet excusso libeat tibi ludere versu
10 atque fatigatam meditando absolvere mentem.
    Non hic fallaci tinguetur barbitus unda,
Pegasus unde leves praevertens motibus auras
fingitur assumpto pendens hinnisse volatu,
dum ferretur equi gravis ungula praepete pinna.
15 Sed nec Pierio ducent hic cantica ludo,
quas sibi ter ternas mentitur fama sorores.
Dat tibi germanum sed verax musica plectrum
et Christum resonans claudetur fistula Phoebo.
    Edidit ut quartam genetrix Audentia prolem
20 teque dedit generi partu fecunda supremo,
confestim parcam promittit ducere vitam
ac deinceps paribus castum servare cubile
constituit votis carorum cura parentum.
Et quia principium tam sancti foederis esses,

Receive in your embrace, virgin most worthy of Christ, this gift that your brother Alcimus dispatches to you; though its style is light, respect the weight of its subject matter and let my song, however insubstantial, reveal the strength of my love. For whenever you have completed in proper form the holy service with the sweet singing of responsive psalms— psalms that the living lyre in your heart, made tuneful by your goodness, sounds within you with chaste harmonies— then you may find diversion in my labored verse and by studying it relax your weary mind.

This lyre of mine will not be dipped in the fictitious waters at which Pegasus, outstripping the gentle breezes in his movements, is falsely said to have whinnied as he hung suspended in midflight, when the weight of the horse's hoof was borne aloft by swift-beating wings. Neither will the nine sisters, the subject of lying renown, inspire this song with their playful Pierian strains. Instead it is truthful music that brings you your brother's playing; the pipe that sounds of Christ will be denied to Phoebus Apollo.

When our mother Audentia gave birth to you, her fourth child, and brought you into our family as the last offspring of her fertile womb, she immediately promised to adopt a life of austerity, and our dear parents with shared vows committed themselves to maintain thereafter a chaste marriage bed. And because you were the initiator of so holy a pact,

25 tu simul offerris Christo, qui protinus ipsis
    accipit in cunis lactantia membra dicatis.
    Sic quondam, cum prima novo splendesceret ortu
    terra nitens pulchrasque darent sua semina fruges,
    viventem ducens ad sancta altaria fetum
30 innocuis sonuisse Deo balatibus agnum
    insinuante fide iustus cognoverat Abel
    et capite oblato placuit grex totus ab uno.
        Ergo ubi vitalis fovit te lympha lavacri
    iamque suum peperit caelestis gratia pignus,
35 non tibi gemmato posuere monilia collo
    nec te contexit, neto quae fulgurat auro,
    vestis ductilibus concludens fila talentis,
    nec te Sidonium bis cocti muricis ostrum
    induit aut rutilo perlucens purpura fuco,
40 mollia vel tactu quae mittunt vellera Seres.
    Nec tibi transfossis fixerunt auribus aurum,
    quo dependentes ornarent vulnera bacae,
    et pretiosa quidem malas, sed saxa, gravarent.
    Latius haec vero sanctus describit Esaias
45 ornatusque refert varios, qui membra venustant,
    quae mox pascendis praebebunt vermibus escas—
    et forsan dum vita manet. Nam currere verbis
    morborum tot saeva potest discrimina nemo,
    ante obitum cuncti quae formidare docemur,
50 singula vel totis obnoxia mortibus esse,
    omnia dum proprio solvantur corpora fine
    atque unus praestet reliquos desistere casus.
    En quid quisque cupit perituro comere cultu,
    interior dum sordet homo ac se crimine turpat?

at the same time you too were offered up to Christ, who 25
straightaway received your body, though you were still un-
weaned, to be consecrated in the cradle. In the same way, in
the past when the earth first shone bright with new fertility
and seeds were producing their own beautiful crops, righ-
teous Abel led to the holy altars a living offspring and at the 30
prompting of faith recognized that the lamb with its inno-
cent bleating was calling to God, so that by the offering of a
single head the whole herd won favor.

And so when the life-giving waters of baptism had bathed
you and heavenly grace now had given birth to you as its
own offspring, no one put necklaces strung with jewels 35
round your neck, no dress shining with threads of gold
clothed you, its fabric interwoven with filaments of pre-
cious metal; not for you clothing of twice-refined Sidonian
purple or the brilliant glow of scarlet dye, not for you the 40
fleeces that the Chinese send, so soft to the touch. No one
pierced your ears with posts of gold so pearl pendants could
decorate the wounds and stones—however precious, yet
still stones—burden your cheeks. The holy Isaiah describes
these fineries more fully and recounts the various orna- 45
ments that lend bodies allure, bodies which soon enough
will provide food for worms to eat—perhaps, too, when still
alive. For no one can enumerate in words all the cruel suf-
ferings caused by diseases that every one of us learns to fear
before dying, in the knowledge that each one of them can be 50
responsible for death in all of its forms—that is, until at the
last our bodies fail and that one turn of fate causes all other
maladies to cease. So, see, why would anyone want to beau-
tify themselves with finery that is destined to perish, when
the inner person is gross and besmirched by sin?

55   Sed tibi cum geminum tetigerunt tempora lustrum,
mox stola sincero velat te candida cultu,
virginis os habitumque decens, et concipit omnem
floribus in primis iam mens matura pudorem.
Haud secus exultans sterilis post damna iuventae
60 fecundata novum cum ferret femina fetum,
vestem laeta suo parvam texebat alumno,
disceret ut Samuhel iam tum puer esse sacerdos.
Sic te laeta domus sanctis altaribus aptans
adsueto docuit dignam concrescere templo.
65 Scriberis in thalamos ac magni foedera regis
et cupit electam speciem sibi iungere Christus,
ornatu vario ditat quam gratia pollens.
    Haec ubi respirans pervenit gaudia mater
ac tibi conlatum parvo conspexit in aevo
70 grande bonum, teneris dum virtus creditur annis,
teque reparturiens melius quam corporis alvo
spemque metumque inter, quamquam iam libera voti,
fert tamen attonitas sic laeta, quod anxia curas,
insinuans causam lacrimis tum talia mandat:
75 "Ortu quarta quidem, sacro sed munere prima,
dulcis nata mihi, caelo quam carne fideque
bis genui Christoque rudem de ventre dicavi,
hactenus hoc nostrum fuerat, sed tempore ducto
iam decet esse tuum, nam quod servabere virgo,
80 a me principium, tibi pervenit. Omnia posse

But as soon as your lifetime had reached the span of ten 55
years, a white gown clothed you in the dress of purity, befit-
ting your virgin countenance and demeanor, and your mind,
already mature, devoted itself entirely to modesty in the
first flower of youth. In the same way a woman who was
cursed by barrenness in her youth but afterward became 60
pregnant, when she to her great joy gave birth to an
unlooked-for child, gladly wove for her offspring a small
coat so that already Samuel, while still a boy, would learn to
be a priest. So too your family happily trained you for the
sacred altars and taught you to grow up to be worthy of the
temple you had come to know well. You were enrolled in a 65
marriage alliance with a great king; Christ wished to unite
himself with your signal beauty, which the power of grace
embellished with a multitude of charms.

Your mother took heart in attaining these joys and saw
that a great gift had been bestowed on you at a young age, 70
when virtue had been vouchsafed you, though tender in
years. She had given you a second birth, better than that
from her bodily womb, but she still felt pangs of anxiety,
poised between hope and fear, though acquitted of her vow,
simultaneously happy and concerned. Tearfully pleading her
case, she instructed you as follows: "My beloved daughter, 75
fourth to me by birth but first by virtue of your sacred call-
ing, whom I bore twice for heaven, in flesh and faith, and
dedicated fresh from the womb to Christ, hitherto the re-
sponsibility has been mine, but now time has passed, it is
properly yours, for the preservation of your virginity took 80
its origin from me, but now devolves on you. You will begin

incipies, cum velle subest. Vestigia fervent,
per quae sectato conscendas tramite caelum.
   "Nec desunt exempla domi; nam respice quantas
virginibus florens iam nostrum stemma coronas
85   miserit in caelum, sancto quas dogmate mater
Severiana levans et te coniungier optat.
Nec multum senior gaudens Aspidia, quondam
sacratum velata caput, tua munia sumpsit
bis senos iungens sanctis altaribus annos.
90   Quam licet hinc celeri tulerit sors ultima leto,
nil tamen est subitum semper migrare paratis.
Aspice nunc columen, gemina quod virgine fulget,
eximiumque decus, cuius tu iure propinqua:
Fuscinam, Fuscina, refer. Nec segnius illam,
95   quae pietate potens, Graia si voce sonetur,
significat propriam sumpto de nomine mentem.
Quis licet emeritum cedant sua saecula culmen
vitaque sublimi cunctis praepolleat arce,
has generosa tamen matres si corde sequaris,
100   gaudebunt vinci, dum proficis, ac tibi summam
sponte dabunt palmam superanti vota magistrae."
Haec dicens sancto teneros hortamine sensus
impulit accendens ad virginitatis amorem.
Sic mater fecunda utero, fecundior actu
105   Machabaea potens et prolis funere felix,
orbari gaudens animo vincente senectam,

to achieve whatever you want, once you summon up the will. The trail glows bright before you on the path you will follow in mounting to heaven.

"There is no shortage of models in our family; just see how many our house, so resplendent with virgins, has already sent to be crowned in heaven, inspired by our holy mother Severiana's pious teaching; you too she wishes to join them. Aspidia was not much older than you when in the past she took up the holy veil, rejoicing to undertake the role you now perform by pledging herself to the sacred altars at the age of twelve. Although her final destiny was to be quickly carried away by death, yet nothing is premature for those always ready to pass from this life. Look now too to the renown and extraordinary glory that shine with a double virginity, a glory that is rightly yours by kinship: Fuscina, take as your model Fuscina. And no less readily imitate the woman, eminent in holiness, who indicates by her name, if it is pronounced in Greek, the quality of her mind. Though in their lifetimes these women were accorded supreme merit and their manner of life endowed all with the greatest prestige in high heaven, yet if in nobility of heart you follow them as your spiritual mothers, they will rejoice to be outdone as you advance, and those teachers will readily present you with the highest palm for surpassing their wishes for you." With these words your mother by her pious exhortations inspired a daughter's youthful feelings, firing you with the love of virginity. In the same way the formidable mother of the Maccabees, fertile in her womb but still more fertile by her deeds, was blessed in the death of her children; rejoicing with triumphant spirit that she was

edocet hortanti subolem non cedere mundo
inflammatque pios ad fortia facta furores.
    Quid tua nunc repetam, tenero quae fortior aevo
110   ante annos animumque gerens responsa dedisti?
Non haec parva tuam suscepit pagina laudem.
Exitus impleto veniet cum tempore victor,
laus melius canitur, cum iam clamante triumpho
consummata tuis reddentur praemia factis.
115   Nunc decet attonitos cauta te voce monere,
sollicitas tecum partiri ac volvere curas
atque iuvare tuos hortantia dicta labores,
dum pugnat varius per crebra pericula casus,
lubrica dum fragili currit sub tramite vita,
120   dum tua calcatus captat vestigia serpens,
ascendens dextro quem conterat aggere planta.
Nil non incertum praesentia saecula ducunt
nec secura datur requies in carne caduca.
Vertuntur nam saepe boni, perit obruta virtus
125   partaque transactae decedunt praemia laudis.
At plerumque solet subito succensa calore,
frigida quae nuper fuerat, mens linquere mundum
atque repentino restringere crimina freno.
Sic alternantem commutant fata rotatum,
130   impius ut speret veniam iustusque timendo
proficiens cumulum magnis virtutibus addat.
Nam studium sancti laxet si forte laboris
pigraque consuetas dissolvant otia curas,
labitur in praeceps damnosae gloria vitae.

left childless in old age, she instructed her offspring not to succumb to the world's promptings, inflaming them with a righteous passion for heroic deeds.

Why should I now record the answer you gave, showing boldness beyond your tender years and belying your age in your resolute spirit? This modest page has not assumed the task of praising you. In the fullness of time, when your life comes to a victorious end, then there will be a better song in your praise; then to the shouts of triumph your deeds will receive their rewards in full number. But now it is right for those who feel concern to counsel you with words of caution, to share and discuss with you their anxieties, and to aid your endeavors with words of encouragement, as various dangerous challenges repeatedly assail you, as your life runs unsteadily on a treacherous track, and as the serpent, though trodden down, is still at your heels; may your foot crush him down as you mount up on the road that leads to the right. The present world brings nothing that is not uncertain and no secure peace is granted for perishable flesh. For often the good are overthrown, virtue is subverted and perishes, and the rewards acquired by former glory pass away. On the other hand, it is frequently the case that a mind that only recently had been chilled in lethargy, inflamed by a sudden heat, leaves behind worldly things and puts an instant check on its sinning. In this way the inconstant wheel of fate works its changes, so that the impious man can hope for forgiveness and the just man, profiting by his fear, add still further to his great virtues. For if the desire for the struggle for holiness happens to slacken and idle relaxation undermines one's customary commitment, the glory of a life become corrupt suffers precipitous decline.

135 Stare nequit meritum: si non acquirit eundo,
amittit rediens; nitendum est viribus amplis,
ut satis angustum servent vestigia callem.
Nam qui diffusam spatio laxante plateam
mundanis ludens facili nunc aggere currit,
140 strictior hunc carcer crudeli sorte ligabit.
　　Tu modo da veniam, qui te exhortatur, amori
currentemque monens, cum vix tamen ipse sequatur,
suadet veloci tardus compendia gressus.
Namque ad doctrinam, canimus quam paupere versu,
145 tu melius iam docta venis, quae iunior ortu,
religione prior vivendi iura dicasti
annorumque sequens meritorum sorte superstas.
Et si consequimur, iam nostrum forte putetur;
quod sequimur tamen, hoc tuum est. Conversio fratrum
150 exemplo debenda pio; te respicit auctor
primitiasque in te sacris de fructibus offert,
indicit sed sancta fides, ut corde propinquo
participata levet fraternum sarcina pondus.
Tu germana, pium quem ducis ab ubere fascem,
155 non carnis, sed legis habes cervice fideli
subdita ferre iugum nec vincla in coniugis ire,
mundanas odisse vias, percurrere mundas,
illinc nolle toros, hinc sponsum quaerere Christum,
sic taedas tempsisse, pio quod amore calere,
160 pigra voluptati fervescere corda labori,
ignorare virum, fetus tamen edere tales,
quos numquam tristis possit tibi tollere casus.

Merit cannot remain stationary: whoever does not acquire   135
it by moving forward loses it by regressing; one must strive
with all one's strength to continue to tread the all too
narrow path. For whoever now hastens on the easy highway,
indulging in worldly affairs in the ample expanses of wide
boulevards, will find in the future that the narrow confines   140
of a prison will cruelly shut him in.

I only ask you to make allowances for the love that in-
spires these counsels. You hurry on ahead—your instructor
can scarcely keep up—yet despite his slowness of step, he
offers advice to one fleet of foot on the best course to take.
For you already bring greater learning to the doctrine I sing
of in my poor verse; junior by birth, yet superior in holiness,   145
you have sanctified the practice of your life, superior in your
virtues, though inferior in years. If we catch up with you,
that then is perhaps to be accounted to our credit, but that
we follow is due to you. The conversion of your brothers is   150
owed to your pious example; our father turned to you and
offered in you the firstfruits from his sacred harvest, still
holy faith declares that a burden shared with a kindred heart
lightens the sibling load. My sister, you who have under-
taken this sacred burden since you were a babe in arms, you   155
must bear in submission on your devout neck the yoke of
the law, not the flesh: to refuse to enter the bonds of mar-
riage, to hate the ways of the world and to pursue the ways
of purity, to shun the marriage bed and to seek Christ as
your betrothed, to scorn the wedding torches, because you
are fired with holy love, to have a heart insensible to plea-   160
sure, but fervent for hardship, to have no knowledge of a
husband, but yet to give birth to offspring that cruel fortune
can never take from you.

Non orbata gemes fecundae pignora vitae
nec viduam sponso metues superesse perenni,
165 expers ipsa mali, nec te sententia tangit,
qua prolis mortisque parens percellitur Eva,
occisam pariens subolem vivente reatu.
Quae subiecta viro, dominum passura cubilis
servit in obsceno tolerans conubia lecto.
170 Sic captiva tori, cum portet nomen inane
coniugis et vana dicatur imagine consors,
sola iugo premitur non aequam ducere sortem.
    At cum longa decem complent fastidia menses
perfectoque gravis fetu distenditur alvus,
175 semina quae patris fuerant, haec pondera matri
infligunt duros utero turgente dolores.
Nam cum luctato solvuntur viscera partu,
una luit tanto carnis discrimine pendens,
quod coiere duo. Spes palpat forte dolentem,
180 editus in lucem si vivat filius; atqui
contingit plerumque, gemens ut mortua fundat.
Saepe etiam suboli nec mortis tempore natae
dant geminum matris commortua membra sepulchrum.
Illud iam levius quotiens intervenit, ipsa
185 ut pereat tum sola parens ac pondere fuso
emittat cum prole animam? Quid forte levatum
nutritumque diu rapitur si funere pignus,
unica quod crebro spes respicit, et perit omne,
quod sibi conceptis spondebant gaudia votis?
190 Omnibus his illud gravius, si forte carentem

You will not grieve the loss of children, the tokens of your fertility, nor will you fear living on as a widow, for your spouse lives forever; you will be free too of suffering your- 165 self. That sentence will not affect you that was passed on Eve, a parent both of children and of death, giving birth to offspring doomed to die while sinfulness continued to live. Subjected to a husband and destined to suffer a master over her bedchamber, she endures marriage as servitude in the lewd marital bed. In this way, as bond servant of the couch, 170 though she carries the empty title of spouse and is called by a specious form of words a partner, she alone is subjected to the yoke, enjoying no equality of fortune.

But when her long and weary pregnancy fulfills its ten months, and her laden belly is swollen with a fully formed baby, what had been the father's seed becomes a weight on 175 the mother, inflicting on her cruel pains as the stomach distends. For when in the travail of childbirth her womb sheds its charge, only one pays in the extreme peril to her body for what two came together to do. Perhaps some hope consoles her for her pain, if a living child is born to the light; but yet it 180 often happens that she grieves for stillborn offspring. Often too the dead body of a mother shares a common tomb with her child, who was not even born at the time of his death. How often, moreover, does that lesser misfortune occur, when only the mother perishes and in discharging the 185 weight in her womb she surrenders her life with the birth of her child? And what if the child does happen to be raised up and long nurtured, only to be snatched away by death—a child frequently looked to as a one and only hope? Then everything that joy and cherished wishes had anticipated comes to nothing. But more grievous than all these occur- 190

caelesti lavacro tenerum mors invida natum
praeripiat dura pariendum sorte gehennae,
quique, genetricis cesset cum filius esse,
perditionis erit. Tristes tunc edita nolint,
195 quae flammis tantum genuerunt, membra parentes.
   Quis memorare queat tanti discrimina casus,
in quae pertrahitur dilectae gloria carnis?
At late longeque tuam discernere sortem
libertas cum lege potest, qua necteris, ut te
200 impia fallentis non stringant vincula mundi.
Tu Mariam sequeris, dono cui contigit alto
virginis et matris gemina gaudere corona,
conciperet cum carne Deum caelique Creator
intraret clausum reserans mysteria ventrem.
205 A genetrice satus, sed quam formaverat ipse,
elegit nitidam, de qua procederet, alvum,
solus qui carnis propriae disponeret ortum
praesciretque diem longe tempusque videret,
quo pariendus erat: praecessit membra voluntas.
210 Ipse Deus Verbum vestitur viscere sumpto;
qui cum patre iubet, materno in corpore servit
suscipit et famulum, Dominus quod iusserat, aevum,
tempora per patrem, per matrem semina nescit.
Illa quidem fecunda fuit, quae pondere casto
215 factorem portare suum Dominumque perennem
edere promeruit, sed nec tibi gloria tanti
defuerit facti, si Christum credula corde
concipiens operum parias pia germina caelo.

rences is if envious death snatches away the tender child without heaven's baptism, so that he is born only to suffer harsh sentence to hell. When he has ceased to be the child of his mother, he will become the child of damnation. Then his grieving parents would regret the birth of a body that they bred only for the flames. 195

Who could recount the extreme seriousness of the perils into which those glorying in devotion to the flesh are enticed? But in the freedom you enjoy a great and far-reaching distinction can be made between you and them; your freedom may come with a rule that constrains you, but only so that the unholy bonds of the deceitful world not have you in their grip. You follow Mary, who was granted by a gift from on high to rejoice in crowns both of virginity and motherhood, when she conceived God in the flesh and the Creator of heaven entered her closed womb, thereby revealing a mystery. Born from a mother, but one he had fashioned himself, he chose to emerge from an unsullied womb; only he planned his own birth in the flesh, knew far in advance the day and foresaw the time at which he was to be born; his will preceded his bodily existence. God himself took on flesh and clothed the Word; he who gives orders with his father, but was a servant in his mother's body and submissively took on life as the Lord had ordered, through his father was free of time and through his mother exempt from generation. She certainly was fruitful, for she won the right to carry the chaste burden of her own creator and to give birth to an eternal Lord, but the glory of such a great deed will be open to you as well, if with full belief you take Christ into your heart and produce for heaven holy offspring in your works. 200 205 210 215

    "Si quis," ait, "nostram compleverit ordine legem,
220 hic mihi semper erit frater materque sororque."
Aspicis, ut sexu careat caelestis imago,
interior sortitus homo quam mente retentat?
Praebuit exemplum surgens a morte Redemptor,
femineum maribus cum sic praeponit honorem.
225 Gustabat sumptam nostro pro crimine mortem
in crucis excelso pendens sine crimine Christus
atque animam, vivos quae mox remearet in artus,
fixus adhuc sancto clavis efflaverat ore.
Deseruit populi spectacula talia coetus
230 signaque ferre nequit, caelum quae triste minatur.
Nam sol obductus vultumque retortus ab orbe
cesserat iniustas nocturnis luctibus horas
atque peregrinis aditum dabat ipse tenebris.
Temporibus magno mutatis cardine rerum
235 nox erat in superis lucemque inferna videbant.
Intremuit tellus et nisu moenia magno
concussis celso nutabant vertice cristis.
Senserunt motum priscis discedere saxa
iussa locis sonitusque novos collisa dederunt.
240   Hos inter strepitus cunctis fugientibus illae
decernunt quamquam trepidae persistere matres,
pervigil ut sancto sic vivens cura sepulchro
serviat et voto praesens persolvat honorem.
Pinguia fragranti componunt illita suco
245 quae salvans salvum servarent lintea corpus.
His amor expensis lugubria dona parabat
supremum credens semet persolvere munus.

His words are: "If anyone fulfills in proper form my law, that person will be brother, mother, and sister to me." Do you see how the heavenly image that the inner man has received and holds fast in his mind lacks distinction of sex? The Redeemer in rising from death showed an example of this, when in so doing he gave preference to honoring women rather than men. Christ, in hanging high on the cross, though sinless himself, was tasting the death he took on for our sinfulness; while still held there by nails, he had breathed out from his sacred mouth the life that was soon to return to his revivified body. The mass of people shunned such a sight, unable to endure the portents that the grieving heavens threatened. For the sun was obscured and, turning its face from the world, had surrendered that period of time to an untimely night and to grief; it was itself giving place to an unseasonable darkness. In this crucial turning point for the world time had reversed: there was night in the realm above, but the underworld saw light. The earth quaked, walls swayed with the violent impact, and battlements shook on the topmost ramparts. Bidden to quit their ancient locations, rocks felt the motion and, colliding with each other, produced a sound unheard before.

Amid this commotion everyone else fled, but those women, though fearful, were determined to stay where they were so that by their vigil the devotion of the living should attend the holy sepulcher and by their presence pay it honor with their prayers. They prepared dressings richly infused with fragrant unguents to preserve in safety a body that itself brought salvation. With this expenditure their love offered up its mourning gifts, fulfilling what it believed was its final obligation. And although shortly before by his

Et cum sic breviter praevenerit ista resurgens,
quod credebatur servandum poscere funus,
250   quo non indiguit, placatur munere Christus.
Pro quo respondens confestim gratia praestat,
angelicos cernant humana ut lumina vultus.
Splendida candebat caelesti in corpore vestis
et vultum rutilus resperserat undique fulgor,
255   matribus ut dignis verbum caeleste sonaret,
angelus alloquitur sancto quas taliter ore:
"Femineo sexu mentes transite viriles
nec trepidate novo, fortissima corda, tumultu.
Adversos haec signa petunt; vos nulla timendi
260   causa manet, quas cura pii confirmat amoris.
Quaeritis, agnosco, pretiosi in sede sepulchri
sollemni nuper tumulatum funere Iesum.
Sed meminisse decet quod praescius ore fideli
dixerit ante obitum duplici non amplius ulla
265   servandum se nocte neci. Iam tertius hic est,
qui complet promissa, dies. Patet ecce sepulchrum,
deseruit vacuum victa quod morte resurgens."
    Taliter excelsus iusso sermone minister
sparsurus mundo vitalis dona triumphi
270   has primum gaudere dedit luctuque levavit.
Ibant impavidae laeto iam pectore matres
credula conceptae servantes corda saluti,
cum medium Christus sese gradientibus offert
agnoscique iubet blando et sermone salutat:
275   "Ite," ait, "et nostris haec iam mandata referte
discipulis, norint ut surrexisse magistrum."
Illae complexis defigunt oscula plantis
atque ad discipulos alacri cum mente recurrunt

resurrection he had rendered those offerings unnecessary, Christ was pleased by the gift believed needed to preserve a body, though in fact he had no need of it. In return grace granted straightaway that their human eyes catch sight of an angel's countenance. The clothing shone bright on the angel's heavenly body, and a shimmering radiance suffused his whole face to sound out the message from heaven to those deserving women, whom he addressed as follows in sanctified tones: "Outdo with your female sex the resolution of men and do not tremble, bravest of hearts, at this strange commotion. These portents are directed at enemies; for you there is no cause for fear, the devotion of your holy love gives you strength. You are looking for Jesus, I know, at the site of his precious tomb, who was recently buried with due funeral rites. But you should recall the trustworthy prophecy he gave before he died, that death would have a hold on him for no more than two nights. Now the third day is here, which fulfills his promise. Look, the tomb lies open that he left unoccupied when he rose again, triumphing over death."

These were the words God's servant from on high was bidden to speak, to communicate throughout the world the gifts of that life-assuring triumph. He gave the women first cause to rejoice and relieved their grief. They were going on their way, now fearless and rejoicing in spirit, maintaining in their hearts belief in the salvation they had received, when Christ showed himself in their midst as they walked, bade them recognize him, and greeted them with affectionate words: "Go," he said, "and report what you have now been told to my disciples so that they may know that their master is risen." The women embraced his feet and planted kisses upon them, then eagerly hurried away back to the disciples;

doctoresque docent et, quae spargenda per orbem,
280 primum femineis instructi discere verbis
agnoscunt animum potius quam vincere sexum.
   Communis virtus igitur, commune periclum
matribus atque viris, nulla est distantia cordis.
Rectum velle subest, si gratia constet, utrisque,
285 cui tamen attento desudet vita labore.
Aut quid dona iuvant hominem, si mente soluta
torpida collatum disperdant otia munus?
Auxilium conatus amat; quis namque vacantem
adiuvet aut somno virtutem iungat inerti?
290   Caelestis Rex ille parans discedere terra
argentum famulis, ut quis virtute valebat,
quinque minas primo, duplicem dat sorte secundo
atque inpar magnis suscepit tertius unam.
Tunc sic discedens famulos simul instruit omnes:
295 "Nunc ut quis vestrum devota mente fidelis
experiar, fuerit quaestu noscendus ab ipso,
qua quis sit virtute potens, qua praeditus arte.
Thesauros geminate meos usuque polite,
livida ne facies pulla robigine tinguat,
300 accipitis nitidum pura quod fronte metallum.
Si redeam, meritis reddentur praemia iustis."
   Dixit et abscessu caelestia regna petivit.
Incubuere duo studii certamine vernae.
Faenerat ille citus partem splendentis acervi
305 pauperibus largo dispensans plurima dono,

they became teachers of those teachers, and the disciples,
who received from the words of women their first instruc- 280
tion in a message destined to be broadcast throughout the
world, came to recognize that it is one's mind that bestows
preeminence rather than one's sex.

Virtue, therefore, is common to both women and men,
and peril likewise; there is no difference in their hearts. If
grace is present, they are both capable of willing the good,
provided their life is one of exertion and diligent struggle. 285
Otherwise how will God's gifts benefit anyone, if with dis-
solute mind they allow enervating sloth to waste the bounty
they have been given? Effort attracts assistance; for who
would help the lazy or ally his virtues with idle sleep?

The heavenly King, when preparing to leave the earth, 290
gave money to his servants in accordance with each one's
merits: to the first he gave five *minae,* to the second in order
of rank two, while the third, who was no match for his supe-
riors, received one. Then on his departure he gave the fol-
lowing instructions to all his servants together: "In order to 295
discover which of you is devoted and faithful to me, let it be
determined from the profit you make how resolute each of
you is in virtue, how skillful and talented. See that you dou-
ble my wealth and keep it bright by usage, lest its appear-
ance become discolored and stained by dark rust, for the 300
coinage you are receiving shines with a clear surface. On my
return rewards will be given you in accordance with your
just deserts."

With these words he departed and made his way to the
heavenly kingdom. Two of the servants then set to work in
eager rivalry. One quickly turned to profit a part of that glit-
tering wealth, generously distributing large quantities to the 305

crescit et in cumulos, quidquid confertur egenis.
Exponens alter sacri mysteria verbi
usuras sancto gaudet concrescere lucro
et cupidus recti vitam, dum praedicat, addit.
310 At solus, minimo qui sumpsit pondere libram,
defossis scrobibus marsuppia mersa locavit
degenerique fluens elegit vivere luxu.
Sed Iudex tandem finito tempore mundi
regreditur, cuiusque moram despexerat, excors
315 contremuit servus reditum. Tunc omnibus ille,
ut doceant ratione, iubet, quem tempore tanto
poscenti reddant operata negotia fructum.
Argentum gemini geminata mole ministri
promunt et laeto referunt commercia vultu.
320 Tertius ille piger dragmam tellure latentem
promit, quae iuncti sorbens contagia caeni
perdiderat proprios incluso lumine vultus.
Illum terribili Dominus tunc increpat ore:
"Tantane te nostri tenuere oblivia segnem,
325 serve piger, reditusque mei sic cura refugit?
Argentum, nitida quod purum luce tulisti,
en taetrum pressumque refers. Nam cognita quondam
delituit nec respondens, ut saepe solebat,
forma mihi vultusque mei non paret imago
330 adsignata tibi. Sed si ferrentur ad usus
altarisque mei tetigissent credita mensam,
cresceret inscriptus nostro de nomine nummus.
Nunc igitur famuli vos totum ferte fideles,
addat et utilibus sors ultima, tollat inerti.

poor; all that was bestowed on the needy amassed a still greater return. The second by expounding the mysteries of the holy word rejoiced to accumulate interest righteously gained; eager for virtue, he acquired eternal life as he preached it. But the lone exception was the servant who had received the currency of least weight, who dug a hole and buried the money bags there, for he chose to live a dissolute life of corrupt indulgence. But at the end time of the world the Judge finally returned and the foolish servant, who had grown negligent at the Judge's long absence, trembled at his return. Then that Lord bid them all give him an accounting of the profit their so long practiced transactions had yielded, for he was calling it in. Two of the servants, who had doubled their stake, set their silver before him and with joyful countenances recounted their dealings. But that third idle one produced the drachma he had concealed in the earth, which had been defaced by coming into contact with the mud that surrounded it and had lost its natural appearance with the obliteration of its sheen. The Master then rebuked him with a terrifying speech: "Have you so forgotten me in your idleness, lazy servant? Are you so unconcerned about my return? Look, the silver which you received from me brilliantly shining and clear, you give back to me defiled and dulled. For the previously familiar outline has disappeared and no longer conforms to mine, as it regularly used to do; the image of my face bestowed on you no longer is visible. But if the money entrusted to you had been put to use and invested on the exchange of my altar, the number of coins inscribed with my name would show increase. So then, my faithful servants, take all there is for yourselves; let the final reckoning enrich the industrious, but deprive the lazy.

335 Improbus in paucis hic dignus non erit ullis:
Quisque voluntatem noscens contemnit erilem,
caeditur hic multis; paucis, qui nescius errat."
    Ergo age, succinctis ad fortia proelia lumbis
armata cum mente veni nec femina bellum
340 formides, quod mens peragit. Nam gloria dudum
sexus ista tui nota est tibi saepe legendo.
Nec dubium te nosse reor, cum Debbora quondam
duceret instructas post fortia classica turmas
et mulier sumpto praecederet agmina signo
345 mirantes hortata viros, quos ipsa ducatu
exemplo verboque monens accendit in hostem.
Sed postquam ducens princeps animosa catervas
impulit accendens vegetata furoribus arma,
barbaricae cecidere manus: dissolvitur omnis
350 hostilis virtus et, qua se femina monstrat,
palantes dant terga viri latebramque petentes,
si vivant, vicisse putant. Tunc maximus ipse,
forma giganteae iunxit quem corpore moli
immensaque levans produxit verticis arce,
355 rex Sisarra fugam telorum fasce reiecto
incomitatus agit metuens sublime notari
corpus et excelsa fugitivum prodere massa.
Sed postquam latuisse putans tectoque receptus
mollia perpetuo demisit lumina somno,
360 hunc etiam sternit mulier terraque iacenti
malleus infixo transfodit tempora clauo.
Femineus sic ille fuit per cuncta triumphus.

This man who has proved untrustworthy in small things will   335
not be worthy of trust in anything. For he who knows his
Lord's will, but neglects it, will suffer many a beating; but he
who errs in ignorance receives few strokes."

Come then, gird yourself for a fierce battle, march for-
ward with a martial spirit and, though a woman, have no fear
of a war that is waged by the power of the mind. For the   340
glory of your sex has long been well known to you; you have
read of it often. I have no doubt you are familiar with the
time in the past when Deborah took the lead of battalions
marshaled behind the warlike trumpet's blast, and, march-
ing at the front of the column, standard in hand, though a   345
woman, urged admiring men to battle. She challenged them
by her leadership, example, and words, and fired their zeal
against the enemy. For after that spirited leader at the head
of her troops drove her men forward, igniting their warlike
valor fired by their passions, the barbarian troops suc-
cumbed: the courage of the enemy vanished entirely, and   350
wherever that woman made an appearance, men turned tail
in disarray and sought out refuge, believing they had won a
victory if they lived. Then the greatest of them all, the king
Sisera, who in physique was endowed with the build of a
giant surmounted with the immense crown of a head,
cast off the weight of his weapons and took to solitary flight,   355
fearing that his massive body would be conspicuous and
that by its enormous bulk it would betray him as he fled. But
after he thought he had found concealment and, on receiv-
ing shelter in a house, had let his drooping eyelids close in a
sleep that was to be forever, a woman laid him low. As he lay   360
on the ground a hammer drove a nail through his skull. In
this way that triumph was entirely woman's work.

At tu, virgo Dei, sanctis quam moribus ornant
hinc pudor, inde fides, internis fortior armis
365 bella geris, iustis saevus quae commovet hostis.
Spes tibi fida foret felix in vertice cassis,
contineat lumbos pretiosi zona pudoris,
iustitiae lorica tuos constringat amictus,
pro gladio semper Verbum teneatur acutum.
370 Has virtutis opes, haec sic solacia belli,
describens mentis varias cum corpore pugnas,
prudenti quondam cecinit Prudentius arte.
Namque ibi bellatrix et pleno robore pollens
Virginitas armata venit, quam foeda Libido
375 appetit et casso vocat in certamina nisu.
Sic bellatricem te sentiat aemulus anguis
cumque lacessitae concedent proelia palmam,
laeta feras summum calcato ex hoste tropaeum.

Nam quidquid sacrae divina volumina legis
380 eloquio sensuque docent, quod praedicat ipse
antiquus mundi replicans exordia vates,
seu ille historias texat seu forte figuras,
quod diversa retro multorum tempora regum
post Ruth succiduo gesserunt ordine magnum,
385 vel quos post reprobum Davitica regna Saulem
ter quinquageno scripserunt carmine psalmos,
pacificus quidquid lata inter sceptra Salomon
obscurum sensu per clara proverbia duxit,
quodque bis octoni post se videre prophetae,
390 quod clausum Iob mitis ait cum vulnere aperto—
Hester quid memorem et castae mendacia Iudith,

But as for you, virgin of God, whose ornaments in your saintly way of life are modesty and faith, you are all the stronger in the wars you wage because your weapons are within you, those wars the savage enemy rouses against the just. Let confident hope be the secure helmet for your head, the girdle of precious chastity encircle your loins, and the breastplate of justice surround your garments; let the incisiveness of the Word always take the place of the sword. This is the armory of virtue, these the resources for war that once Prudentius sang of, when prudently and skillfully he described the various battles of the mind with the body. For there Virginity advances bearing arms, a warrior woman, powerful and full of vigor, to be met by vile Lust, who with misplaced aggression challenges her to combat. May the envious serpent find you to be an equally warlike woman; when you meet the challenge and the battle bestows on you the victory palm, after trampling your enemy underfoot may you joyfully carry off the supreme trophy.

Let your reading be all that the holy books of the sacred law teach, both with their eloquence and their substance: the words of the ancient prophet, recounting the first beginnings of the world, whether composing a historical narrative or a figural; the great deeds that the different reigns of many past kings saw in constant succession after the story of Ruth, and the hundred and fifty poetic psalms that king David wrote, when he succeeded the rejected Saul; all the obscurities of sense that Solomon the peacemaker, wide in his sway, made clear by his proverbs; all that the sixteen prophets foresaw was to come and the concealed meaning that patient Job declared by his open wounds. Why need I mention Esther and the deceit practiced by chaste Judith,

ornati cum fraude satraps accenditur oris,
cum manet illudens obscenum femina lectum
desectoque feros compescit vertice visus,
395 quod melius cernens caecato in corpore Tobit,
quae secreta videns perscripsit conditor Esdras,
quidquid post priscam succedens gratia legem
intonat atque novi miracula testamenti
hinc hominis clamat facies, ast inde leonis
400 et pernix aquila et fortis certamine taurus?—
inde quater terni puris quod mentibus agni
egerunt toto spargentes semina mundo,
bis septena pii quod spargit epistula Pauli,
quod Petrus Iacobusque docent, quod Iudas et ipse
405 qui conspecta refert caeli secreta, Iohannes,
quin et veridici quae plurima tractatores
exposuere suis mysteria digna libellis—
haec tu cuncta tenens animo sitiente bibisti.
Nec, si quid sacrum nostri cecinere poetae,
410 te latet; agnoscis leges et commata servas
atque aliena tuo commendas carmina cantu.
Quid totum replicem? Tu sensibus utere doctis
et quae nota tibi vel quae percursa legendo,
ad virtutis opus studio converte virili.
415 Nam nisi doctrinae iungatur vita fidelis,
agnosci gravius non observanda nocebit.
    Esuriit quondam Dominus, cum forte vianti
conspicitur diffusa levi ficulnea fronde,
nec iam maturum praedicta ex arbore fructum
420 carpere tempus erat. Quam mox ut repperit ille
indutam tantum foliis, sed germine nudam,
prorsus inane virens ornatus inutilis horret;

when a lord was enflamed by the seductive allure of her countenance, and that woman made a mockery of his indecent desire to bed her, checking the aggression of his gaze by cutting off his head? Why mention Tobit, who saw better after he was blinded, the secret visions that Ezra the author recorded, and all that grace, superseding the old law, thunders forth or the New Testament miracles that the symbols of a man and a lion, a swift eagle, and a bull, strong in the fray, proclaim? Then too there are the actions of the twelve lambs, pure in spirit, who spread the seeds throughout all the world, the messages broadcast by the fourteen epistles of saintly Paul, the teachings of Peter and James, of Jude, and of John, who recounts his vision of the secrets of heaven, and furthermore the many precious mysteries that truth-telling exegetes have set forth in their writings. All these you have imbibed in your thirsty soul and firmly embrace. Nor are you ignorant of all the sacred songs our poets have composed; you understand their meter, observe their phrasing, and win praise for others' poems by the way you sing them. But why should I enumerate everything? Only be sure that you make good use of your learning and apply all of your knowledge and all of your reading with a manly zeal to the practice of virtue. For unless your learning is accompanied by a life of true holiness, to know what is right but not practice it will only harm you more.

Once the Lord felt hunger, and as he journeyed by chance he caught sight of a spreading fig tree with a light growth of leaves—it was not yet the time for plucking ripe fruit from that tree. As soon as he found that it was clothed only in leaves and devoid of fruit, instantly the useless display of quite purposeless greenery shriveled up, the tree's roots

percutitur subito radix afflata calore
aruit et posito ramorum tegmine truncus.
425 Instruimur tali legem cognoscere signo:
ne Christi famulum solo sermone fatenti
nomine conficto vivens operatio desit.
Nam si Christicolas nosmet sanctosque putemus,
aggravat hoc etiam, ni dictum facta sequantur.
430 Sic et virginitas sacro devota pudori
indiget adiunctis virtutibus et, nisi mentem
intactam servans casto cum corpore iungat,
concumbit vitiis nec castam dicere carnem
iure potest, animus quam sic corrumpit adulter.
435 Ira, furor, maeror, livor, discordia, luxus,
lingua duplex, constricta manus, laxata voluntas
moechantur cum corde hominis, tum semine turpi
fetus mortis alunt. En quo perducitur omnis,
nomine virgineo quae se dum iactitat, intus
440 criminibus gravidam nescit turgescere mentem.
Ecce tibi e multis unum, quo cetera noscas
exemplo.
          Dominus plebem cum forte doceret
pervigili cura supremum noscere tempus,
expectare diem, quo Iudex imminet orbi,
445 virginibus sancto signatos chrismate confert
hasque decem nobis documenti in vertice monstrat.
Quarum quinque tamen sapientia dives adornat,
ast aliis stolidum lentavit inertia sensum.
Sopitas pariter requies complectitur una
450 atque obitum signans depressit lumina somnus.
Transierat medium vix forte quietis et illud
tempus noctis erat, quo Christus carne recepta

were struck by a sudden blast of heat, and the trunk, stripped of its covering of branches, withered away. By this   425
image we are taught to acknowledge the rule not to declare oneself Christ's servant in words alone, when the title is counterfeit and not put into practice in life. For if we think ourselves pious Christians, it intensifies the fault if deeds do not correspond to words. In the same way virginity too,   430
when it has taken a vow of sacred modesty, needs to maintain the accompanying virtues and, unless it preserves a pure mind along with a chaste body, succumbs to vice and cannot rightly call the flesh chaste that adultery of the mind has so corrupted. Anger and passion, grief, envy, discord, and lux-   435
ury, a deceitful tongue, a tight fist, a dissolute will, all commit adultery with the human heart, and from a vile insemination nurture death as their offspring. See what the end is for all who exalt themselves with the name of a virgin, but are unaware that within their mind is swollen, pregnant   440
with sin. Here is one example from many, from which you can understand the rest.

When the Lord was teaching the people to anticipate the end of time with watchful care and to prepare for the day when the Judge would come upon the world, he compared   445
those sealed with the holy chrism to virgins, ten of whom he cited as the best of examples for us. Five of these were adorned by the riches of wisdom, but laziness dulled the others' foolish wits. A common repose lulled and took possession of all of them, and a sleep that symbolized death   450
came over their eyes. The middle of their nighttime slumbers had only just passed; it was the time of night when Christ, after taking on human flesh, had already broken

fregerat obstructas perrupto cardine leti
iam portas, Inferne, tuas spretoque sepulchro
455   devictis laeta remeabat luce tenebris.
Perstrepuit subitus rumpitque silentia clamor:
"Tandem sponsus adest; nocturnus corpore torpor
cedat et abiecto vegetentur membra cubili!"
   Protinus exiliunt omnes stratisque relictis
460   aptavere suas quaesito lumine flammas.
Tunc sed quinque, quibus cordi sollertia maior,
quamvis festinent, oleum tamen addere sumptis
sollicitudo fuit vasis pinguique liquore
ignibus armatis squalentem rumpere noctem.
465   At quae neglectum liquit pars altera sucum,
sumens flammigeras nequiquam sustulit hastas.
Emicat exiguus commoti luminis ignis,
sed virtute carens languentem lampada fervor
deserit et siccam percurrit flamma papyrum
470   atque inter picei nebulosa volumina fumi
canescunt pigra crescentes mole favillae.
Ut sese indignas tali videre paratu,
occurrant sponso quae comminus advenienti,
tarda movet lentis pudibundum cura dolorem.
475   Quae prece submissa stultis tum vocibus orant,
ut porrecta manus torpentes suscitet ignes
dividat et proprium sapientia pinguis olivum.
Respondent pariter tali sermone sorores:
"Est miseranda quidem vestrorum causa malorum,
480   sed tamen hic oleum non plus, quam sufficit, affert
unusquisque sibi; constat iam copia vasis
et perfecta suum servat mensura liquorem.
Nec fas quaesitum partiri aut perdere sucum,

down your barred doors, Hell, and burst open death's hinges,
when in defiance of the tomb he was returning to light's joy- 455
ful welcome, having overcome darkness. Then a sudden
shout rang out and broke the silence: "The bridegroom is
here at last; throw off your nighttime lethargy, abandon your
beds, and set your bodies to work!"

Immediately they all leaped up and, leaving their couches,
made ready to set their lamps aflame in the search for light. 460
Then five of them, who showed the greater intelligence, de-
spite their hurry took care to add oil to the lamps they had
picked up, so as to dispel the gloom of night once the fire
was fueled by the rich liquid. But the second group, who left 465
the provision of oil neglected, grasped and raised up their
flaming lamps to no avail. A feeble flame flickered into life,
giving wavering light, but the lamplight faded as the heat,
lacking sustenance, left it, the flame skittered along the dry
wick, and amid curling wafts of sooty smoke the ash piled 470
up, white and smothering. When they realized that with
such preparations they were unworthy to meet the arriving
bridegroom face-to-face, slowly anxiety aroused a sense of
shame and grief in them, however tardily. Then with abject 475
prayers they foolishly begged that the other virgins lend a
hand to resuscitate their failing fires, that wisdom, rich in
resources, share with them its oil. As one the sisters replied
with this speech: "Certainly the reason for your suffering is
worthy of pity, but each of us has only enough oil to suffice 480
for herself, no more; the supply is now perfectly matched to
our lamps; each holds an amount of liquid precisely mea-
sured to its capacity. It is not right to share out or squander

ne dispersa cavis desint fomenta lucernis,
485 cumque lucrum vobis dispendia nostra parabunt,
tota simul fessis torpescant lumina flammis."
Talibus abiectae dictis tristique repulsa
perlustrant, quocumque loci commercia fervent
venalesque manus, sed dum disceditur, ecce
490 introiit sponsus thalamum duxitque paratas
atque vagas linquens exclusit porta sorores.
     Cernis virginei pereat quod nomen honoris,
ni fertur sanctus thalamis caelestibus ignis.
Felix illa manus, largis quae provida donis
495 accensum pura fovit pinguedine lumen.
Tantum namque olei vasis diffunditur amplis,
quantum poscenti miserans porrexit egeno.
Hinc Dominus palmis ardentes ferre lucernas
admonet; hoc opus est, haec clarae gloria vitae.
500 · Suppetat ergo tibi pietas, patientia, virtus—
sed virtus animi—fragiles nam carne puellas
protulit interdum caelo constantia mentis.
     Eugeniae dudum toto celeberrima mundo
fama fuit, dum dat Christi pro nomine vitam.
505 Ante tamen mulier fortes processit in actus,
cum stipante choro sanctorum fieret abbas
atque patrem complens celaret tegmine matrem.
Sed postquam sancto cunctis perclaruit ore
et meritis annisque graves longaque verendos
510 religione senes iuvenali rexit in aevo,
impatiens recti toto qui tempore serpens

the oil we possess lest the fuel run out and the wells of our lamps run dry, or lest, though our loss will bring you benefit, all the lamps give out together as the flames in them die down." With this denial and bitter rejection, they roamed the streets in search of anywhere where there were shopkeepers and the bustle of business, but while they were away, behold, the bridegroom entered the bridal chamber, took with him those who were ready, but left the errant sisters outside the door.

And so you see that the name and honor of a virgin counts for nothing, unless the fire of holiness is brought to heaven's bridal chambers. Happy is that hand that by providently bestowing abundant gifts keeps a light alive and sets it aflame with a pure, rich fuel. For the quantity of oil that is poured into those capacious lamps corresponds to the amount of alms given in pity to the pleas of the needy. That is why the Lord instructs us to carry in our hands lamps that are alight; this is the task, this the glory of a life of renown. Summon up piety, endurance, and virtue—virtue of spirit, that is—for from time to time mental resolution has elevated girls to heaven despite the fragility of their flesh.

Eugenia, of highest renown through the whole world, won fame in the past when she gave up her life for the name of Christ. At first she advanced to deeds of bravery as a woman, but then in the company of a band of holy men she became an abbot and in fulfilling the role of a father concealed her motherhood by her clothing. But after she won universal fame by the holiness of her words and at a young age had presided over old men who were eminent for their virtues and years and revered for their long religious devotion, the serpent, impatient of goodness, who at every

mille nocendi artes stimulis inflammat amaris,
quod famam violare cupit, dedit inde coronam.
Commovet insano qui fingat amore puellae
515 accendi Eugeniam motuque ardere virili.
Turba senum turbata coit, quod crimine tanto
tam rigidam nuper potuisset solvere vitam
mens deiecta viri, viduataque praesule summo
nil non posse dolet titubans perfectio carnem.
520 Ducitur ista foro iuvenis saevumque tribunal
intrat adhuc monachus. Vincit concordia fraudis
et iam iamque reum secreti ignara tenebat
publica vis odio tantum flammata sinistro,
conscia cum sexus proprii cordisque pudici
525 vincitur, ut vincat iam prodens femina fraudem.
Quamvis exterius carnem compulsa fateri,
interiore tamen servato permanet heros.
Semper tuta fuit casti custodia voti.
Quamlibet impugnet miseri fraus callida mundi
530 extendatque dolis laqueos, mendacia nectat,
non venit ad pronam mens culpae ignara ruinam
quosque fremens hostis fallaci tribulat astu,
purgandos sancto patientia discutit igni.
  Vendiderat quondam iuvenem manus aemula fratrum
535 et famulum Ioseph tellus Memphitis habebat.
Pertulit ille quidem dominam cum crimine falso
confictus voluisse nefas, quod triste refugit.
Sustinuit tolerans ergastula, vincla, catenas,

moment incites with his stinging goads a thousand ways of doing hurt, in seeking to sully her fame, instead gave her a crown. He suborned someone to claim falsely that Eugenia was inflamed by crazed love for a girl and burning with a manly emotion. At this the old men *en masse* gathered together, in alarm that a man's resolution could be overcome and with so grievous a sin abandon a life hitherto so austere. Deprived of the greatest of leaders, perfection faltered, distressed that there was nothing flesh could not accomplish. The young person then was led to the forum and, still in monk's attire, came before the seat of judgment. The conspiracy to deceive was winning the day; increasingly public hostility, unaware of her secret and violently inflamed by a perverse hatred, was finding her guilty, until she was proved to be avowedly female in sex and possessed of a pure heart, so that the revelation of her womanhood won out over deceit. Though compelled to confess her outward physical form, yet she preserved her inner nature and remained a hero. The observance of her vow of chastity always was secure. However much the cunning wiles of the unhappy world launch their assaults, however many snares they treacherously set or lies they contrive, the mind innocent of fault does not succumb to disaster, while patient endurance puts to the test those whom the fierce enemy afflicts with deceptive guile to cleanse them with holy fire.

In the past a jealous group of brothers sold the young Joseph, who became a slave in the land of Egypt. There he suffered at the hands of his mistress, when he was alleged with a false accusation to have sought a crime which in fact he fled as repugnant. He was forced to endure prison, fetters, and chains for as long as the sun, redoubling the period of

    dum spatium replicans geminos sol iungeret annos.
540 Oblitus iam lucis erat, iam crine fluenti
    nutritus macie tangebat terga capillus;
    Sed vegetante Deo mens nullis clausa tenebris
    praevidet arcanum quidquid post exitus implet.
    Denique producto certatim gloria fertur,
545 non tantum venia, et precibus tunc ipse rogatur,
    ut diadema libens captivo in vertice sumat,
    exilium regno commutet, principe servum.
    Praemia servati cordis sic percipit iste.
      Susannam post hunc dignis quis laudibus umquam
550 excolat, infirmis quondam quae vicit in annis
    improba vota senum coniuratosque furores?
    Primum disiuncto quos cepit causa viritim
    consilio solusque sibi promisit uterque
    spem culpae, sed turpe calens in cordibus ignis
555 conflavit mentem sceleris fornace duorum.
    Conveniunt, nam forte die sic contigit una,
    abscessu ficto diversa ut parte redirent,
    inque nemus venere simul. Vulgata vicissim
    proditur alterno flagrans in corde voluptas.
560 Ilicet incautam fallentes fraude puellam
    appetiere simul; poscunt, consentiat ante,
    dedecoris tantum moveat quam fama rebelli,
    moxque retorquendum facinus, ni cedat, in ipsam.
    Confessi ardorem pariter mendacia produnt
565 disposita et laqueos pandunt, quos nectere vellent.
    Anceps illa diu secum luctatur et haerens
    fluctuat, incertae quo vergat pondera mentis:

time, added to the first a second year. He had already forgot-   540
ten the daylight, already his hair was flowing in long braids
down to his back—it was thriving, though he was wasting
away. But his mind, inspired by God, could not be confined
in darkness; he saw in advance all that was hidden but that
afterward would come to happen. Finally, when he was re-
leased he was eagerly offered not just pardon but honors,   545
with the prayerful request that he willingly take the diadem
on his formerly captive head and exchange exile for a king-
dom, slavery for being a prince. And so in this way he re-
ceived the rewards for his steadfastness of heart.

After him, who could ever properly celebrate with praise
Susanna, who in the past, though tender in years, defeated   550
old men's wicked desires and their conspiracy in passion? At
first the impulse seized each of them individually without
mutual consultation, and each alone held out to himself the
prospect of crime; an obscene fire burned in their two hearts
and set ablaze their sensations in a furnace of wickedness.   555
But then they met, for it happened one day that after pre-
tending to go away they both retraced their steps and came
together from different directions in the one grove. They
told their story in turn and revealed the desire that burned
in each of their hearts. Straightaway, with devious cunning   560
together they made their approach to the unwitting girl;
they demanded that she consent before rumor spread tales
to her great disgrace if she resisted, saying that the crime
would immediately be cast back on her if she did not yield.
They both confessed their passion, uncovered their treach-
erous plan, and revealed the snares they were ready to set.   565
For a long time she struggled with herself, hesitant as she
wavered which way the balance of her uncertain mind

lex peccare vetat rursumque infamia terret.
Nunc iterum duros precibus mollire furores
570 temptat et obscenas lacrimis restinguere flammas.
Sed postquam nullis precibus monitisve remotos
obstrictosque senes vicit cognata libido,
femina praeclaro mentem succensa pudore
decrevit tum casta mori, ne crimine tanto
575 ambirent miseram carnis commercia vitam.
Caelum teste vocat famamque recusat inanem
iudicio contenta suo, cum conscia cordi
commendat se pura fides servatque futuris.
Maluit ille tamen secreti inspector apertum
580 examen praestare loco facinusque reclusum
pandere et obtectas laqueis producere fraudes.
　　Spectabat vanis commotam fletibus urbem
iunior ille puer, pueris tribus ipse futurus
post comes, undanti quos iecit Parthica flammae
585 contempto imperio flammis ferventior ira.
Arsit contrario pariter crescente calore
hinc furor, inde fides, sanctis dum mollior ignis
serviit et tepido collusit pruna rubore,
donec miratus cessare incendia satraps
590 sentiret tantos, quantos succenderat, ignes.
　　Hos meritis aequans Danihelis proxima virtus
horrida frendentum compescuit ora leonum,
dum prius accensi stimulis famis atque furoris
frenatoque simul sternentes corpora rictu
595 incolumem lambunt inter ieiunia pastum,

should incline: the law forbids sin, but on the contrary dis-
grace inspires fear. Time and again she tried to alleviate their
cruel passion with her prayers and to extinguish their flames   570
of lust with her tears. But after a shared desire kept those
old men fast in its grip, proof against all prayers and urging,
that woman, her heart on fire with a glorious devotion to
chastity, determined to die still pure, lest because of such
a crime trafficking in the flesh take over her life and make it   575
miserable. She called on heaven as a witness and defied false
infamy, secure in her own self-judgment, for the purity of
her heartfelt faith was its own recommendation and contin-
ued to be so into the future. But that divine observer of
what is hidden chose to have the men's cross-examination   580
conducted in the open, to reveal the crime they had con-
cealed, and to entice their covert treachery into a trap.

The young boy Daniel saw the city moved to unavailing
tears at Susanna's fate. Later he himself was to be a compan-
ion for three boys whom Parthian fury, itself hotter than
flames, cast into a sea of flame for scorning a royal com-   585
mand. Two opposing forces were afire, each with increas-
ing heat, on the one side rage, on the other faith, until the
weaker fire abated in obeisance to the saints and the coals
conspired to cool their glow. Finally the ruler, amazed that
the flames had lost their force, felt fires as strong as he   590
had set.

A like virtue, in merit equal to that of those youths, al-
lowed Daniel to control the fearsome jaws of roaring lions.
At first they were goaded to a frenzy by hunger and rage, but
then they all stretched out on the ground—it was as if their
mouths were muzzled—and, famished though they were,
only licked the man they had been given as food without   595

cum sumat tamen ipse cibos, quos vertice pendens,
angelica librante manu per inane citatus,
subiectas calcans immotis gressibus auras,
intulit illatus fascis cum fasce propheta.
600 Excepit Danihel transmissas desuper escas,
fercula longinquis mirans ferventia terris
adservare suos peregrina in sede sapores.
  Hic ergo impubis Susannam forte videbat
in tormenta rapi, veri quam nescius ante
605 vulgus inauditam damnaverat, et simul omnes
insontis sontem certabant cernere mortem,
cum subito in medium iuvenis se proripit agmen,
accensum tenera castigans voce tumultum,
cur tanto ex coetu nullus rem iudicet, ac se
610 liber ad iniustum clamat non currere letum.
Protinus ad verbum pueri permota repressit
turba sequax animos. Iudex decernitur ipse
censetorque senum, per quem via vera patescat.
Consulit avulsos, quisnam sit criminis ordo,
615 sed dum discordans responsum praebet uterque,
coniunctum facinus disiuncta voce fatentur.
Tunc omnes pariter timor accipit; undique clamor
tollitur, auctores sceleris plebs obruit omnis
laudaturque Deus, qui numquam vota bonorum
620 deserit auxiliumque suum pro tempore monstrat.
  Ettamen his prior est, quae virginitate pudica
intactum perfert vota ad caelestia corpus.

doing him harm. Meanwhile he was being fed himself, for a prophet brought him food, who owed his movement to the supporting hand of an angel holding him up by the head and propelling him through the empty air, so that he trod underfoot the breezes without moving his feet; one cargo carried another. Daniel welcomed the food conveyed to him from on high, but was astonished that dishes coming from such distant lands were still warm and retained their flavor in a foreign location.

When young, Daniel happened to see Susanna being carried off to torture, for the populace, still ignorant of the truth, had condemned her unheard and were all vying to see the guilty death of an innocent. At that moment the young man suddenly burst into the midst of the throng, castigating the frenzied commotion of the mob in boyish tones, and asking why no one from so large a crowd was bringing the matter to trial; he declared that he, while free to act, would not have recourse to an unjust death. Immediately the crowd was moved by the boy's words and in response checked their passion. He himself was appointed judge, to interrogate the old men and reveal the proper way to proceed. He questioned them separately about the circumstances of their charge, when by giving inconsistent responses they both confessed with their disparate reports their complicity in conspiracy. Then fear gripped all alike; a shout rose up from every side and all the people denounced the authors of the crime, while praising God, who never abandons the prayers of good men and makes plain his assistance as the occasion requires.

Yet superior to all these is the woman who as a chaste virgin brings an unsullied body to a marriage in heaven. For

Nam si terrena nubentem lege puellam
adservasse toros atque unum nosse cubile
625   mortali tantum laudatur iudice coetu,
conice, virgineis quantum disponitur illic,
quo Christus vocat hinc, meritis, ubi sede superna
humanum in partes dirimet genus Arbiter orbis,
agnis dextra levans, laevis condemnet ut haedos.
630   Stabunt angelici mirantes facta bonorum
laudantesque chori, cunctis commune patebit
decursae carnis meritum; fraus nulla tenebris
abdere vel notas poterit subducere culpas.
Illic tota tibi substantia, vita petatur,
635   quo iustus ditat dispensans praemia Iudex.
Quondam succincte quod dictum est ore Magistri,
dum viget officio famulans sollertia Marthae
attentamque tenet verbi virtute sororem
cura cibo melior, pastu quia digna perenni.
640   Tunc vacuas Domino deponens Martha querellas,
"O doctor, non cernis" ait, "quod sola paratu
vexor et haec nullum confert germana levamen?"
Cui Christus sic forte refert: "Sunt plurima, quae te
obstrictam retinent, melior sed causa quietae
645   lectaque nec poterit Mariae pars optima tolli."
   Sic, germana, suis dum flagrant saecula curis,
electam servare tibi non desine partem.
Te meruit primam cognatio tota patronam,
iam te signiferam sequimur vexillaque Christi,
650   te portante libens sectatur stemma parentum.
Quos licet antiquo mundus donasset honore

if a girl who marries according to the law of this earth is so
highly praised in the judgment of human society for keeping   625
her wedding vows and knowing only one marriage bed,
imagine the reward those will receive in that place to which
Christ summons them for their virtues as virgins, when as
Judge of the world on his high throne he separates the hu-
man race into two parts, elevating the lambs to the right to
condemn the goats to the left. Choirs of angels will stand   630
there singing the praises of the good, full of amazement at
their deeds; all will share the knowledge of a virtuous life in
the flesh. But for the others no deceit will be able to cloak in
darkness or suppress their well-known guilt. You should
seek all your wealth, your very life, in that place where the   635
righteous Judge distributes his rich rewards. This was pro-
nounced concisely in the past by the words of the Master,
when Martha's busy solicitude paid him devoted service,
while her sister pursued diligently by the authority of his
word a more important concern than food, because she was
deserving of eternal nourishment. Then Martha, voicing her   640
groundless complaints to the Lord, said, "My teacher, don't
you see that I alone am busied with housework, and my sis-
ter here brings me no relief?" To her Christ replied as fol-
lows: "There are very many concerns that keep you in their
grip, but in her repose Mary's is the better cause; she has   645
chosen the best role and it cannot be taken from her."

So, my sister, when the world flares up with its own
anxieties, never fail to maintain the role you have chosen.
All of your kin have won you as their chief patron; it is you
now we follow as standard-bearer, your whole family line   650
eagerly marches behind you as you raise the banners of
Christ. Though the world has long presented those men

et titulis monstret generoso semper ab ortu,
plus tamen ornavit divinum insigne gerentes,
ordine quod proprio sanctas meruere cathedras.
655 Non et avos tibimet iam nunc proavosque retexam,
vita sacerdotes quos reddidit inclita dignos;
pontificem sacris adsumptum respice patrem.
Cumque tibi genitor vel avunculus undique magni
post fasces placeant populorum sumere fascem,
660 suscipe, quos humiles patrum ad consortia fratres
officio simili nectens Ecclesia iunxit.
Pro quibus assiduas Christo persolvere grates
fundere vel fletus non taedeat, ut tibi nullus
fratrum de numero desit, dum praemia sumes
665 factis digna tuis materque effecta parentum
virgineae victrix sociabere laeta catervae.

with honors and by the titles it bestows always demonstrates their noble descent, yet it is the divine badge of honor that conveyed more distinction on those who wore it, in that by their own promotion they won holy sees. I will not now enu- 655 merate for you your grandparents and great-grandparents whose distinguished lives made them respected priests; look instead to your father, who was promoted to hold sacred office as bishop. And since you take pleasure in the actions of your father and uncle, who, eminent in every way, assumed responsibility for God's people after the responsibilities of a magistracy, receive to your care your lowly brothers, whom 660 the Church has united in close ties with their fathers by their holding a like office. Do not flag in giving continuous thanks to Christ and pouring forth your tears, so that none of your brothers is absent when you receive worthy reward for your actions and, made mother to your kinsmen in 665 victory, you joyfully join the virgin company.

Abbreviations

CSEL = *Corpus scriptorum ecclesiasticorum Latinorum* (Vienna, 1866–)

ILCV = Ernest Diehl, ed., *Inscriptiones Latinae Christianae veteres,* 3 vols. (Berlin, 1925–1931)

OLD = P. G. W. Glare, ed., *Oxford Latin Dictionary,* 2nd ed. (Oxford, 2012)

PCBE = André Marouze, Charles Pietri, and Luce Pietri, eds., *Prosopographie chrétienne du bas-empire,* 4 vols. in 6 (Paris, 1982–2013)

PL = *Patrologiae cursus completes, series latina* (Paris, 1841–1865)

PLRE = A. H. M. Jones, J. R. Martindale, and J. Morris, eds., *Prosopography of the Later Roman Empire,* 3 vols. in 4 (Cambridge, 1971–1992)

ThLL = *Thesaurus linguae Latinae* (Leipzig, 1900–)

Note on the Texts

I follow Rudolph Peiper's *Monumenta Germaniae historica* edition of Avitus as my base text, with occasional minor changes of punctuation and orthography. In particular, in accordance with DOML series practice, I assimilate prefixes and regularize spellings to the most common classical form. Other variations from Peiper's text are listed in the Notes to the Texts. Peiper strongly preferred readings from the Gallic family of manuscripts. The vast majority of emendations to his text derive from the alternative German tradition.

Sigla

Arweiler = Alexander Arweiler, *Die Imitation antiker und spätantiker Literatur in der Dichtung "De spiritalis historiae gestis" des Alcimus Avitus,* Untersuchungen zur antiken Literatur und Geschichte 52 (Berlin, 1999)

Beikircher = Hugo Beikircher, "Spezereien aus dem Paradies (zu Prud., cath 5,120 und Alc. Avit., carm. 1,292f.)." *Wiener Studien,* n.s., 20 (1986): 261–66

Chevalier = Ulysse Chevalier, ed., *Oeuvres complètes de Saint Avit* (Lyon, 1890)

Dittmann = *Thesaurus linguae Latinae,* vol. 6, part 3, *H–hystrix* (Leipzig, 1936–1942), col. 3050, lines 79–80

Gärtner 1 = Thomas Gärtner, "Zur Bibeldichtung *De spiritalis historiae gestis* des Alcimus Avitus," *Jahrbuch für Antike und Christentum* 43 (2000): 126–86

Gärtner 2 = Thomas Gärtner, "Untersuchungen zum Text und zu den literarischen Vorbildern der Dichtungen des Alcimus Avitus," *Jahrbuch für Antike und Christentum* 44 (2001): 75–109

Hecquet-Noti = Nicole Hecquet-Noti, ed., *Éloge consolatoire de la chasteté (Sur la virginité)*, Sources chrétiennes 546 (Paris, 2011)

McDonough = Christopher J. McDonough, "Notes on the Text of Avitus," *Vigiliae Christianae* 35 (1981): 170–73

Nodes = Daniel J. Nodes, "Further Notes on the Text of Avitus," *Vigiliae Christianae* 39 (1985): 79–81

Peiper = Rudolph Peiper, ed., *Alcimi Ecdicii Aviti Viennensis episcopi opera quae supersunt*, Monumenta Germaniae historica: Auctores antiquissimi 6, part 2 (Berlin, 1883), https://www.dmgh.de/mgh_auct_ant_6_2

Ramminger = Johann Ramminger, "Zu Text und Interpretation von Alcimus Avitus' *De spiritalis historiae gestis*," *Wiener Studien* 101 (1988): 313–25

Sirmond = Jacques Sirmond, ed., *S. Aviti archiepiscopi Viennensis opera* (Paris, 1643)

Notes to the Texts

Book 1

76	cui est artis in usu *Hecquet-Noti*: quibus artis in usu est *Peiper*
79	segni *McDonough*: signi *Peiper*
220	excelsus *Gärtner 2*: sic celsus *Peiper*
221	densante *Hecquet-Noti*: densente *Peiper*
292	flamina *Beikircher*: flumina *Peiper*

Book 2

22	vitii *Gärtner 2*: vitio *Peiper*
157	miror magis ut tamen *Ramminger*: miror magis. Ut tamen *Peiper*
158–59	tactus. / Scire velim *Ramminger*: tactus, scire velim *Peiper*
159	dura *Ramminger*: dira *Peiper*
162–63	clausit? / Cum serpente *McDonough*: clausit / cum serpente *Peiper*
163–64	bruto / non pudet *Peiper correction*: bruto? / Non pudet *Peiper*
284	discere *Hecquet-Noti*: dicere *Peiper*
356	quos vita tibi. Solacia *Nodes*: quos vita. Tibi solacia *Peiper*

Book 3

17	quosque pavit *Hecquet-Noti*: quosque rapit *Peiper*
69–70	a Iudice flectis, / te Iudex *Hecquet-Noti*: a iudice flectis? / Te iudex *Peiper*
89	quae *Gärtner 2*: quia *Peiper*
147	pendas *Gärtner 1*: pendat *Peiper*
148	prolis *Hecquet-Noti*: proles *Peiper*

195   His *Gärtner 1*: Sic *Peiper*
347   quos *Hecquet-Noti*: quod *Peiper*

Book 4

125   quem *Gärtner 1*: quae *Peiper*
247   discreta *Chevalier*: dispersa *Peiper*
299   committit *Gärtner 2*: cum mittat *Peiper*
441   albus *Peiper, correction*: alvus *Peiper*
445   locum fecit *Gärtner 2*: facit luctam *Peiper*
472   salsis *Chevalier*: falsis *Peiper, misprint*
604   fatiscat *Gärtner 2*: patescat *Peiper*

Book 5

50   hae *Gärtner 1*: haec *Peiper*
61   plebem *Hecquet-Noti*: gregem *Peiper*
83   darent, hos talia *Dittmann*: darent hostilia *Peiper*
163   aera flatu *Gärtner 1*: aere flatus *Peiper*
216   ista haec *Gärtner 1*: istaec *Peiper*
343   secum dimissa ferant *Hecquet-Noti*: tecum dimisse feras *Peiper*
367   tenebris *Gärtner 2*: tenebrisque *Peiper*
435   respergine flatum *Gärtner 2*: respergere flatu *Peiper*
633   abeant *Arweiler*: habeant *Peiper*
646   arva *Arweiler*: arma *Peiper*

In Consolatory Praise of Chastity

title   De consolatoria castitatis laude *Hecquet-Noti*: De virginitate *Peiper*
90   sors *Hecquet-Noti*: fors *Peiper*
101   superanti *Gärtner 2*: superantes *Peiper*
102   sancto teneros *Peiper correction*: teneros sancto *Peiper*
197   in quae *Sirmond*: in quos *Peiper*
234   cardine *Chevalier*: ordine *Peiper*
315   contremuit *Hecquet-Noti*: contemnit *Peiper*
329   non *Hecquet-Noti*: nunc *Peiper*

379   sacrae divina volumina legis *Gärtner 2*: sacrum divina volumina
   verbis *Peiper*
419   nec iam *Gärtner 2*: et iam *Peiper*
485   parabunt *Gärtner 1*: negabunt *Peiper*
590   tantos *Gärtner 1*: totus *Peiper*
596   ipse *Chevalier*: iste *Peiper*

Notes to the Translations

Spiritual History

Dedicatory Letter

Apollinaris: Avitus's brother, Apollinaris, was bishop of Valence.

a minor work: The Latin *opusculum* literally means "a small work," implying a work of modest ambition.

the sequence of their subjects and chronology: That is, Avitus was planning to arrange his epigrams according to the criteria of subject matter and chronology. It is possible, but unlikely, that Avitus includes the books of the *SHG* in his "quantity of epigrams."

that most notorious disturbance: The reference is to the fighting between the brothers Gundobad and Godegisil in 500 for the city of Vienne.

names and titles: Listed by Isidore, *De viris illustribus* 36, as "The Beginning of the World" (*De origine mundi*), "Original Sin" (*De originali peccato*), "The Sentence Passed by God" (*De sententia Dei*), "The Flooding of the World" (*De diluvio mundi*), and "The Crossing of the Red Sea" (*De transitu Maris Rubri*). The manuscripts give the title of book 1 as *De initio mundi*.

touch on other matters: Avitus here refers to his practice of incorporating material into his poem extraneous to the immediate biblical narrative.

the freedom to lie, which is granted to painters and poets alike: The accusation that poets lie is longstanding, going back to Hesiod (probably late eighth century BCE). When Christian authors make this charge, they particularly have in mind the mythological subject matter of pagan poetry. For the comparison of poets and painters in this respect, see Horace, *Ars poetica* 9–10.

a transference of meaning: The language is used of various tropes in the grammatical and rhetorical traditions. Perhaps Avitus has in mind the metonymy whereby the name of a god is substituted for a concept or object with which he or she is associated (for example, Mars for war, Vulcan for fire, Venus for love); Michael Roberts, "The Prologue to Avitus' *De spiritalis historiae gestis*: Christian Poetry and Poetic License," *Traditio* 36 (1980): 399–407. Such words would be doctrinally as well as stylistically offensive.

if men will be made . . . have spoken: See Matthew 12:36.

Book 1

1   The first line echoes the programmatic statement of Juvenal's first satire, "All the actions of human beings . . . will form the mishmash of my book" (*quidquid agunt homines . . . nostri farrago libelli est*, 1.85–86).

7   *first father*: That is, Adam.

10   *the blasting of its stock*: With "by sowing the seed" *(semine)*, "growth and life" *(vitalia germina)*, and "the blasting of its stock" *(percussa in stirpe)*, Avitus sustains a metaphor from vegetation.

14–16   Genesis 1:9.

17–23   Genesis 1:14–18.

24–29   Genesis 1:11–12.

30–41   Genesis 1:20–25.

41   Avitus identifies as agents of creation the Word (*Verbum*, 14 and 27) and Wisdom (*Sollertia*, 41; *Sapientia*, 51 and 75). Both allude primarily to the role of Christ in creation. See Daniel J. Nodes, *Doctrine and Exegesis in Biblical Latin Poetry*, Arca 31 (Liverpool, 1993), 62–65.

48–50   Genesis 1:25.

55–68   Genesis 1:26 and 1:29–30.

59   *upright countenance . . . downward-looking*: Traditionally, humans

are distinguished from animals, whose gaze is turned to the earth, by their upright stance on two feet, implying for Avitus an affinity to heaven (1.69–72).

73–81   Genesis 2:7.

87–89   The metaphor is from the lyre. The human tongue corresponds to the plectrum, producing the articulate sound, the palate of the mouth to the lyre's sounding box.

91   *branching hands*: The branches of hands are presumably fingers.

96   *as the work of the same single creator*: Avitus's point is that though the body has two sides, front and back, one creator is responsible for both.

110   *The fixture of the spleen*: According to Aristotle, the spleen and the liver served as anchors for blood vessels. See D. Kuijper, "Lienis regula," *Vigiliae Christianae* 9 (1955): 50–55.

121–27   Genesis 2:7.

133–37   Genesis 1:28–30.

138–43   See Exodus 20:3–5; Deuteronomy 4:16–19.

144–45   Genesis 1:31.

146–57   Genesis 2:21–22.

162–67   See John 19:34.

163   The verbs *pendēret*, "was suspended," and *pendĕret*, "was paying off," differ only in the quantity of the second *e*. I have been unable to represent the play on words in my translation.

168–69   Just as Eve comes out of a part of Adam's body *(membrum)* when he is at rest to be his wife, so the Church, in the sacrament of baptism, comes from Christ's flank *(lateris membrum)* when he is resting to be his bride. See Augustine, *De civitate Dei* 22.17.

170–79   Genesis 1:28.

175   *I have granted you unlimited offspring*: Avitus adapts Virgil, *Aeneid* 1.279, "I have granted unlimited empire" *(imperium sine fine dedi)*, Jupiter's promise of Rome's future greatness.

182–87   Genesis 2:24. See also Matthew 19:5–6, Ephesians 5:31–32.

198–99   *with the proximity of the heavens . . . preserve a native darkness*: Literally, "preserve a native night," a paradoxical expression; their blackened bodies bring night to the light of day. "Native darkness" means here the darkness with which they were born. Avitus imagines paradise as a place where heaven and earth are in close proximity (1.212). In the land of the *Indi* the two are already becoming close, perhaps because of the country's mountainous nature.

217   *heaven's ministers*: That is, angels.

238   The Sabaeans were a people of Southern Arabia, a land known for its perfumes and spices.

239–44   The mythical bird, the phoenix, was extraordinarily long-lived, but when finally weakened by age, it would collect spices and perfumes to build its own funeral pyre, on which it was to be cremated. From the ashes the phoenix was reborn.

249   *healthful flowers*: Presumably they have medicinal uses.

258–59   Genesis 2:10.

260–63   Genesis 2:13–14.

262   The identification of Geon with the Nile is widespread in patristic exegesis; so too Physon with the Ganges (1.290).

268   *fertility is enhanced*: The verb *taxo, -are* means "to estimate the value of." It normally has a neutral sense but here has positive connotations: the fertility of the land after the Nile flood is valued highly.

269   *a terrestrial inundation*: As opposed to an inundation by rain.

272   *nullified*: Literally, "leveled" or "made equal." If the land demarcations are thought of as boundary stones or other physical objects, the word could mean that these objects were leveled to the ground. Alternatively and more abstractly, it could mean that the distinctions they mark out were "made equal" and thereby "nullified."

299–319   Genesis 2:15–17.

Book 2

5   *however small the plot of land*: The significance of *tenui de caespite* is not immediately clear. I take it in opposition to the richly teeming *(opimi)* bushes. A continual abundance of produce is produced from a small area of land.

6–9   The logic of the passage suggests that the "trees" of line 7 are vines. Once their fruit is ripe and ready to be picked, immediately the process of producing new fruit begins. These lines illustrate the principle formulated in what precedes, that the production of crops is continuous.

11   *spangled grass*: That is, grass picked out with colorful flowers.

22   *guilt of wrongdoing*: Following Thomas Gärtner, I adopt the reading of the German family of manuscripts here, *vitii* (wrongdoing); Thomas Gärtner, "Untersuchungen zum Text und zu den literarischen Vorbildern der Dichtungen des Alcimus Avitus," *Jahrbuch für Antike und Christentum* 44 (2001): 79–80. I take *causa* to mean "guilt, responsibility, blame" (*OLD, causa*, 11a).

120–21   The "rebel" is Satan, who as a fallen angel has an "airy body."

123   The serpent's "neck" extends the length of its body.

134–35   *Then it pretends . . . tongue*: These lines describe the physical appearance of a snake, but the details are chosen with an eye to the deceitful character of Satan.

144   *bit with coaxing words*: The snake's speech to Eve is the equivalent of a poisonous bite from a snake.

157–60   Genesis 3:1.

157   *For my part I feel no envy, but rather marvel*: A direct quotation of Virgil, *Eclogues* 1.11.

161   *hissed words*: Literally, "hissings." Again, the word is chosen to reflect the speaker's serpentine nature.

162–65   *What folly, O woman . . . your language*: In Christian Latin poetry the poet frequently apostrophizes an actor in the narrative with indignant words in this way.

172–80   Genesis 3:2–3.

186   Genesis 3:4.

199   *a law*: That is, the commandment not to eat from the tree of the knowledge of good and evil.

200–203   Genesis 3:5.

209   *title and high abode of the gods*: The reference is to 2.201–2.

212–31   Genesis 3:6.

222   By "love" Avitus means Eve's ambitious desire to be equal to the gods.

231 *only to be swallowed herself*: Avitus describes the serpent's speech tempting Eve as his bite (2.144). Now that she has succumbed, he has consumed her. The choice of language also refers to the introduction at the Fall of death, which is regularly said to "swallow" or "devour" its victims.

242 There is irony in Eve identifying the tree of the knowledge of good and evil as a "life-giving tree" (*vitali . . . germine),* since in the introductory lines to book 1 (1.8) Avitus describes the Fall as precluding *vitalia germina* (life-giving growth) for the human race.

243 In the Christian Latin poetry of late antiquity, God is frequently "the Thunderer" *(Tonans).*

244 For the sentiment, see 2.200–202.

252–60 Genesis 3:6.

252 *securing its victory*: I have translated *victurae* as the future participle of *vinco,* "conquer." It could also be from *vivo,* "live." The sense then would be that the Fall allowed death to live (that is, exist). The paradox would be to the taste of late Latin poets.

258 Another ambiguity. The Latin translated "in response to his unfortunate wife's urging" *(miseraeque ex coniugis ore)* could also mean "from his unfortunate wife's mouth," since she took first bite of the fruit.

259 *betraying his past pledge*: This is a rather wordy translation for *inconstans,* which, I take it, is referring to the contravention of the covenant that the first parents entered into at the end of book 1 not to eat of the tree of good and evil. Adam's inconstancy in this contrasts with his unwavering resolve *(constanter)* to eat the fruit Eve offers him.

264–66 By emphasizing that after the Fall Adam and Eve possess a "new way of seeing" *(novos . . . visus)* and by insisting that they already possessed eyesight at the creation, Avitus counters a reading of the biblical text "their eyes were opened" (Genesis 3:7) that might suggest they could not see before the Fall. See Augustine, *De Genesi ad litteram* 11.31. I owe this reference to Nicole Hecquet-Noti, ed., *Histoire spirituelle,* 2 vols., Sources chrétiennes 444 and 492 (Paris, 1999–2005), vol. 1, p. 22n5.

271–74 Genesis 3:7.

274   *ashamed or shameless*: It is shameless to feel such novel instincts, but it also arouses shame to feel them.

276   See Romans 7:23.

280   *depths of the fearsome abyss*: I follow Hecquet-Noti, *Histoire*, vol. 1, 222–23n6, in taking this as a reference to necromancy (compare 2.319–20).

285–87   It is a common objection against astrology in pagan and Christian authors that twins born at the same time can have different fates.

288–91   Avitus has in mind the planets that share the names of pagan gods and constellations named after mythological heroes. He adopts the euhemeristic view, common in Christian apologetic, that the gods were once living humans who, because of their merits, were hailed as gods after death.

295–98   See Exodus 7:19–22 and 8:1–7. Moses received from God the order to initiate the plagues. In the case of the first two, rivers of blood and frogs, the Egyptian magicians were able to duplicate the miracles, in so doing intensifying their own sufferings.

303–5   *the Marsi*: A central Italian tribe renowned for their ability to tame and handle snakes (see Augustine, *De Genesi ad litteram* 11.28). They can call up snakes from their lairs.

307   See Psalms 57:5 for the closed ears of the asp. According to Augustine (*Enarratio in Psalmos* 57.7), they press one ear to the earth and cover the other with their tail in an attempt to avoid hearing the spell of the Marsi.

314   *the first mother*: Eve, who spoke to a snake and had firsthand knowledge of its deceitfulness.

319–20   Both snake charmers and necromancers have in common that they attempt to engage in forbidden conversations.

329–37   Genesis 18:20.

349–51   See Genesis 19:28.

353–54   Genesis 19:12–13.

359–62   Genesis 19:17.

365–70   Genesis 19:24–25.

373   *in raising himself up*: The serpent had spoken to Eve from high in a tree (2.142–43).

379–80   *Whoever has come to know evil has already left the ranks of the good*: The point here is not immediately clear. Presumably, Lot's wife, in turning back, "comes to know evil" and thereby condemns herself.

385–94   Genesis 19:26.

398   *though senseless*: Avitus is playing on the two senses of *sapit*: "have a taste," which Lot's wife as a pillar of salt does, and "be wise," which she isn't, since she is *sine mente,* literally, "without a mind."

399   *salt of her example*: Salt is used by Christian authors as a literary term for spiritual substance that seasons a text or, in this case, an image (see Colossians 4:6).

416   *commingle wrong with right*: Literally, "join left with right," where "left" has the sense of "ill-omened, harmful." Avitus is perhaps also playing on the *dextrarum iunctio,* the joining of hands, a rite that formed part of the Roman marriage ceremony.

Book 3

4–16   Genesis 3:7.

14   *using the moist inner fiber of the tree*: Apparently the strands of this inner bark serve to attach the leaves to each other.

19   *ominously*: *Gravius* literally means "more heavily," in antithesis to *tenui,* "light, thin." Adam's clothing was made of a light covering of leaves, but it bore a heavy burden of significance, as embodying his fallen state.

20–21   *the latest Adam*: That is, Christ, who will destroy the power of death by his own death on the wood of the cross (see 1 Corinthians 15:45).

24–26   Moses's setting up of a brazen serpent in the desert to heal the Israelites who suffered snake bites (Numbers 21:8–9) prefigures Christ on the cross (see John 3:14). The poison is that of death, brought into the world by the Fall and redeemed by Christ's death on the cross.

27–31   Genesis 3:8.

35   *if a sentence of death had already been passed on them*: God has not yet passed judgment on the first couple, and so they are not yet subject to death.

44–45   See Revelation 11:15, *Et septimus angelus tuba cecinit,* "And the sev-
          enth angel sounded the trumpet."

46–47   See Matthew 25:32–33.

48   *with a gulf between the two*: See Luke 16:26.

50–54   See Genesis 19:24. Avitus insists on the metaphor implied in
          the biblical phrase "the Lord rained sulfur and fire" *(Dominus
          pluit . . . sulphur et ignem).* The words *nimbo* (storm cloud), *gut-
          tatim* (literally, "in drops"), *plueret* (rained), and *stillarent* (liter-
          ally, "dripped") all contribute to the image.

55–56   The comparison here is between the destruction of Sodom and
          Gomorrah and the destructive effect of sinfulness in later gen-
          erations.

60–64   These lines refer to the revival and second death of sinners at
          the time of the resurrection of the flesh (see Augustine, *De civi-
          tate Dei* 20.9).

66–68   Genesis 3:8.

74–81   Genesis 3:9–11.

90   *in the clear light of day*: Adam had earlier feared daylight (3.30–31)
          and sought out darkness (3.68).

98–101   Genesis 3:12.

108–13   Genesis 3:13.

112   *its lofty seat*: That is, the head, the seat of reason and mental
          powers.

116–36   Genesis 3:14–15.

116   *final decree: Finalem . . . legem,* in contrast with the "first law / dis-
          pensation" *(prima lex,* 3.99, 3.138) that governed human rela-
          tions before the Fall (Hecquet-Noti, *Histoire,* vol. 1, p. 274n1).

124–25   *your body will curve in pursuit of itself*: This is a description of a
          snake's sidewinding motion. The same word *(lapsus)* is used of
          the snake's sliding motion and the Fall of the first couple, fol-
          lowing the principle of the *lex talionis,* that the punishment
          matches the crime.

137–52   Genesis 3:16.

155–76   Genesis 3:17–19.

160   *following your example*: The earth disobeys humans, as Adam dis-
          obeyed God.

169 *the allure your appetite exerted on you*: A reference to the fruit the first couple were tempted into eating.

177–89 Avitus refers to the murder of Abel by Cain (Genesis 4:1–8), both of whom were sons of Adam and Eve.

195–96 Genesis 3:21, 3:23.

197 *a new land*: That is, the land outside paradise. Avitus imagines paradise as higher than the rest of the earth, but not as a separate realm. They do not literally fall, but they have come down in the world because of their "Fall" in the theological sense.

212 *their now-receptive cheeks*: The poet, I suspect, has in mind the analogy with late repentance that he makes in the following lines: only now (too late) do their tears show the first parents to be sensitive, responding to their sinfulness and its consequences. The phrase *attentis genis* is modeled on the more familiar "with receptive ears" (*attentis auribus*); here the tears flowing down their cheeks demonstrate their receptiveness.

220–305 See Luke 16:19–30.

255 *depths of Avernus*: Christian poets regularly use titles for the pagan underworld of the Christian hell.

258–59 *not far away . . . the outcome shows*: Avitus's language reflects the exegetical problem that, despite the distance between heaven and hell, the two figures are able to communicate.

261 *recently received into the light of God*: A reference to the reward that the virtuous receive after death. Hecquet-Noti (*Histoire*, vol. 1, p. 294n1) compares a sepulchral inscription (*ILCV* 3444, *cuius spiritus in luce Domini susceptus est,* "whose spirit has been received in the light of the Lord").

273 Avitus plays on the words for "throat" (*guttura*) and "drops of water" (*guttas*). I have not been able to preserve this in my translation.

280 *the noble patriarch*: That is, Abraham.

301 *someone be sent*: In the Bible it is Lazarus whom the rich man requests as go-between (Luke 16:27). Avitus leaves the identity of the messenger indefinite. Later (3.307–8), Adam plays that role for the people of the poet's day.

335 *a hundred tongues*: A poetic cliché for inexpressibility, deriving in

Latin from Virgil's *Aeneid* (6.625), where it refers to innumerable crimes and punishments.

336–37 *the poet from Mantua or Maeonia*: That is, Virgil or Homer. Maeonia is a poetic name for Lydia, one of the alleged birthplaces of Homer.

361 *perils . . . evil*: Avitus plays on the Latin words *discrimen* (danger) and *crimen* (crime).

363–64 See Romans 9:21.

365–66 See Luke 15:8.

367–70 See Luke 15:4–6.

370–83 See Luke 15:13–24.

380 *finest of clothing*: The phrase *vestis . . . prima* comes from Luke 15:22 (for the sense, see Hecquet-Noti, *Histoire*, vol. 1, p. 309n3). Avitus plays on the literal sense of *prima*, "first," contrasting it with *ornatus . . . secundos*. I take this latter phrase to be, on the literal level, a reference to the fine garments the prodigal son wore before he descended into poverty and which he now assumes for a second time. For the figural sense, see 3.390–95.

384 *In your case*: The language suggests a contrast with the father of the prodigal son, perhaps because he suffers a loss by being bereaved of a son, whereas God is incapable of diminishment.

385 *enjoy the assurance of salvation*: The sense of *constare* with the dative is difficult to determine here. I take it to mean literally something like "conform to."

395 *give your returning offspring, Father, his first mantle again*: The language picks up on the parable of the prodigal son, who receives "the finest of clothing" on his return (*vestis . . . prima*, 3.380; *stolam primam*, Luke 15:22). In this new context the "first mantle" points metaphorically to the original condition of Adam before the Fall, which the poet here prays to God to restore; Manfred Hoffmann, trans. and ed., *"De spiritalis historiae gestis" Buch 3: Einleitung, Übersetzung, Kommentar* (Munich, 2005), 268–69.

396–406 See Luke 10:30–35. Avitus interprets the Good Samaritan as Christ and his care for the wounded man as an allegory of the redemptive action of the incarnate Christ.

409–19   See Luke 23:40–43.

422   *the wicked robber*: That is, the devil.

424–25   Avitus's emphasis on the role of divine grace reflects his opposition to contemporary Semipelagianism. See Daniel J. Nodes, "Avitus of Vienne's *Spiritual History* and the Semipelagian Controversy: The Doctrinal Implications of Books I–III," *Vigiliae Christianae* 38 (1984): 185–95. The last two lines of book 3 anticipate the redemptive content of books 4 and 5.

Book 4

5–6   See Ovid, *Metamorphoses* 1.414–15. In the Ovidian flood story the sole surviving couple, Deucalion and Pyrrha, create a new human race from stones.

10   *still in its infancy*: Literally, "still suckling, unweaned" *(lactantem)*.

59   *the originator of sin and the exemplar of guilt*: That is, Adam.

62   *issuing first from a small pitcher*: In ancient art river gods were regularly represented with a pitcher, symbolizing the source of their waters.

78–80   See Genesis 5 for the longevity of the pre-Flood generations.

86–87   Genesis 6:4.

94–100   In Greco-Roman mythology the Olympian gods had to fight off assault by hybrid-formed giants. Ovid (*Fasti* 5.35–38) describes these creatures as having snakes in place of legs.

101   *the high Thunderer*: The Latin noun *(Tonans)* is regularly used in Christian authors of the Christian God (see 2.243), but here it refers to Jupiter.

102–3   Avitus here draws attention to the implausibility of the giants' serpentine undercarriage. The snakes form the legs and feet of the giants but continue to behave in their traditional manner.

104   *Phlegrean war*: The plains of Phlegra were the location of the mythical battle between the giants and the Olympian gods.

113–28   See Genesis 11:3–9.

129–32   Avitus imagines that the biblical giants also practiced impious building activity before the Flood but that the Flood eliminated all evidence of it.

141–42   Genesis 6:6.

160–63   See 1.15–16.

163   Genesis 6:17.

166   *brandished with his right hand a flood*: The flood is described as if it
were a weapon to hurl at the earth, comparable to Jupiter's
thunderbolt (see Ovid, *Metamorphoses* 2.308).

167–71   See Genesis 6:8–9.

172–73   *distinguished great-grandfather*: That is, Enoch. For Enoch's as-
cent to heaven, see Genesis 5:24.

176   *a greater deed*: That is, Enoch's ascent to heaven without experi-
encing death was no greater than Noah's glorious deeds.

179–84   See 2 Kings 2:11.

183–84   Avitus may well have in mind the contrast with the mythologi-
cal Phaethon, who was unable to control the fiery horses of the
sun chariot.

200   *one that stands out*: That is, the angel Gabriel.

203–5   The reference is, of course, to the Annunciation to Mary (Luke
1:26–38).

205   *with his words as wedding gift*: The phrase wedding gift (*dotali
verbo*) finds a parallel in Avitus's *Contra Eutychianam haeresim*
(*verbo dotavit*), suggesting *verbo* here is not the Word, in the
theological sense, but just his (that is, Gabriel's) words; see Ru-
dolph Peiper, ed., *Alcimi Ecdicii Aviti Viennensis episcopi opera
quae supersunt*, Monumenta Germaniae historica: Auctores an-
tiquissimi 6, part 2 (Berlin, 1883), p. 17, lines 34–35.

206–12   Avitus's account of Gabriel's announcement to Elizabeth of her
future pregnancy and of the subsequent striking dumb of Zach-
ariah (Luke 1:8–25, 1:57–64) is somewhat compressed, relying
on his readers' familiarity with the story.

206   *as a messenger*: In classical Latin, "messenger" is the normal trans-
lation of the word *nuntius*. Its Greek equivalent is *angelus*. But
just as the Greek word in Christian usage comes to mean "an-
gel," so the Latin *nuntius* may carry that sense too. I have pre-
ferred "messenger" in my translation, because in the present
context that is the role Gabriel is playing.

213–24   The employment of Gabriel to bear God's message to Noah departs from the biblical text, where God communicates directly with Noah. Avitus here adopts the convention in classical epic of the divine messenger; Paul-Augustin Deproost, "La mise en oeuvre du merveilleux épique dans le 'De diluvio mundi' d'Avit de Vienne," *Jahrbuch für Antike und Christentum* 43 (1991): 92–93. The best-known case is that of Mercury, dispatched by Jupiter to Aeneas in *Aeneid* 4.

224   *his face in fear averted its gaze*: I take *pavidi . . . vultus* as nominative. Avitus emphasizes that the reactions to the angel's presence are not choices willed by Noah, but instinctive natural impulses prompted by the brightness of the angel's appearance.

237–38   See Genesis 6:17.

238   *the abyss*: See Genesis 1:2, where *abyssus* refers to the primal waters of creation.

239–52   Genesis 6:14–16, 6:18.

253–54   *let life begin to take you in as its own*: This phrase contrasts with both the preceding and the following clauses. The wickedness of the human race sets Noah apart *(exclusit),* while life is to take him in *(includere);* the "life" that takes him in is opposed to the "deaths" that will rage around him. On the literal level Noah will be "shut in" inside the ark.

255–56   Genesis 6:18.

255   *the partner of your side*: The language is chosen to recall the creation of the first wife, Eve, from Adam's side.

262–68   See Genesis 6:19–20.

292   *that my feeble hand can build so vast a structure*: That is, the ark. But the Latin could also mean "that my feeble hand can perform so mighty a task," that is, the work of salvation.

293   *hope . . . for life*: The language conveys a double meaning. "Life" means both surviving the Flood and securing eternal life through the work of salvation that the Flood narrative prefigures.

295–305   Description of the felling of trees for shipbuilding (or sometimes for other purposes) is a traditional theme in Latin narrative poetry (Ovid, *Heroides* 5.41–42 and 16.107–12; Claudian, *De raptu Proserpinae* 3.363–69; Sidonius Apollinaris, *Carmina* 5.442–45).

299–301   Pelion, Ossa, and Pindus are all mountains in Thessaly. Pelion traditionally supplied the timber for the first ship, the Argo.

302   *Atlas*: The mountain in North Africa. Like the other mountains mentioned, it is personified in offering service for the building of the ark.

323–26   *from the waters*: But the Latin *(ab undis)* could also be translated "by waters," with a reference to the role of baptism in bringing salvation. The Flood is regularly interpreted as a figure of baptism (1 Peter 3:20–21).

336   *rich in expectation*: The Latin word translated "rich" *(beatum)* can also mean "blessed." Both senses are present here.

337–45   See Matthew 24:37–39 and Luke 17:26–27. With "the various activities of the world," Avitus has in mind the reports of Matthew and Luke that the inhabitants of the earth continued eating, drinking, and marrying right up to the Flood.

359   *a man . . . much buffeted by land and sea*: The language is taken directly from Virgil's characterization of Aeneas at the beginning of the *Aeneid* (1.3).

361   *feared a flood*: The Bible does not specify what form the destruction of Nineveh will take.

363–71   See Jonah 2:1 and 2:11.

371   *his prison*: That is, the sea creature.

its chastened would-be dinner: Jonah is chastened for initially refusing God's command to go to Nineveh. In late Latin the word *castigatus* can also mean "purified." Like the story of the ark, that of Jonah in the belly of the sea creature can be interpreted as a figure of baptism, from which the candidate for baptism emerges "purified."

373–76   See Jonah 3:3–4.

380   See Jonah 3:8.

384   *strange to relate*: The strangeness lies in overcoming dangers by fear rather than by more vigorous measures.

388–90   See Jonah 3:10.

395–400   Genesis 7:2. The reference to "wild animals" (*silvestres . . . feras*) echoes the earlier mention of "wild animals" (*silvarum . . . feris*) in Gabriel's instructions to Noah (4.264), though there the archangel makes no mention of special treatment for clean animals. Avitus is unusual in understanding the biblical text as referring to seven clean animals in total, not seven pairs. He may be following a variant Old Latin text (Deproost, "Mise en oeuvre," 90n10).

402–3   Genesis 7:7.

406–12   Genesis 9:21–22, 9:25–27.

414–15   See John 8:34, "Everyone who commits a sin is the slave of sin" (*omnis qui facit peccatum, servus est peccati*).

425–28   Genesis 7:11.

428   *then already*: The destruction of the Flood prefigures the Last Judgment.

436   *strange new waters*: The Egyptians were used to the annual flooding of the Nile, but this was something different.

437–38   *Garamantes . . . Massylian Syrtes*: The Garamantes were a tribe of the Sahara Desert; the Syrtes was a coastal region in North Africa of sandbanks and sandflats, inhabited by the Massylians, a Numidian tribe.

441–42   *Don . . . Riphaean range*: The river and the mountain range from which it rose were located in Scythia, in the extreme north of the Roman world.

462   *an elemental force*: Scholars and translators differ on the sense of the phrase *vertex rerum*. I take it to mean that the ocean is one of the principal forces of the world (so Hecquet-Noti, *Histoire*, vol. 2, pp. 89–90n5). Avitus adopts the traditional classical view of the ocean as surrounding the earth and marking its outer limit. This sense of the ocean as an extreme boundary to the earth may also contribute to the meaning of *vertex rerum*.

468   *new forces*: Avitus stresses the novelty of the situation. Normally rivers flow into the sea, not vice versa.

497   *Charybdis-like*: A dangerous whirlpool off the coast of Sicily encountered by Odysseus and subsequent seafarers, Charybdis is

here used metaphorically of the dangerous and destructive teachings of heretics.

506–9 The thought that one may surrender to the assaults of the world, provided the soul remains inviolate, is Stoic in origin (Deproost, "Mise en oeuvre," 91).

511–13 The metaphor is financial. Avitus imagines the occupants of the ark, the "source of new life," as a deposit, stored for safekeeping in that vessel's protection; at the proper time, when peace returns to the earth with the end of the Flood, that deposit will be repaid.

514–15 Genesis 7:19.

516–19 *Othrys*: A mountain in southern Thessaly. Parnassus is the mountain in Phocis where Delphi is situated, Lycaeus a mountain in Arcadia, sacred to Zeus and Pan. Avitus chooses them for their literary resonances.

524 Genesis 7:17.

527–35 Genesis 8:2–3.

537–40 Genesis 8:4.

544–52 Genesis 8:6 and 8:8–9. Avitus reverses the biblical order of events, having Noah send out the dove (though he doesn't identify the species of bird) before he sends out the raven.

563–67 See Genesis 8:6–7. The detail that the crow was detained by feeding on carrion is not biblical but is common in patristic texts; Nicole Hecquet-Noti, "Le corbeau nécrophage, figure du juif, dans le *De diluvio mundi* d'Avit de Vienne: À propos de l'interprétation de Gn 8, 6–7 dans *carm.* 4, 544–584," *Revue d'études augustiniennes et patristiques* 48 (2002): 297–320.

568 *in his shared refuge*: The ark and its inhabitants prefigure the Christian community from which the raven, in Avitus's reading prefiguring the Jews, is excluded.

573 *transgressed that first agreement*: Perhaps a reference to the "sacred pact of peace" (*placidum … foedere pactum,* 4.289) promised by Gabriel to Noah before the Flood.

579–82 Genesis 8:10–11.

590–98 Genesis 8:20–21.

600–604 Genesis 8:21.

608–12   Genesis 9:1–2.

613–14   Genesis 9:11.

625   *Thaumantis*: A patronymic; Thaumas was Iris's father. The name is used by the Roman poets Ovid and Statius.

628–30   Avitus's emphasis on the difficulty of determining the individual colors in the rainbow owes something to a simile in Ovid's *Metamorphoses,* which speaks of the problems in distinguishing where one color ends and another begins (*Metamorphoses* 6.65–67).

634   *different elements*: The cloud represents water; the sun, fire; the heavens, air; and the earth, of course, earth.

636   *image of the rainbow*: As an expression of harmony in diversity, the rainbow embodies the harmony between heaven and earth that God promises for mortals; Daniel J. Nodes, "Noah's Rainbow in Early Jewish and Christian Exegesis," *American Benedictine Review* 42 (1991): 243–46, and Nodes, *Doctrine and Exegesis,* 70.

637   *a sky that was cloudless*: *Nube serenum* refers both to the cloudless sky that would follow the Flood and, metaphorically, to the mental serenity that humans would enjoy as a result of God's promise.

640   *observe this sign that other signs serve to figure*: Presumably the double nature of Christ, signified by the rainbow, is also represented by other figures.

643–47   For the rainbow as intermediary between heaven and earth, God and man, see Nodes, *Doctrine and Exegesis,* 71–72.

650–51   See 1 Peter 3:20–21. The "eight souls" are, of course, Noah, his wife, his three sons, and their wives.

653   *He won for himself that gift*: I take *ille* to refer to Noah, and *comparat* in the sense of "acquire." Others take *comparat* to mean "grant, furnish" and understand *ille* of God or Christ.

Book 5

10–18   In these lines Avitus rings the changes on the opposition between, on the one hand, the events of the Red Sea crossing (*gesta*) and the narrative of those events (*series, historiae*), and on the other, their more important figural significance (*signa, praemissae forma salutis, figurae*).

18   *from its fertile encasement*: *Gravido . . . de tegmine* is a difficult phrase to translate; literally, it means "from its pregnant covering." Avitus adopts a metaphor from childbirth to describe the relation between the historical and the figural senses. The literal narrative conceals within itself the spiritual sense. It can therefore be said to be pregnant (as we say, "pregnant with meaning"), and from it the full figural sense of the passage can be conceived and brought to birth.

19–23   For the circumstances of the Israelites' servitude, see Exodus 1:14, and for its intensification, 5:8 and 5:18–19. Some of Avitus's language derives from the latter passages.

25–29   Exodus 1:16–17. Avitus's account differs from that of the Bible in that he has their mothers saving the children, whereas in Exodus the midwives play that role.

31–32   Exodus 1:12.

35–36   Exodus 3:2.

37–39   Avitus interprets the burning bush as a figure of the human soul. "The thorns of the spirit" (*spinas . . . mentis*) would normally refer in Christian texts to sins, which are here subject to the purifying fires of Christian devotion (Hecquet-Noti, *Histoire*, vol. 2, pp. 152–53n1). See *In Consolatory Praise* 532–33.

40–47   Exodus 5:1.

40   *chosen prophets*: Avitus's account of the antecedents to the expulsion of the Israelites is very compressed. He does not explain how the "prophets," Moses and Aaron, were "chosen," nor describe their receiving instructions from God.

43   *the baskets they must carry*: I have added "they must carry" for clarity's sake. The language shows the influence of Psalms 80:7.

49   See Exodus 5:2.

    sends omens: It is unclear what Avitus is referring to here. At this stage in the narrative God has given various signs to Moses of his chosen status, but there is no reason to think the pharaoh is aware of these.

55   See Exodus 5:17.

56–59   See Exodus 5:8–9.

63   *Pharos*: Strictly, an island lying off Alexandria famous for its lighthouse. Here, it stands by synecdoche for Egypt as a whole.

64–65   *Anubis . . . fiercely baying*: Anubis was a dogheaded Egyptian divinity.

67–70   See Exodus 7:9–10, although there it is Aaron who throws the staff to the ground.

80–91   Exodus 7:11–12.

84   *dismal muttering*: The pejorative language for the spells of the *magi* reflects Avitus's own perspective. The pharaoh would not have used such language.

86   *with its own familiar phantom*: Augustine (*De civitate Dei* 10.8) explains that the *magi* use "enchantments and magic spells" (*veneficia et incantationes magicae*), the particular weapons of demons (*mali angeli, hoc est daemones*), to work their illusions.

96   *priest of God*: Avitus gives Moses the title of priest (*sacerdos*) only here and when he refers to the miracle of bringing forth water from a rock (Exodus 17:5–6; *SHG* 5.462).

98   *inflamed by knowledge of the truth of what had happened*: I have added a few words to the translation to try to make clear what I take to be the sense. Avitus's language (*conscius ardor*) suggests that the violence of the pharaoh's response to Moses and Aaron derives from an unacknowledged awareness that they have right on their side, prompted by the miracle of Moses's staff.

104   *God's past instructions*: See line 40 and note.

109–13   Exodus 6:6–7.

113–15   Exodus 6:6, 7:3–4.

118–19   Exodus 6:8.

127–29   Exodus 7:17, 7:19–21.

139–46   Exodus 7:18, 7:21.

142   *the fatal disaster to come*: The reference is to the destruction of the Egyptian host in the Red Sea.

145   *Canopus*: A city in the Nile delta, perhaps here standing by synecdoche for the delta itself, since Avitus refers to its "broad extent" (*patet ampla*).

151–52   Avitus uses two cognate Latin words for "whip" (*flagellum* and *flagris*) to refer metaphorically to the scourge that the Egyp-

tians endured (that is, the rivers of blood) and the literal whip-
ping the Israelites continued to suffer.

157–60   Exodus 8:3.

162–67   Exodus 8:17 and 24. Avitus has conflated the third and the fourth
plagues, taking *scinifes* (gnats) and *muscae* (flies) as the same in-
sects (see Psalms 104:31, which omits the third plague).

173–74   Exodus 9:3 and 9:6.

177–78   Exodus 9:9–10.

178   *a holy fire*: This is the literal meaning of the Latin phrase *sacer
ignis,* but in medical parlance it refers to "various diseases af-
fecting the skin, including in human beings erysipelas and her-
pes, and in animals anthrax" (*OLD, ignis,* 7b). Here both the lit-
eral and the medical senses are appropriate.

181–89   Exodus 9:23–25.

193–94   See Exodus 10:13–15. Avitus's reference to *bruci,* a type of locust,
which I have translated "grasshoppers," derives from Psalms
104:34.

214–15   Exodus 10:22.

216–17   While the Egyptians are plunged into darkness, the Israelites
enjoy full daylight (Exodus 10:23).

222   *mystical victim*: The lamb is a figure of the crucified Christ,
whose blood, like the lamb's, secures salvation for his people
(5.247–53). It is this that makes the lamb "mystical" and its sac-
rifice especially holy *(sollemnem)*.

223   *laments the consequences of its guilt*: *Reatum . . . gemat* would nor-
mally mean "laments its guilt," that is, "regrets it," but that
does not fit the present context.

234–37   Exodus 12:2–3 and 12:6. Nisan, the first month of the Hebrew
year, corresponds to the month of March (named after Mars).

238–41   Exodus 12:5, 12:7.

243–45   Exodus 12:12–13.

250–53   I take it that "the seething mortality of the failing world" refers
to the destructive effect of worldly pleasures that bring spiri-
tual death and ultimately damnation to those unprotected by
the sign of Christ.

250 *when taken in our mouths*: A reference to the taking of wine in the Eucharist.

254–56 The sudden address to the reader is unexpected here.

258–59 See 1 Corinthians 5:7.

261–62 Exodus 12:28.

263–64 Exodus 12:14.

265–66 Exodus 12:29, "and it came to pass at midnight" (*factum est autem in noctis medio*).

272–76 Exodus 12:29.

297–99 Exodus 12:30.

301 *Business was rightly suspended . . . to grieve*: A free translation, which I hope conveys the sense; more literally, "a just suspension of business constrained those deserving to grieve." Avitus plays on *iustitium* and *iustum* (a just suspension of business) and *maerere* and *merentes* (deserving to grieve), which perhaps explains the obscurity of the language.

308–9 Exodus 12:33. The following speech corresponds to one in the Bible containing only two words, *omnes moriemur* (we will all die).

315–17 In their agitated state the speakers equate the reversal of nature in the plagues with a collapse of the world order.

333–39 Exodus 12:35–36.

352–56 Avitus has in mind here Joseph's words of reconciliation with his brothers after Jacob's death: "you plotted evil against me, but God turned that evil to good" (*vos cogitastis de me malum, sed Deus vertit illud in bonum*, Genesis 50:20). Hence, presumably, the reference to a brother in line 356. The relevance of these lines to the immediate context is not immediately apparent. I suspect the point is that the hardships of the Israelites and their mistreatment by the pharaoh will eventually turn out to their advantage and to the detriment of the Egyptians. (The taking of the Egyptian treasure is a first example of this.)

352 *against the good works to their advantage*: Or "against what is right works to its advantage," depending on whether *rectis* is taken as masculine or neuter plural.

357–59 Exodus 12:39.

361   *almost five hundred years*: Avitus rounds up. Exodus 12:40 records that the Israelites spent 430 years in Egypt.

362–65   For Jacob's migration to Egypt, see Genesis 46:1–27. Genesis 46:27 reports that Jacob's household numbered seventy souls. When the Israelites left Egypt, they had about six hundred thousand men of military age (Exodus 12:37).

368–69   Exodus 12:42.

373–74   Exodus 12:51.

401   Exodus 13:20.

403–20   Exodus 13:21.

405   *a fire shines ominously in the restless sky*: The reference is to thunder and lightning.

419–20   *holy elders . . . leaders*: That is, Moses and Aaron.

450–57   See Deuteronomy 8:2–4.

458–64   See 1 Corinthians 10:3 for the typological parallel between manna and the Eucharist (Nodes, *Doctrine and Exegesis*, 66–67).

459   *a body . . . pure without seed*: Manna is a form of nourishment that, unlike the crops of earth, does not grow from seeds; Jesus was born from a virgin, and so too without seed.

460   *from the celestial abode*: Corresponding to the origin of manna from the skies. Jesus is "the living bread, who came down from heaven" (John 6:41).

462–63   See Exodus 17:6, Numbers 20:8–10. The "highest priest" is Moses.

464   See 1 Corinthians 10:4, "and the rock was Christ" (*petra autem erat Christus*).

465   See John 19:34.

469–96   Exodus 14:5.

480–81   *Taskmasters*: See Exodus 5:14, 5:18.

485–86   Avitus (5.371–88) imagines that the Israelite company includes an armed force *(manus)*, as well as the unarmed populace *(plebs)*.

493   *let the ground be invisible . . . corpses*: The disappearance of the earth under piles of corpses is a commonplace of the epic battle narrative. See Michael Roberts, "Rhetoric and Poetic Imitation in Avitus' Account of the Crossing of the Red Sea (*De spiritalis historiae gestis* 5.371–702)," *Traditio* 39 (1983): 44–45.

496	See 5.334–39.
497–500	See Psalms 2:1–4.
501–3	See Exodus 14:6–7.
507–13	Avitus here describes two types of Roman body armor, the one breastplate made of interlocking iron rings (507–9), the other made of overlapping, interlinked thin metal plates (510–13).
514	*impassioned*: The Latin *(ardentum)* could also refer to the blaze of light from the Egyptians' armor and weapons.
518	*set off their dark and angry features against the brilliance of their weaponry*: More literally, "surrounded their angry darkness with the light of weapons." Avitus again refers to the dark skin of the Egyptians.
526–27	Exodus 14:2.
530	*clouds of dust*: Premonitory clouds of dust are also a standard element of the epic battle narrative (Roberts, "Rhetoric and Poetic Imitation," 68).
531	Exodus 14:10.
538–39	Exodus 14:20.
544	Exodus 14:10.
547	*Oh thrice and four-times happy*: *O terque quaterque beati* is a direct quotation of Virgil, *Aeneid* 1.94, where Aeneas, facing shipwreck, regrets that he did not have the good fortune to fall at Troy.
548–53	See Exodus 14:11.
558	See Exodus 14:13.
559	*do not despair*: In Horace, *Odes* 1.7.28, the fugitive Teucer similarly rallies the spirits of his crew with the words "no need to despair" *(nil desperandum)*. They too are traveling to a promised land, a new Salamis on Cyprus ("for unerring Apollo has promised," *certus enim promisit Apollo*).
564	*your chastened foe*: That is, the pharaoh.
566	*an interposed column*: I am translating the word *mediatricis* (interposed) as a reference to the physical location of the column, between the two armies, but it is also appropriate to the column as a *mediator* between God and man, and thereby a prefiguration of *Christus mediator* (*SHG* 4.645; Hecquet-Noti, *Histoire*, vol. 2, p. 213n4).

569   Exodus 14:13.

577–78   Exodus 14:21.

579   *counter to nature*: God hurls his scorching winds like a thunder-
            bolt *(fulminat)*, but one that ignites water, not land.

581–83   Exodus 14:24.

582   *jagged shafts of sunlight*: The Latin is difficult and has been vari-
            ously understood. There is some evidence of *acies* being used of
            rays of the sun *(ThLL,* vol. 1, col. 400, lines 50–53).

589–94   Exodus 14:22.

592   *wall*: Scaena is literally the stage building in a theater, in front of
            which is the stage.

626   *the torrid zone of the sky*: Corresponds to the zone of the equator
            on earth.

627   The constellation Scorpio is associated with summer heat, the
            Bear with northern cold.

642   *by the name of Cencres*: Avitus probably derives this information
            from the second book of Eucherius of Lyon's *Instructiones*
            (CSEL 31:142.2).

645–47   Exodus 14:23.

646   The text is difficult here. I have adopted the reading of the Ger-
            man family of manuscripts, *arva,* which I understand as em-
            phasizing the illusion the Egyptians are under that they are ad-
            vancing on dry land. See Hecquet-Noti, *Histoire,* vol. 2, p. 225n5,
            and Alexander Arweiler, *Die Imitation antiker und spätantiker
            Literatur in der Dichtung "De spiritalis historiae gestis" des Alcimus
            Avitus* (Berlin, 1999), 189–90.

650–52   Exodus 14:24.

657–58   Exodus 14:26.

659–70   Exodus 14:27.

661   *wood's special mystery*: The salvific associations of wood extend
            not just to the cross but also to the ark (4.542).

663   *the waves first massed*: The waves here are described in terms ap-
            propriate to military maneuvers (see too 668–69).

672–76   The equivalent speech in the Bible (Exodus 14:25) is spoken by
            the Egyptians as a whole, not by the pharaoh.

680   See Ecclesiasticus 17:27 and Romans 10:9.

693   *both equally red in color*: The text could mean either that the wa-

ters of the Red Sea became red, the color of blood, thus living up to the omen of its name, or more likely that the waters of the Red Sea were thought of as naturally red, and now the color is matched by the blood shed in them (see 5.588).

702–3   Exodus 14:31.

704–5   *described that glorious event . . . throughout the world*: Alternatively, "described in a celebratory song that glorious event which is hymned throughout the world." (The final relative clause can either refer to *carmine*, "song," or *factum*, "event"). See Exodus 15:1.

706–8   For the crossing of the Red Sea as a figure of baptism, see 1 Corinthians 10:1–2.

708   *the ancient crimes Eve had committed*: The verb I translate here "had committed" *(edidit)* could also mean "gave birth to," suggesting the secondary meaning that Eve's fall gave birth to a sinful race.

716   *the true Israel*: In supersessionist theology the Christian Church and its people embody the fulfillment of the events prefigured by the historical experiences of the Israelites in the Old Testament, and so can be described as the "true Israel."

718–19   *achieve consummation*: Avitus is presumably describing the crossing of the Red Sea as the culminating and perhaps most important prefiguration in the narrative of the Pentateuch (the "five volumes" of the following line). "The holy prophet" is Moses, to whom the Pentateuch was traditionally attributed.

IN CONSOLATORY PRAISE OF CHASTITY

Dedicatory Letter

Apollinaris: The addressee is again Avitus's brother, the bishop of Valence.

an epigram: Avitus calls his 666-line poem an epigram apparently out of modesty, although there is some evidence that Sidonius Apollinaris also uses the word of longer compositions.

step back: Literally, "withdraw my foot." The word "foot" *(pes)* is also used as a unit of verse, a metrical foot. I was unable to preserve the play on words in my translation.

In Consolatory Praise of Chastity

title   *In Consolatory Praise of Chastity*: An unusual title. Speeches of praise and consolation are normally separate genres of epideictic oratory (see Introduction to this volume).

9   *my labored verse*: The sense of *excusso* is unclear. I follow, though not with complete confidence, *ThLL*, which suggests that the meaning here is "harsh" or "bold" (vol. 5, part 2, col. 1314, lines 13–15 and 27–28).

11   *fictitious waters*: The reference is to the spring Hippocrene, on Mount Helicon, a source of poetic inspiration that according to the myth first opened up when the earth there was struck by the hoof of the winged horse Pegasus.

15–16   *nine sisters . . . Pierian*: The nine sisters are the Muses; the region of Pieria in Thessaly was said to be their home.

29–32   See Genesis 4:4.

38   *twice-refined Sidonian purple*: Sidon, in modern Lebanon, was renowned in the ancient world for its production of high-quality purple dye, made from the crushed shell of the *murex,* a shellfish. The phrase I have translated "twice refined" *(bis cocti muricis)* literally speaks of "*murex* boiled down twice".

40   *the fleeces that the Chinese send*: That is, silk.

41   Avitus plays on *auribus* (ears) and *aurum* (gold). I have not been able to represent the wordplay in my translation.

44–45   See Isaiah 3:16–24.

59–62   See 1 Samuel 1:5, 1:20, 2:19. The "small coat" was a miniature priestly vestment.

72   *acquitted of her vow*: See lines 24–26. Fuscina was dedicated to Christ at birth.

86   *our holy mother Severiana's pious teaching*: Hecquet-Noti suggests that Severiana may have been an abbess and tentatively accepts her identification with Sidonius Apollinaris's daughter of the same name; Nicole Hecquet-Noti, ed., *Éloge consolatoire de la chasteté (Sur la virginité)*, Sources chrétiennes 546 (Paris, 2011), 44.

87   *Aspidia*: Not known elsewhere; presumably, a member of Avitus's family. Peiper (*Aviti opera,* 309) wrongly understands her

to be "not much older" than Severiana, rather than Fuscina. The point rather is that Aspidia took the veil at the age of twelve, Fuscina at the age of ten.

94   *Fuscina*: The elder Fuscina, whom her namesake is to model herself on, is otherwise unknown. The "double virginity" is that of the two Fuscinas.

95–96   Peiper (*Aviti opera*, 313) records a gloss giving the woman's name as Eusebia, which roughly corresponds to "eminent in holiness" (*pietate potens*).

104–5   *the formidable mother of the Maccabees*: 2 Maccabees 7 records the story of seven brothers who were put to death for rebelling against the Seleucid rule of Judea; their mother looked on and urged them to steadfastness in the face of death.

120   See Genesis 3:15. The serpent is, of course, the devil with his wiles.

137–39   See Matthew 7:13–14.

150–51   Hecquet-Noti (*Éloge consolatoire*, 137) understands *auctor* (father) of God, but normally firstfruits are offered to God, not by him. I take the "sacred harvest" to be Fuscina and her siblings, from whom Fuscina is offered to God as the "firstfruits."

152   *still holy faith declares*: Hecquet-Noti (*Éloge consolatoire*, 137n2) compares Matthew 11:29–30, but the language is not very close, and the point somewhat different. The sequence of ideas is that Fuscina blazed the trail, but when her siblings too adopted some form of religious life, the burden for all became lighter.

168   *Subjected to a husband*: Although grammatically this should describe Eve, in what follows Avitus is clearly thinking of the lot of married women in general, pursuing a commonplace in Christian writing on virginity.

181   *for stillborn offspring*: Avitus's language (*mortua fundat*) is more brutal: literally, "that she pours forth dead things."

198–200   I have translated these lines somewhat freely to bring out what I take to be the sense. The virgin enjoys a paradoxical freedom from the ties of the world by accepting restraints, that is, by submitting herself to the rule of virginity.

219–20   See Matthew 12:50.

231–35   See Matthew 27:45, Mark 15:33, Luke 23:44.

236–39   See Matthew 27:51.

244–47   See Mark 16:1 and Luke 24:1.

253–67   See Matthew 28:2–6.

263–65   See Matthew 16:21, 17:22.

271–77   See Matthew 28:7–10.

290–337   See Matthew 25:14–30.

290   *heavenly King, when preparing to leave the earth*: The Bible refers to a lord departing for a foreign land. Avitus's language reflects his interpretation of the parable.

292   *minae*: The *mina (mna)* was in origin a Greek unit of currency. In the Vulgate New Testament it is used interchangeably with *talentum* (see Luke 19:13 and Matthew 25:15; *ThLL*, vol. 8, col. 991, lines 50–53).

302–12   See Matthew 25:16–18.

313–17   See Matthew 25:19.

323–25   See Matthew 25:26.

331   *the exchange of my altar*: The word translated as "exchange" (*mensa*, literally, "table") is used both of a banker's or money changer's counter and of the surface of an altar on which offerings were made. Avitus here interprets the words of the master in the biblical parable that the third servant should have entrusted the money to money changers and brought him the profit (Matthew 25:27). I understand his point in this passage to be that talents righteously expended in good works have the capacity to multiply spiritual credit, just as money invested with a banker realizes financial profits, hence my somewhat free translation. The analogy between spiritual and material finances informs Avitus's treatment of the parable throughout.

333–34   See Matthew 25:28–30.

336–37   See Luke 12:47–48.

338   See Luke 12:35.

342–62   See Judges 4.

350   *courage*: *Virtus* in Latin; the word derives etymologically from *vir*, "man." The enemy host loses its "manliness" in combat with a woman.

352–57   The detail of Sisera's gigantic stature is not biblical.

360   *a woman*: Her name was Jael (Judges 4:18–22).

366–69   For spiritual weaponry, including the "breastplate of justice,"
           see Ephesians 6:14–17.

372   *Prudentius*: The reference is to Prudentius's *Psychomachia*, in
           which he recounts combats between the personified virtues
           and vices in and for the human soul. In it, Prudentius (*Psychoma-
           chia* 40–108) describes the conflict between Modesty (*Pudici-
           tia*) and Lust (*Libido*).

379–408   The succession of relative clauses in this passage depends syn-
           tactically on the verb "you have imbibed" (*bibisti*) in line 408;
           "all these" (*haec cuncta*, 408) summarizes the content of the
           previous enumeration. In English such a construction is not
           sustainable, and I have had to introduce a couple of neutral
           phrases and sentence breaks to manage the sequence. The rhe-
           torical question beginning "Why need I mention" (*quid memo-
           rem*, 391) introduces a further complication, since it breaks the
           syntactical structure. I have punctuated it as a kind of paren-
           thesis, though it has primarily a stylistic purpose, to intro-
           duce variation into the list of biblical books. I have followed
           Hecquet-Noti in continuing the question to line 400, but it
           could equally end at line 394 (so Peiper).

381   *the ancient prophet*: That is, Moses.

387   *Solomon the peacemaker*: "The peacemaker" (*pacificus*) translates
           the meaning of the name Solomon.

391–94   See Judith 10–12:12.

396   Ezra was a scribe. His visions are recorded in the apocryphal 2
           Esdras.

399–400   *man . . . lion . . . eagle . . . bull*: The symbols of the four evangelists,
           respectively Matthew, Mark, John, and Luke.

401   *the actions of the twelve lambs*: The apostles are often represented
           iconographically as lambs (see the apse mosaic of Sant'Apol-
           linare in Classe, Ravenna). The reference is to the Acts of the
           Apostles.

410   Avitus here uses the technical language of meter and style. He
           refers to the "laws" (*leges*) that govern metrics and the short

units of sense *(commata)* that make up a line of verse. The reference to singing in the next line suggests that Avitus may have in mind Christian hymns.

417–24 See Matthew 21:18–19 and Mark 11:12–14.

445–91 See Matthew 25:1–13.

445 *sealed with the holy chrism*: That is, baptized. The reference is to anointing with oil.

489 *shopkeepers*: The word *venales* (more usually, "for sale") seems to have an active sense here, though I can find no parallel for it.

501 *virtue of spirit, that is*: The qualification perhaps owes something to Avitus's sensitivity to the etymological sense of *virtus* (see the note to line 350).

505 *Eugenia*: A Roman martyr, who according to the legend was executed in the mid-third century in the reign of Valerian.

512 *a thousand ways of doing hurt*: A Virgilian phrase (*Aeneid* 7.338), used of the Fury Allecto and often applied by Christian authors to the devil.

514–15 The *Vita S. Eugeniae* 11–15 tells the story of a woman of good family in Alexandria, Melanthia, who, after being healed by the saint of a sickness, falls in love with her (she thinks Eugenia is a man). When she is rejected, she denounces the saint for making sexual advances to her (*PL* 73.612B–615A). Consequently, Hecquet-Noti (*Éloge consolatoire*, 179n4) takes the "crazed love for a girl" to be that of Melanthia for Eugenia and translates accordingly, substituting for the masculine relative pronoun (*qui*) the feminine (*quae*), which also has manuscript authority. While it is grammatically possible for the phrase to describe Melanthia's motivation for her false denunciation, qualifying *fingat* (claim falsely), it is more natural to take it with *accendi* (was inflamed). It is also awkward to describe Eugenia as a girl (*puella*), when she has been described as a woman (*mulier*, 505) a few lines earlier. If my translation is correct, Avitus recounts a simplified but still internally coherent version of the story.

516 *the old men en masse . . . in alarm*: The Latin plays on *turba (en masse)* and *turbata* (in alarm).

518–19 The phrasing is oddly abstract. Hecquet-Noti (*Éloge consolatoire*,

179n5) takes the perfection in question to be that of Eugenia and these lines to express the painful belief of the old men that she had faltered, understanding the "greatest of leaders" (*praesule summo*) as Christ. But the language is more naturally taken as a statement of fact rather than of opinion. I'm tentatively inclined to identify the faltering aspiration for perfection as that of the old men and the "greatest of leaders" as Eugenia. The clause would then expand on their disturbed state of mind referred to at the beginning of the sentence.

533   *holy fire*: See *Spiritual History* 5.37–39, where Avitus, in his interpretation of the burning bush, speaks of "the devout fire of passion in the hearts of the holy" that has the power to consume sins. Augustine (*Enarratio in Psalmos* 96.7) also speaks of a "holy fire" (*sanctus ignis*) burning off sinful devotion to things of the world—in his case to the theater. (I'm grateful to Adam Trettel for discussing this passage with me and supplying the Augustine citation.)

536–38   See Genesis 39:7–20. The wife of Potiphar, an officer of the Egyptian court and Joseph's master, attempted to seduce Joseph and, when he rebuffed her, accused him of assaulting her.

539   That is, Joseph was in prison for two years (Genesis 41:1).

541   *it was thriving, though he was wasting away*: Avitus's wording (*nutritus macie*), literally, "nourished by (his) emaciation," points to the paradox of the luxuriant hair in company with an emaciated body (see Genesis 41:14).

543   A reference, of course, to Joseph's ability to interpret prophetic dreams (Genesis 40:5–41:39).

544–47   Avitus somewhat exaggerates Joseph's status in Egypt. Joseph's elevation prefigures the joyous reception the committed virgin will receive in heaven.

549–81   The story of Susanna is told in Daniel 13.

552–55   See Daniel 13:10–11.

558   *in the one grove*: The Bible speaks of Susanna walking in an orchard (Daniel 13:7). The two old men spy on her there. In an attempt out of embarrassment to conceal their desire for her

from each other, they both leave the orchard, only to sneak back again, where they encounter each other and confess their passion (Daniel 13:11–14).

560–63   The two men threaten to accuse Susanna of being unchaste (Daniel 13:21).

580–81   At the intervention of Daniel the two men were separately cross-examined, and the disparity in their stories revealed their guilt, as described in lines 614–16 (Daniel 13:45–59).

582   See Daniel 13:33.

583–90   See Daniel 3:13–23, 3:93–95.

584   *Parthian fury*: The reference is to the Babylonian king Nebuchadnezzar (Daniel 3:13 and 19).

590   The (metaphorical) fires that Nebuchadnezzar experiences are presumably those occasioned by the frustration of his attempt to punish the three youths, compelling him to recognize the God of the Israelites (Daniel 3:95).

591–602   Avitus's account of Daniel in the lions' den follows Daniel 14:30–38 rather than the version in chapter 6 of the same book.

593   For the detail that the lions were starved to make them hungrier, see Daniel 14:31.

599   *one cargo carried another*: The two cargos are the prophet Habakkuk, carried by the angel, and the food, carried by the prophet.

603–20   Daniel's intervention on behalf of Susanna is recounted in Daniel 13:45–64.

608–10   See Daniel 13:48–49.

617–20   See Daniel 13:60.

629   *elevating the lambs to the right*: Literally, "raising up the right for the lambs." The awkwardness is occasioned by the desire to introduce a play on words between *levans,* "raising up," and *laevis,* "to the left." The first syllable of each word would be pronounced identically in this period. For the sentiment, see Matthew 25:32–34.

637–45   See Luke 10:38–42. Lines 641–45 paraphrase quite closely the exchange between Martha and Christ in Luke 10:40–42.

638   *by the authority of his word*: I understand this to mean that Christ's words authorize the higher value of Mary's actions.

Hecquet-Noti takes *verbum* in the theological sense here, but not at 3.366, where the same phrase occurs.

657–59 Avitus's father, Hesychius, preceded him as bishop of Vienne. He presumably earlier held a secular magistracy ("Hesychius 11," *PLRE*, vol. 2, pp. 554–55; *PCBE*, vol. 4, part 2, p. 1072). The uncle in question may be Sidonius Apollinaris, if, as has been suggested, Avitus's mother, Audentia, was his sister. Author of three imperial verse panegyrics, a collection of poetry, and an extensive corpus of letters, Sidonius was city prefect of Rome in 468 and subsequently bishop of Clermont ("Gaius Sollius [Modestus?] Apollinaris Sidonius 6," *PLRE*, vol. 2, pp. 115–18; *PCBE*, vol. 4, part 2, pp. 1759–1800).

660–61 In addition to Avitus's episcopacy, his brother Apollinaris was bishop of Valence.

Bibliography

Editions and Translations

Arweiler, Alexander. *Die Imitation antiker und spätantiker Literatur in der Dichtung "De spiritalis historiae gestis" des Alcimus Avitus, mit einem Kommentar zu Avit. carm. 4,429–540 und 5,526–703.* Untersuchungen zur antiken Literatur und Geschichte 52. Berlin, 1999.

Chevalier, Ulysse, ed. *Oeuvres complètes de Saint Avit.* Lyon, 1890.

Hecquet-Noti, Nicole, ed. *Éloge consolatoire de la chasteté (Sur la virginité).* Sources chrétiennes 546. Paris, 2011.

——, ed. *Histoire spirituelle.* 2 vols. Sources chrétiennes 444 and 492. Paris, 1999–2005.

Hoffmann, Manfred, trans. and ed. *"De spiritalis historiae gestis" Buch 3: Einleitung, Übersetzung, Kommentar.* Beiträge zur Altertumskunde 217. Munich, 2005.

Morisi, Luca, trans. and ed. *Alcimi Aviti "De mundi initio."* Testi e manuali per l'insegnamento universitario del latino 44. Bologna, 1996.

Nodes, Daniel J., ed. *The Fall of Man: De spiritalis historiae gestis libri I–III.* Toronto Medieval Latin Texts 16. Toronto, 1985.

Peiper, Rudolph, ed. *Alcimi Ecdicii Aviti Viennensis episcopi opera quae supersunt.* Monumenta Germaniae historica: Auctores antiquissimi 6, part 2. Berlin, 1883. https://www.dmgh.de/mgh_auct_ant_6_2.

Schippers, Abraham. *De mundi initio.* Kampen, 1945.

Shanzer, Danuta, and Ian Wood, trans. *Avitus of Vienne: Letters and Selected Prose.* Translated Texts for Historians 38. Liverpool, 2002.

Shea, George W., trans. *The Poems of Alcimus Ecdicius Avitus.* Medieval and Renaissance Texts and Studies 172. Tempe, 1997.

Sirmond, Jacques, ed. *S. Aviti archiepiscopi Viennensis opera.* Paris, 1643.

Further Reading

Deproost, Paul-Augustin. "La mise en oeuvre du merveilleux épique dans le 'De diluvio mundi' d'Avit de Vienne." *Jahrbuch für Antike und Christentum* 43 (1991): 88–103.

———. "La mise en scène d'un drame intérieur dans le poème 'Sur la péché originel' d'Avit de Vienne." *Traditio* 51 (1996): 43–72.

Döpp, Sigmar. *Eva und die Schlange: Die Sündensfallschilderung des Epikers Avitus im Rahmen der bibelexegetischen Tradition.* Speyer, 2009.

Fontaine, Jacques. *Naissance de la poésie dans l'occident chrétien: Esquisse d'une histoire de la poésie latine chrétienne du IIIe au VIe siècle.* Paris, 1981.

Gärtner, Thomas. "Untersuchungen zum Text und zu den literarischen Vorbildern der Dichtungen des Alcimus Avitus." *Jahrbuch für Antike und Christentum* 44 (2001): 75–109.

———. "Zur Bibeldichtung *De spiritalis historiae gestis* des Alcimus Avitus." *Jahrbuch für Antike und Christentum* 43 (2000): 126–86.

Homey, Helge Hanns. "Evas Schuld (Alcimus Avitus *De spiritalis historiae gestis* 2,145–182)." *Hermes* 137, no. 4 (2009): 474–97.

Nodes, Daniel J. "Avitus of Vienne's *Spiritual History* and the Semipelagian Controversy: The Doctrinal Implications of Books I–III." *Vigiliae Christianae* 38 (1984): 185–95.

———. *Doctrine and Exegesis in Biblical Latin Poetry.* Arca 31. Liverpool, 1993.

Roberts, Michael. *Biblical Epic and Rhetorical Paraphrase in Late Antiquity.* Arca 16. Liverpool, 1985.

———. "Rhetoric and Poetic Imitation in Avitus' Account of the Crossing of the Red Sea (*De spiritalis historiae gestis* 5.371–702)." *Traditio* 39 (1983): 29–80.

Roncoroni, Angelo. "L'epica biblica di Avito di Vienne." *Vetera Christianorum* 9 (1972): 303–29.

———. "Note al *De virginitate* di Avito di Vienne." *Athenaeum* 51 (1973): 122–34.

Vinay, Gustavo. "La poesia di Sant'Avito (I *Poëmatum libri*)." *Convivium* 9 (1937): 431–56.

Wood, Ian N. "Avitus of Vienne: The Augustinian Poet." In *Society and Culture in Late Antique Gaul: Revisiting the Sources,* edited by Ralph W. Mathisen and Danuta Shanzer, 263–77. Aldershot, 2001.

Index